SEWANEE IN STONE

SEWANEE IN STONE

David Bowman

For Jack Blackwell
— Hope this agrees
with your Sewanee
memories!
David Bowman
(Dec. 4, 2003)

PROCTOR'S HALL PRESS
SEWANEE, TENNESSEE

Published by
Proctor's Hall Press
Sewanee, Tennessee

Library of Congress Card Number 2003110267

ISBN 0-9706214-6-9

The cover photograph of
Convocation Hall and Breslin Tower is by Latham Davis.
Many photographs and illustrations in the text pages have been provided by the University of the South Archives as indicated in the captions, in some cases with the name of the photographer Spencer Judd. Other photographs, when not credited, are by Latham Davis or the author.

Printed in the United States by Thomson-Shore, Inc.

SEWANEE

IN STONE

Lichen-covered sandstone in Hawkins Cove

PREFACE

Back in the mid-1950s I had essentially two views of what academic architecture could be.

There was the campus of Memphis State College, which started life as a "normal school" for turning out teachers, and gave its name to our neighborhood, Normal-Buntyn. Its buildings were redbrick, squat, and rather uninteresting, even to an architectural naif like me. Much later—when I was writing and publishing my weekly civic research newsletter, *Citywatching* (1978–1982)—when I was attuned as to how such public building contracts were delivered, frequently to favorites of powerful state politicians, there was no longer any mystery why these buildings were so remarkably unremarkable.

There was also Sewanee.

My introduction to the University of the South campus came in the summer of 1955, when I attended Camp Gailor-Maxon, the Episcopal camp held at the DuBose Conference Center in Monteagle. I was 14—and just getting intrigued about the pretty girls who swirled about the place like summer breezes—but I remember what a strong visual impression the university buildings made as our bus drove down the tree-lined arc of University Avenue and parked in front of All Saints Chapel.

Our counselor pulled us off the bus, and bullied us into a semblance of silence, to explain that the Chapel was not finished, and that the "temporary" wooden roof had been sitting on top of its half-finished walls for nearly 50 years.

The inside of the Chapel was cool, and somehow alive with sounds, not just of our noisy giggly bunch, but also with the whispers of history, emanating from flags and banners, marble plaques and epitaphs.

Back outside, we followed our leader up the path towards the great stone tower, with its pointy spires spiking the sky, and we entered the University Library, a wonderful dark-wood paneled hall with high stained glass windows, like some cathedral for learning.

Otey Parish Church (Judd)

Fast-forward nearly 50 years: I am a semi-retired gentleman with high-brow tastes and low-brow expectations.

The former was formed by growing up in St. John's Episcopal Church, a wealthy parish that literally overlooks the Memphis Country Club, and by going to Dartmouth College, a snooty Ivy League institution, all-male like Sewanee was, until they both took the co-educational plunge about ten years too late for me.

The latter reality, sinking expectations, was the result of my being forcibly retired, at 55, by having our daily newspaper shut down, shot out from under 22 wonderful employees, in 1996. In fairness to the Newhouse media empire, we were offered the choice of taking a job with the city's surviving daily or a generous severance package. I took the buyout, firmly convinced if I went to our stepsister paper, still angry, within two weeks, I would shoot off my mouth, and get myself fired.

Taking the buyout proved fortunate, as well, for it allowed me to take care of my aged parents, in the three last years of their lives, over in the Arkansas Ozarks. Being there also led to my teaching a "Writing About Architecture" course, in the fall of 1999, at the University of Arkansas's School of Architecture in Fayetteville.

Thanks to a leap-in-the-dark decision by UA/SA's chairman, architect David Buege, I got to teach a course that I had only dreamed about, as an architect wannabe. For nearly 30 years, I have been writing about architecture, urban environment, historic preservation, and livable places as often as my editors allowed it. Since 1975, I have written on all these closely-tied topics for magazines like *Memphis*, *Mid-South Business*, *Place*, and *Southern Exposure*; since 1989, I have written columns, editorials, and features on such topics for newspapers like the *Huntsville News*, *Baxter Bulletin*, *Morning News of Northwest Arkansas*, and the *Giles Free Press*.

Writing a book about Sewanee's architectural stonework is proving to be something else again.

Sewanee in Stone should probably not be a book at all, but a color videotape, with the camera swimming over the wonderful sandstone surfaces, in a graceful adagio, like the white-robed soul who does tai-chi in a towering circle of old oaks and tulip poplars in Manigault Park each morning. Even more interesting, for the future, would be a CD-ROM, offering 360-degree pans in exciting spaces like St. Luke's Chapel, or a DVD, whatever that is.

But books are what I do. I've written eight novels and assembled a dozen annual compilations of my newspaper commentaries. I've penned several arrogant theory-of-everything critiques, three literary monographs, one play, and three local histories. All these 30 titles have been published in micro-editions, of five to 100 copies, through my own imprint LaGrange Books (founded in August 1983 in LaGrange, Tennessee); they are like 30 small airplanes, waiting on the tarmac, some of them ready to take off after this one.

So here goes something. The moment is sentimental; in the palindrome year of 2002, it is the 40th anniversary of my first commentary writing for *The Dartmouth*, once a six-day daily, published on a campus as amiable in its own way as Sewanee, but without its benign weather or its lovely southern exposure.

The book idea was given me by Raneé Pruitt, a Huntsville archivist, who grew up in Sewanee, and whose grandfather worked on university buildings during the 1890s. Chief among those who have continually helped me, on this quixotic project, are Carl Reid, master stone mason, now retired, after a lifetime of building, superintending, and understanding what makes a really good sandstone building; Waring McCrady, retired French professor and local historian extraordinary, who read the final draft and caught innumerable bloopers of fact or lapses of judgment; and Annie Armour, University archivist who seems to have a mental map of where every map, document, or photo should be. Together, these three, and so many others, have answered my nagging questions about how the Sewanee community evolved in the charming ways it has.

As I said to you good folks, back in February 2002 when I started this project, all of you could do the book without me, but I could not do the book without you. Thanks very much.

Finally, four caveats for readers, scribbled on the last day of 2002, now that the final draft is in the hands of Sewanee book designer Latham Davis:

■ While it's true that architectural histories have a fetish about building dates, please remember that such dates can vary considerably, depending on whether we are talking about a groundbreaking; a cornerstone laying; dates on architects' plan drawings, specifications, or contract agreements; an actual contractor's completion date; or a dedication ceremony date. Note, for example, that All Saints' Chapel bears an MCMV (1905) date on its cornerstone and was "finished" in 1959, but wasn't actually dedicated until 1975, when the debt on it was paid off. So when, for example, Sewanee's college catalog tags buildings with dates, they may vary with some of the dates hereinunder.

■ I want to apologize in advance for omitting from discussion virtually all of the distinguished residences in and around the Sewanee Domain. To give them their due would (and should!) require another book nearly as longwinded as this one. So I would like to offer a loving litany of some names or nicknames here: Rivendell, The Cliffs (AKA Claramont Castle), St. Mary's Cloisters, Morgan's Steep, Bairnwick, The Goodsteins's House, Vice-Chancellor Hall's House (AKA French House), Plum Tree Cottage, Kappa Sigma (Gilchrist House) and other old stone fraternity houses, Crash Landing (the remarkable Kirby-Smith house done in 1949 by James Fitzgibbon), Glen Antrim, Otey Rectory, and others yet unexplored by this shy inquirer. Most egregious in this list of "those things we have left undone," as the old prayer of general confession so eloquently says it, is not dealing with the Otey Parish Church (1891), the small-is-beautiful stone parish church now agonizing over possible alterations to accommodate more parishioners. By way of partial atonement, let's at least pay homage to Otey with Spencer Judd's formal portrait (p. x) of the structure soon after its completion. Note the wooden steps and the tree stump not yet removed from the building site.

■ Sewanee's buildings are *sui generis*—eccentric, quirky, expressing strong individual style. We talk loosely about a "Collegiate Gothic" as being the dominant stylistic mode here. But as we shall see, in the pages that follow, Sewanee's architectural style can be anything from Romanesque (University Supply Store) to "Early English" (H. H. Holly's term for the 1878 Hodgson Library) to "Stockbroker's Tudor" (my term for the three delightful dormitories—Cannon, Johnson, and Tuckaway—done by Tilton & Githens in the money-roaring 1920s). Anything else—such as the "Eisenhower Gothic" tag on Sessums Cleveland Hall—is apt to be pure whimsy. The "Tudoresque" arches on the front of Guerry Hall don't make it a Tudor building, any more than the marvelous north-facing Tudoresque bay windows on duPont Library. This exuberant eclecticism is 100-percent-pure American in spirit. Not surprisingly, perhaps, architect W. H. Wood tried to popularize the term "American Gothic" about the time he designed Convocation Hall (1886).

■ *Sewanee in Stone* may be a work less of "architectural history" than of "artifact-based history." Sewanee's buildings are a strong expression of its mountaintop individualism. They don't adhere blindly to the "Collegiate Gothic" line. What ties this university's diversity together is its 125-year tradition of sandstone cut and set by four or more generations of stone masons. This book aims to celebrate that art of fact.

David Bowman
31 December 2002

CONGLOMERATES

A GOOD SPOT TO GRASP THE ASSOCIATED IDEAS of "Sewanee" and "Stone" is to stand across the street from the University's Forestry and Geology Building. There, at the northeast corner of the intersection of Alabama and St. Augustine, is a low shoulder of what the geologists have dubbed the Sewanee Conglomerate.

If you adjust your vision from the macro to the micro, by getting on your knees and examining the surface of the low rock outcropping, you will see a whitish sandstone studded with white quartz pebbles the size of peas or lima beans. (Ignore passersby who believe you're either crazy or are looking for a lost contact lens.)

This, my friends, is the rock that the Episcopal Church founded its university upon, quite literally.

Unlike sites elsewhere—one thinks of antebellum New Orleans having to put its building foundations on cotton bales to keep them from rotting away and sinking into the marshy soil there—all of Sewanee's buildings enjoy the assurance of a firm bedrock usually only a few feet below the structure's ground line.

If you refuse to stoop, for anyone, there is another great place to view this Sewanee bedrock. It is where U.S. 41A from the direction of Monteagle makes a graceful curve into University Avenue. You can park your car, truck, or bicycle on the paved shoulder and gaze at a 10-foot-high escarpment of Sewanee Conglomerate. It appears to have been creased, and scored, possibly by a bulldozer carving it away, back when the Dixie Highway (more of this important development in a later chapter) was cut through here in 1919–1920, or when the highway was widened in 1937, or when the merging lanes for the new highway bypass were created a few decades ago. An alternative theory, certainly worth considering, is that the scorings are the result of wind erosion; after all, the stone is softer and more erodable than the Warren Point Sandstone (next chapter) out of which the majority of Sewanee buildings are constructed.

Regardless of the true explanation for this scored sculptural surface, this corner makes a natural billboard saying you are now in Sewanee, a domain that is by law and tradition billboard-free.

The word conglomerate may seem odd to the non-geologist. For most of us, it means one of those gigantic U.S. corporations like Gulf & Western, or latter-day giants like RJR Nabisco, which can swallow up remarkably diverse types of companies, and run them as if their products were all of a kind. Geologically speaking, however, conglomerate is simply a rock composed of different sized aggregates, large or small, with some kind of binder like an iron compound to cement it all together.

Here is a much more precise definition, taken from an article by two Sewanee geology professors, Martin A. Knoll and Donald B. Potter, and published in the 1998 *National Speleological Society Guidebook* (p. 148), when the NSS held its convention here:

> The Sewanee Conglomerate (up to 130 feet thick), the oldest member of the Crab Orchard Group, is a white to yellowish-gray to yellowish-brown and locally pale red sandy conglomerate (Moore 1983). Quartz content is commonly above 98 percent. Rounded quartz pebbles are up to 2 inches long, and intraclasts of gray shale, brown shale, and siderite are up to 16 inches long. It is medium- to very thick-bedded, and crossbeds are planar or trough-shaped. The base is commonly rich in liesegang bands and is well cemented with limonite. The formation locally forms most of the bedrock surface on top of the Cumberland Plateau.

Since embarking on the Sewanee in Stone project, in February 2002, I have been intrigued with several other conglomerates worth a stoop-and-study in this small and beautiful university town.

■ There are the washed-concrete finishes on the sidewalks here. This slightly more expensive finish exposes the concrete aggregate, mostly brown flint river gravel, of varying screen-sizes.

My favorite sidewalks have large stones, an inch or sometimes more across; their surfaces have been polished by untold years of being tumbled in sand-grit, like a colossal gem tumbler, and more recently, by the scuffing of many well-shod feet.

In general, the smaller the aggregate, the less agreeable the paving, since there is correspondingly more dishwater gray cement visible, and far less of those lovely polished brown pebbles.

One of those most knowledgeable about Sewanee's buildings and grounds, Dr. Gerald Smith, a religion professor and secretary of the University's Board of Regents, recalls that though this tradition of washed-gravel walks began in the 1930s, many were constructed about a decade ago, when the campus was being wired for fiber-optic cable for its computer and telecommunications system. That cyber-age system was laid in trenches and concealed a good bit of the time by the reworked network of sidewalks.

■ There is also the wonderful conglomerate called University Avenue. It is a venerable concrete surface, 32 feet curb to curb, dating from 1938, when the highway through town was widened to federal standards. For about 65 years, now, vehicular traffic has been grinding away the paving, rather like those terrazzo floor-grinders , exposing the gray limestone aggregate chips. They are almost as elegant as the marble chips on a bank lobby terrazzo floor.

Better night visibility on University Avenue was a good reason to excuse the installation of center-line reflectors, in the summer of 2002, though the bonding cement could have been slathered on a bit more carefully.

Preservationists should be clear as to the significance of protecting this surface from defacement, including too much yellow paint thou-shalt-nots, or ugly cement patch-jobs, or an abominable asphalt cover-up, or (according to the new campus master plan by MacLachlan Cornelius & Filoni) the proposal of a median strip and bicycle lanes.

The new MCF study, released in May 2001, has many sensible recommendations. The avenue-fix is one of its few goofies. In this case, we should follow the ancient conservative principle: If it ain't broke, don't fix it.

CAVES, SPRINGS, & BLUFF SHELTERS

IT SEEMS APPROPRIATE, IN A REGION SO BLESSED with natural beauty as the Sewanee mountaintop, to point out just a few of the astonishing "architectural" creations here—particularly, its caves, springs, sinks, and bluff shelters—before getting into our main topic—the remarkable collection of sandstone buildings created from the 1870s to now.

The best tour guide of the Sewanee area published so far, *Under the Sun at Sewanee* (1967), spends a remarkable number of its 117 pages describing the architectural wonders sculpted by Mother Nature. The guide's charming text—written by Waring McCrady with photos by Bruce Rodarmor and Mazie McCrady—takes readers on a scholarly adventure that emphasizes, among other things, that the best things in life are free and fairly accessible.

Here, for example, is McCrady's description of Dry Cave (p. 20):

> This relatively small cave consists essentially of one tremendous room (40' high and 75' x 250' on the floor; the Vice-Chancellor's residence would fit in easily) with a few very short side passages. It is an ideal cave to take children to, as no one could possibly get lost in it, and it can be thoroughly explored in an hour.

Dry Cave is one of dozens of caves in the Sewanee-Monteagle area; others, often descriptively named, include Kirby, Peebles, Wriggle, Stream-Bed, Lost Cove, Monteagle Saltpeter, Multilevel, Salt River, Sinking Cove, Soda-Straw, Walker's Spring, Wet, and Wonder. Together they lured the National Speleological Society to Sewanee for its 1998 convention.

Caving is clearly not for everyone. (The author, for example, gets severe panic attacks when put in tight spaces like crowded elevators, overbooked airplanes, small crawl spaces under houses, etc.) But as a science lesson illustrating the slow but steady workings of thousands or millions of years of

Sewanee's Natural Bridge in the 1890s (Judd)

geologic time, the interactions of water and rock, and the resultant accretions (stalactites, stalagmites, etc.), caves are one of the best destinations for family outings yet devised.

One of my favorite nature-made architectural wonders is the Natural Bridge. Follow the signs on Tennessee 56 south from U.S. 41A until you get to Natural Bridge Road, naturally, and follow it out to the bluff-edge.

Wow! This is Sewanee-in-Stone at its most awesome.

It's not as big as Virginia's Natural Bridge, over which the old roadway of U.S. 11 still goes, but it's splendid nonetheless, particularly as a picnic spot. Here is a century-old view of Natural Bridge, taken by Sewanee's master photographer, Spencer Judd, with the five figures, dressed in their Sunday best, giving a sense of scale.

The University gave the site to the State of Tennessee in 1976.

Some people immersed in the Sewanee saga, from 1857 onwards, might point to the site of the 1860 cornerstone as the precise center of the old campus. After all, the University's central building was to have gone there, on the Domain's highest point, a knoll circumscribed neatly by Louisiana Circle. (Never mind that a bite was taken out of the circle by the 1937 realignment of University Avenue.) Those laying out the campus no doubt drew the ring road as a kind of symbolic Ground Zero for the new university.

But others would undoubtedly say that the symbolic center of Sewanee's campus is Polk's Spring, also known as Tremlett Spring, located immediately behind the athletic facilities complex of Fowler Center on Texas Avenue.

Tremlett Spring in Abbo's Alley

Anyone who has studied settlement patterns in historic regions like Middle Tennessee, and the placement of the earliest houses in those settlements, knows that the biggest single determiner will be the existence of a good waterspring, what real estate brokers of farm properties still call "an everlasting spring."

In the beginning, long before the Sewanee Utility District presumed to supply piped water to this community, there were a few really good springs. Polk's Spring was—and continues to this day—to be one of the very best. Its function today is primarily scenic, providing a lovely meandering watercourse along Abbo's Alley, the amiable greenway and botanical garden that runs a half mile to the south.

But it seems likely that this spring drew indigenous peoples here, long before the mountaintop was settled by those of Old World ancestry. In their 1998 article, Knoll & Potter follow local historians in identifying this particular spring with one at Rowe's Tavern, a stop on the stage road between Nashville and Chattanooga, which appears on Col. Charles Barney's 1858 plat of the area. It was also referenced, by a Union soldier (on August 7, 1863), as "a very large spring of the clearest and finest I ever drank" (E. L. Pennington, 1950, "The battle at Sewanee," *Tennessee Historical Quarterly*, v. 9, no. 3, pp. 3–29, cited in Knoll & Potter 1998).

My favorite testimonial to the miraculous powers of Polk's (or Tremlett's) Spring comes from the University's historiographer, Arthur Ben Chitty and his wife Elizabeth Chitty, in their *Sewanee Sampler* (1978). They note that the great Sewanee football team of 1899 always took two barrels of Tremlett Spring water with them on road trips. It is difficult to argue with the logic of a team that finished its season undefeated, 12–0, vanquishing all its mighty rivals in the Southeastern Conference.

Not the least impressive aspect of Polk's (Tremlett) Spring is the fact that it issues forth from an immense arc of sandstone, cantilevered out like some airport terminal canopy designed by Eero Saarinen, but in shape rather like the nearly 200 bluff shelters that can be found around the scalloped edges of the Sewanee Mountain.

ATO House

Just to argue that this shape is no fluke, but happens elsewhere, you can step down behind the Alpha Tau Omega House, on University Avenue, and find another historic spring, seasonally dry, with another cantilevered ledge almost as impressive. This, too, has a double name; some call it the ATO Spring, and some call it Otey's Spring, after another great bishop co-founder of Sewanee.

As to the bluff shelters, my friends in the University's archaeology program, Major McCollough and David Michaels, would argue the less said about them the better. Some of the bluff shelters have been attacked, and virtually destroyed, by pot-hunter types. As you might suspect, any and all archaeological significance in such a site can be destroyed by the mining of artifacts built up by sometimes thousands of years of occupants there.

Still, it is coming to be understood, by a century of study in such sites, that a remarkably high level of civilized society existed in these sheltered spots, particularly when we can lay aside our cultural biases, our lurking suspicions that anyone lacking refrigerators, BMWs, and 150 cable TV channels must be primitive indeed.

Until we get better techniques and instrumentalities for understanding (noninvasive when possible) basic facts about what they ate, what they wore, how they functioned as a society, and what they believed about themselves and their world, it is obviously better to leave such bluff-shelter sites alone, for the future of history.

But once again, in understanding the WHY of there being so many bluff shelters, we return to the peculiar geologic fact of the large "cap" of sandstone that tends to stay intact, cantilevering itself out, while erosion of the limestone and other layers beneath it continues. The result is a great stone roof—a great bluff shelter. At some points, of course, the immense tonnage will overwhelm the sandstone, and it will tumble down the mountainside as gigantic peanut-brittle-like blocks.

The most famous of these sandstone blocks is the one on U.S. 41A just inside the stone portals announcing you are entering the University Domain. Stone steps have been thoughtfully provided, as well as some unthoughtful spray-painted graffiti, so you can climb up the backside of the block, to the Angel's Landing lookout, which offers a million-dollar view west towards Winchester, absolutely free.

This sandstone cap, composed mainly of a two-layer cake of Sewanee Conglomerate and Warren Point Sandstone, dates from the so-called Pennsylvanian geologic era, created by the forces of nature roughly 325 million to 285 million years ago.

It is this latter stuff that will become the hero—ta-dah!—of our tale. Here, once again, is Knoll & Potter 1998 (p. 148):

> The Warren Point Sandstone (*30* to *130* feet thick) is light-gray (weathers yellow-brown) fine- to medium-grained, and is thin- to very thick-bedded. Crossbed sets 3–6 feet thick are common, and the predominant dip direction is southwest. . . . The Warren Point Sandstone forms the prominent bluff, and northwest- and northeast-trending vertical joint sets control the shape of the bluff line. Isolated blocks where partial joint separation has occurred include Piney Point and Proctor's Hall.

During a botanical field trip, in July 2002, a small group led by professor-emeritus George Ramseur hiked to Piney Point. Stepping out onto the gigantic sandstone block, with a foot-wide separation between it and the mainland, so to speak, takes an act of considerable faith, taking a stand where non-angels fear to tread. (Wee theological joke.) No one knows when the Piney Point block will decide to head farther west downhill.

Not the least significant effect of these vertical joint sets is the fact that when they do decide to break off, they leave a crisp and dramatic scarp behind.

More importantly, for our architectural tale, these bluff-edge blocks are also the best spots to quarry that gorgeous Warren Point Sandstone.

My introduction to one of these quarries, on May 30, 2002, starts with a one mile walk from the west end of Breakfield Road, where three old rutted roads are closed off by steel barricades.

My guide is Carl Reid, now in his early 80s, retired after a life spent in the service of the University, as a master stone mason, and later as Commissioner of Buildings and Lands, a post that other institutions might call "clerk of the works" or whatever.

The Mountain Goat (Judd)

We walk south, through a considerable stretch of recently timbered-off ground, in the direction of Armfield Bluff. When we re-enter the woods, there is considerable undergrowth, and more poison ivy underfoot than either of us care for. But when we get to the bluff edge, Reid points to a stretch of exposed sandstone, and explains that this is the old High Top quarry, a quarryable ledge of about 400 to 500 feet.

The critical factor, he says, is that the sandstone has to have a "bottom," that is, a bedded horizontal fissure, to work down towards; otherwise, he says, there's no way in the world to dig it out.

The story of Sewanee and the "Mountain Goat" railroad deserves a chapter unto itself. This branch line followed the Nashville & Chattanooga Railroad's main line for two miles from Cowan and then swung over it on a wooden trestle (later a stone arch bridge) near the north portal of the great old Cumberland Mountain Tunnel built in the 1850s. But for our purposes the slicing and tunneling work offer splendid geological profiles worth several field trips.

Let's give Tom Kirby-Smith the witty tour guide's last word:

> When the University of the South celebrated its centennial a few years ago, someone might have pointed out—as additional evidence of the institution's solidity—that its literal foundations are more than 200 million years old. The Sewanee Conglomerate is one of the more venerable formations in the United States; in contrast to this, the glacial till and outwash on which Harvard University stands dates back a mere 25,000 years (*Under the Sun at Sewanee*, p. 38).

ARCHITECT OF THE DOMAIN

About 50 years ago, Sewanee's historiographer Arthur Ben Chitty started referring to George Rainsford Fairbanks (1820–1906) as the "architect of the domain." Fairbanks designed no University buildings, but he had firm and influential ideas about their function and placement. In that sense, the epithet is well deserved, for as the University's first Commissioner of Buildings and Lands, and its unpaid business manager, Fairbanks handled all manner of business matters, practical and financial, leaving no detail unattended.

But what seems most significant for this study is a document delivered to the Board of Trustees of the University of the South, on August 2, 1886. It was authored by Fairbanks and thoughtfully re-printed in Fairbanks's book-length *History of the University of the South* (1905) just a year before his death.

This 1886 statement, running in the book from page 248 to page 261, seems to be aiming to do three very important things: 1) re-state the plans of the founders of the university articulated around 1860; 2) summarize and codify these plans, at the moment when the University was reaching some financial stability and clarity as to its future directions, in the mid-1880s; and 3) preach a lay sermon to those 20th-century readers as to where the University had come from and where it ought to be going.

Fairbanks begins with a rhetorical appeal to authority, namely the University's founding fathers, notably Bishop Leonidas Polk:

> In the whole history of educational institutions in America no other instance is recalled where the conception of a grand landed domain was made so important a feature in the planning and planting of a college or university.... The Sewanee idea was to create its own environment; as Bishop Polk said when asked, in reference to the isolated location of the proposed University, "Where will you get your society?" His answer was, "We will make it; and not only so, but we will sur-

> round the University with such a society as is nowhere else possible in this land." It was not an idle boast, but a sagacious forecast of a future then seemingly distant, but now quite within our sure range of vision (Fairbanks, *History*, p. 249).

Though there have been hard times, for the University and for the South in general, for the past 40 years, Fairbanks notes with some assurance that "the South is today prosperous, united, and well settled in its social, business, and political relations." One symptom of this benign state of affairs, on Sewanee's young campus, is the plan for a handsome new building, now known as Convocation Hall, dating itself from 1886, graced with a magnificent bell tower (Breslin) and soon followed by a utilitarian academic building (Walsh Memorial Hall).

But the Domain's de-facto architect is not talking merely about buildings, and certainly he does not want to ape Oxford and Cambridge in their architectural style, even if the funds were unlimited.

So he quickly articulates the premise that it is the Domain's natural environment that is critical:

> Our landed domain, acquired with much effort and sacrifice, consists of about 9,000 acres of woodland, lying upon the tableland of the Cumberland Mountain plateau, and extending in most instances sufficiently far down the slopes of the mountain to give us control of the bluffs and approaches from the valleys. . . . The only straight avenue planned by Bishop Hopkins extended westerly from the cornerstone of the grand central building about one mile, forming a boulevard some two hundred feet in width as a grand drive, and giving a fine perspective view of the central building and most of the projected college buildings. . . . The soil is a sandy loam lying upon a conglomerate rock, and good roads are easily made by following the sinuosities of the ridges, making handsome drives, easily kept in order. Gentle elevations, rising slightly above the general level, are frequently found, presenting beautiful natural sites for dwellings (Fairbanks, *History*. pp. 250–251).

The paradox of this vision is that it is pastoral, yet it also evokes two of the great cities of the world. There is the grand central boulevard of Paris, as created by the urban planner Baron Haussmann (1809–1891), and there is the distinct idea of New York's Central Park, as designed by F. L. Olmsted (1822–1903) and others.

Fairbanks then quotes with approval remarks by Bishop Stephen Elliott published in 1858:

> The time is not distant when this whole plateau will be covered over with villas and cottages and watering places, and will teem with the most refined society of the South and West.... Wilmington, Charleston, and Savannah will here shake hands with Mobile, New Orleans, Nashville and Memphis, and cement the strong bonds of friendship and love (p. 251).

Though this crystal-ball projection would soon be partially realized, with the creation of summer places like the Monteagle Sunday School Assembly (1882), and the families who have settled in around the University, generation after generation like Elliott's descendants, his view sounds uncannily like the 1990s boom here, the fact that the Sewanee mountain is now one of the hottest destinations for up-scale retirement houses, gated community-seekers (Clifftops and Cooley's Rift), and weekend houses for prosperous citizens from Nashville, Huntsville, and elsewhere.

Fairbanks noted that "as we had no level plain upon which all the buildings of the University could be placed in symmetrical form, the topography must be carefully studied and mapped out, the levels ascertained, and a system of location adopted which should conform to the ground and present a symmetrical plan as a whole."

He recalled Bishop Nicholas Hamner Cobbs's resolution, approved by the board at Beersheba Springs (another summer resort model of real significance) in 1859, to "employ a landscape gardener for the purpose of laying off and arranging the grounds of the University with due regard to convenience, comfort, and taste."

Fortunately, members of the board were close friends with an architect and landscape gardener, Bishop John Henry Hopkins, who agreed to spend the winter of 1859–1860 in a laborious study of the Sewanee domain, with the help of Col. Charles R. Barney's wonderful 1858 topographic map.

One of Hopkins's principal recommendations was a grand drive some 30 miles around the edge of the Domain which he dubbed the Corso. Though in his day such a drive might connote a fashionable procession of carriages, it is fortunate such a route was not created, for it would probably have ended up in our day as an automobile-choked ring road, spoiling all the bluff-edge beauty, as a single oversized off-domain edifice (no names, please!) does now.

Another key issue, settled by a resolution of the Executive Committee in 1860, was how to exercise optimum control over the land uses on the Domain:

> Resolved, that the executive committee be authorized to arrange the reservations required for the use of the University, and around the springs, and also to lay out the public grounds, avenues, streets, etc., and shall give two months' notice of the time of leasing the lots on the domain. The size and shape of the lots, and the terms, conditions, and mode of leasing thereof shall be determined by the executive committee, who shall have full discretionary power in reference to all matters contained therewith (p. 253).

Such matters are today in the hands of the all-powerful Lease Committee, which rules on all related issues, large and small, with the endorsement of the Vice Chancellor (who exercises final authority over the matter ex officio).

As to the actual design of the University of the South campus, the pre-war paradigm was to erect a great central building on a site (circumscribed later by Louisiana Circle) about 500 feet in diameter, gently sloping in all directions, in Fairbanks's words:

> One of the plans furnished by a leading architect gives as the entire length of the building 272 feet, its greatest depth 135 feet; divided into a central portion 70 by 135 feet, containing the theater or a great hall, 70 by 120 feet, to seat 2,500 people; a library wing 41 feet front by 81 feet in depth on one side, and a gallery of fine arts in the other wing, of the same dimensions, the wings connected by corridors 60 feet in length by 20 feet in width—not unlike the general plan of the Capitol at Washington (p. 255).

Again, in some ways, it is fortunate that such a building was not constructed, because it might have dictated an architectural precedent (e.g. Greek Revival) that would have constrained later campus additions. On the other hand, given the unprecedented prosperity of the South in the 1850s, it is exceedingly unfortunate that this wealth, with multi-million dollar sums pledged by the various dioceses, did not arrive in time to be put to good use. After the war, of course, truly humble buildings—cabins of logs, cottages of board-and-batten sawmill lumber, etc.—made a virtue of dire necessity.

Fairbanks's own cottage, Rebels Rest, remains as the best testimony of his own architectural latitude. (He also built a very formal house as his Florida residence.) Rebels Rest is a handsome log house, with three front gables, as rootedly "American" as the 1860 building would have been "imported goods." Actually, immediately after giving the dimensions and character of the 1860 building, Fairbanks commented that the other buildings ought to be "of different styles of architecture, of moderate size, and not to exceed $25,000 each in cost," while the professors' houses and boarding houses "were expected to be built in their vicinity upon some corresponding plan as to symmetry and general appearance."

Rebel's Rest as it appears today

Given the likelihood of fires, which quickly burned down all manner of buildings, enormous and expensive buildings were a bad idea, as other campuses periodically discovered. (When, for example, there was a fire at Martin College, in 1904, it swept through every building and dormitory, because they were all conjoined in a single complex; fortunately, the leading citizens of Pulaski, Tennessee, pledged they would raise funds to rebuild it all, one way or another.) That ugly fact, flammability, may have been the kernel of logic behind the quaint-seeming notion of a 35-foot setoff distance between any building and its property lines.

The final stone in Fairbanks's overarching plan involved trees. Nearly 10,000 acres of them.

The University's founders, he noted, set apart "a campus of one thousand acres" for the University buildings, professors' houses, and boarding houses. Outside of this 1,000 acres, tax-exempt by state charter, would be land available for lease by church families, and those who would erect summer residences. The founders, he asserted, "would create at no distant day a secure endowment, ever increasing in value; leases taken of every available locality, and a large and refined society, brought together here from all parts of the South, centering around these halls of learning, interested in and advancing this great work" (p. 256).

Fairbanks seems to be suggesting, more than a century before it was declared by pundits like sociologist Daniel Bell, that the future of America's post-industrial economy will be "knowledge-based" communities that look like, and often are, college or university towns. Not everyone drawn to places like Sewanee comes to seek knowledge; rather, they are seeking a rural quality of life, enlivened by urbane culture.

Old University Avenue, with Breslin Tower in background (U. Archives)

Such places offer what Simon Schama, in his brilliant book *Landscape and Memory* (1995), describes as the creative tension, enjoyed in classical times, between "otium" (leisure) and "negotium" (business). Cicero has his townhouse in Rome, and his country house at Tusculum, as did most of his cultivated friends:

> Pliny's second villa in Tuscany (was) . . . organized around its farm estate. But virtually all Roman villas that we know of were places devoted to the productive ordering of nature, rather than the contemplation of its pristine beauty. Pliny presents his Tuscan house, tucked into the side of the Apennines (close to the modern Citta di Castello), as a more remote and serious place than the opulent and seductive Laurentinum. Its climate was harsher in winter (when, evidently, its owner was seldom there), the terrain more rugged (*Landscape and Memory*, p. 530).

So at least part of the "secure endowment" Fairbanks seems to be describing involves practical considerations, including an elevation above the so-called "malaria line," a pure "freestone water" supply, abundant quantities of building stone, accessibility by railway and common roads, and a large forest of trees, particularly "these towering oaks":

> It was not the purpose to build up a town, but a large sylvan population, where every home should be surrounded with the leafy shades of the primeval forests, mingling the wildness of nature with the improvements of man, and placed upon wooded knolls with meandering paths upon their gentle slopes, or on bold summits presenting distant scenes of unsurpassed beauty, rich valleys and a boundless horizon stretching far away into purple-hued cloudlands, where clouds and sky are indistinguishable (Fairbanks, *History*. p. 257).

After such a rhapsody, lest the reader think he is off in some cloud-cuckoo-land, Fairbanks nails down another practical matter. The founders, he noted, insisted on the need to "appoint a forester to prevent the cutting down of this valuable forest growth," constantly patrolling the domain, to warn off "trespassers and bark and wood cutters." Unfortunately, in recent years, the tree poachers and ordinary lumbering practices have left "thousands of unsightly stumps," something Fairbanks deplored.

Though he doesn't credit Fairbanks for inviting him to the campus, in the fall of 1898, it seems likely that Carl Schenck came here with the encouragement of Fairbanks's disciples. Schenck is one of perhaps three founders of modern American forestry practices, along with Gifford Pinchot, and ran the nation's first forestry school at Biltmore, North Carolina, operating from 1898 to 1913. Here is his recollection in the delightful memoir published by the Forest History Society in 1974:

> In the fall of 1898 I was invited by the University of the South, in Sewanee, Tennessee, to inspect its woodlands. Some universities, namely Yale and Cornell, were planning at the time to offer forestry courses, and Sewanee, small though it was, was ambitious to outrival them, believing that it was particularly qualified for forestry by its control of some ten thousand acres of surrounding forests. They were indeed glorious virgin forests, on a nonagricultural formation of limestone rock, well watered by noisy subterranean brooks. I made an address on

The box-like tunnel on the bluffedge called Proctor's Hall

> forestry in the university auditorium and promised to submit to the authorities in the course of the next six months, free of charge, a working plan for the Sewanee university forests. The working plan was made, duly submitted, and discussed, but it was never executed, since the university was short of money. Forestry is no go with an owner short of money (p. 81).

George Fairbanks's 1886 peroration is an impassioned plea for the board of trustees to be good stewards of its wonderful assets:

> A period has now arrived when it seems necessary that some decided and systematic action be taken by the board for the preservation of valuable timber and building sites on the domain; for the proper location of University buildings hereafter to be erected; for opening and making available the many suitable sites for residences, so that we may thereby increase our revenues and secure an increase in the number of families having a home and interests here; for laying out judiciously new avenues, and for securing the health of the community by proper sanitary regulations (p. 260).

No surprise, friends, George Fairbanks's appeal could have been made with equal power and greater urgency today. Sewanee has not only the community responsibility for good stewardship of its own best assets: it also has the opportunity to be a strong advocate, with a 10,000-acre example, to help show ALL communities how to veer away from the Road to Uglification and Environmental Waste we seem to be driving down at hellish speeds.

A PRIMER ON STONE-SETTING

WRITING A BOOK IS PRESUMPTUOUS ACTIVITY. It presumes someone wants to read what you're writing. Even more questionable, it presumes you know enough about your subject, certainly more than your reader.

The highest act of presumption is to write a book on something you've never done. *Sewanee in Stone* is one of those books.

Fortunately, I have a panel of experts, including Carl Reid, a third or fourth generation stone mason on the Sewanee mountaintop. He loaned me his *Audels Masons and Builders Guide #4* (1945) so I could photocopy its 57-page and lavishly-illustrated chapter on stone masonry. I've also talked with Houston King, currently the master stone mason at Sewanee, which is continuing its long history with using Warren Point Sandstone, quarried on the mountaintop, in its just-completed $18 million dining hall.

With its oldest surviving stone building, St. Luke's Hall, dating from 1876, the University of the South has roughly 125 years of experience with architectural stonework. The university's stone buildings—about 50 academic halls, professors residences, and other structures, notably the cathedral-like All Saints Chapel—round out my panel of experts and speak eloquently for themselves.

One of the things we stone-lovers (call us lithophiles) need to learn first is how to read a wall.

Assuming the basic choice has already been made as to the kind of stone used—limestone, marble, granite, or sandstone—the designer's first decision is whether to use unsquared (rubble), roughly squared, or squared stone. Another term for this squared-off stone is "ashlar," locally referred to as "cut stone." Raw stone shattered by tools or by nature is termed rubble, and in Sewanee rarely figures on a visible surface.

Much used in Sewanee's residential buildings (dormitories, fraternities, and private residences) is "field stone," or "pick-up stone," i.e., stones found already weathered on the mountainside. Their stained and sometimes even mossy surfaces are set puzzle-like to form an exterior surface that has the instant patina of genuine age.

The next choice is whether to lay the stone uncoursed, random coursed, or coursed.

Uncoursed rubble is described picturesquely by the masons as "cobweb rubble" because that's the way the mortar joints visually express themselves in a wall.

A course, in stonework as in brickwork, is simply a series of blocks laid (bedded) as a horizontal row, with the top and bottom mortar joints forming continuous parallel lines. Most of Sewanee's official University sandstone buildings, old or new, are laid up in coursed ashlar blocks. Their dimensions are typically 12 to 18 inches deep (vertical), and their length (horizontal) is in familiar ratios like 2:1, 3:1, or 3:2, with corresponding wall thicknesses like 18 inches.

It is important, everyone says, for the stones to be set with their bedding planes—that is, the way the stone was formed in beds and tends naturally to split when quarried out—corresponding to their horizontal joints. Stones set vertically are apt to take rainwater into their planes and then spall off in seasonal freeze-thaw cycles.

Coursed ashlar can either be roughly squared, leaving irregularities that require a ½ to one-inch mortar joint, or squared, allowing a tighter joint of ½ to ⅜ inch. It is Carl Reid's considered opinion, after about 50 years of experience with this art-form, that tighter joints will make the wall last longer. The drawback, he concedes, is that with hand-dressed stone, in the days before big cable stone-cutting saws, using carborundum grit, smooth ashlar took 20 times as much labor as the rougher finishes.

Another option to stone setters is what is called "broken ashlar." This simply means, or not so simply, the horizontal course gets broken up, by means of blocks stepping up and stopping a horizontal course.

Needless to say, this is far more difficult to do, even if you agree on a formula for stone-setting like "two against one," where the sum of the two horizontal stones will butt up against the one larger dimension stone, or "two against two," where the big-stone/little-stone combination butts up against the same size two stones inverted as a little-stone/big-stone combo.

The possibilities of this broken-bond stonework are limited only by the virtuosity of the stone-setter. The really cocky stone-setters, like virtuoso jazz musicians, can do "three against two" or other jazzy patterns. Broken-bond stonework also results in a stronger wall, they say, because the stones lock together in tighter three-dimensional patterns.

The worst and weakest walls, if poorly laid, have long vertical joints that can crack if there's any instability or settling beneath the wall. If you see a crack in a wall, somewhere, it will probably follow one of those overlong vertical joints.

There's also the imperative, in the stone mason's trade, of a good bond between the outside wall and the inside wall. Even when the inside wall is going to be uncoursed rubble, or hollow tile, or cement block, or brick, there was a traditional standard of one block turned—so its long dimension spans the entire 18 inch thickness of the wall, like a brick "header"—every four feet in each course. In the second half of the 20th century, this block bonding was replaced by requirements for various "wire bonds" or galvanized fasteners bedded into the mortar so as to hold inner and outer walls together.

The last, but probably most significant, variable in our wall-reading is the remarkable number of finishes available to the one face of each block that we see.

There is the long-repeated exchange between the distinguished Boston architect, Ralph Adams Cram, commissioned to do the All Saints' Chapel nearly a century ago, and some high-ranking University official. The

Four stone-setting styles (Audels Guide)

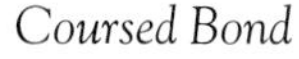

Coursed Bond

Broken Bond; two against one

Broken Bond; two against two

Broken Bond; three against one

exact words, if they are not the stuff of urban legend anyway, have not survived. The gist is that the architect-brahmin noted the rough-pitched faces of all the Sewanee sandstone buildings then in existence—St. Luke's, Convocation, Walsh, Hodgson, University Press, University Supply, ATO House, and so on—and said in essence, that simply will not do, since all high-gothic stonework MUST have smooth facing, as everyone knows. The reply from Sewanee, possibly from the Vice-Chancellor, was equally haughty: Well, that's the way we do it at Sewanee and that's the way we will continue to do it.

One of four doors on the west face of St. Luke's Hall

As Carl Reid explained to me—one day when we were admiring the old stonework on St. Luke's Hall—the heavier the mallet hitting the rock face, the bigger the bite taken, resulting in a stronger "pitch," a more visually dramatic sculptured surface. If you want a lower pitch, a flatter face, you use a lighter mallet for your pitching tool.

In the succeeding years, this craggy face has come to be a Sewanee trademark, rugged and expressive, distinct from the Oxford and Cambridge esthetic to which the antebellum Sewanee so much aspired.

If you want to see what Sewanee could have looked like, as translated into American collegiate gothic, go to the University of Chicago campus, built in the 1890s with about $30 million of Mr. John D. Rockefeller's pre-income tax fortune. JDR ordered his architects to pick out their favorite Oxbridge buildings, make measured drawings, and then build them anew in the fashionable Hyde Park suburb of Chicago.

As the silly old football cheer goes, dating from about 1899, when Sewanee beat all its rivals in the South, YEA, SEWANEE'S RIGHT. Or at least mostly right: these buildings are Oxbridge tempered with Tennessee mountain orneriness.

As to piercing these stone walls—doors, windows, porches, arcades, and so on—that is a large and complex topic for the architects, builders, stone cutters, and stone setters involved.

In the case of Sewanee's stone buildings, beginning in 1875 with the Hodgson Memorial Library, the architect (Henry Hudson Holly of New York City) simply dictated a squared-off opening for the doors and windows, trimmed out in what the specifications called "bluestone," a fine type of limestone that was a la mode in that Gilded Age era, ordered from a company in Nashville.

When the same architect was asked to submit plans for the University's next stone building, St. Luke's Hall, two years later, he ventured putting a

Hodgson Memorial Infirmary (U. Archives)

couple of curved stone elements into its dramatic nine-bay front. The facade consists of four pyramid-capped tower sections alternating with five recessed bays. Each of these latter elements featured two stories of windows capped with an arched and voussoir-segmented sandstone eyebrow. Entry to the four towers was through limestone trimmed archways done in the grand style popularized by Holly's house designs for Thomas Alva Edison and other notables.

Stylistic clues to Holly's firm being involved—even if you didn't know already that he was the same architect who did Hodgson's $10,000 library—lurk primarily in the mansard-chateauesque roof and pedimented dormer details. Happily, St. Luke's survives in fine form, to this day, while the Hodgson Library was unrecognizably transformed in its next incarnation as the Hodgson Memorial Infirmary (1899).

The next major building, Convocation Hall (1886), offers a nice choice of arched openings, including two types of round-topped windows, all cased completely in the native sandstone. On the building's north flank are three windows with a larger diameter top, on the east half; on the west half are four skinnier-diameter tops. (There is also a curious little door, with round-shouldered corners, a few feet west of the 1886 cornerstone.) The total number of windows, if you believe in numerology, or at least architectural symbolism, seem to this writer to be a sure expression of the Seven Liberal Arts, divided into the trivium (three-way, of grammar, rhetoric, and logic) and the quadrivium (four-way, of arithmetic, geometry, astronomy, and music), as any 19th-century scholar worth his or her latin-savored salt would surely know.

Kappa Alpha House

The voussoir segments of the seven arches simply notch in, unobtrusively, with the appropriate stone course they reach.

Later buildings at Sewanee would call dramatic attention to the arch by the voussoir segments having a curved inner segment (intrados) and a curved outer segment (extrados). Examples of this much-more showy arch, fashionable in the ornamental grammar of great 19th-century architects like Henry Hobson Richardson and Louis Sullivan, can be seen in the University Press Building (1903), University Supply Store (1904), and the Kappa Alpha House (1916).

My personal favorite old sandstone building, St. Luke's Chapel (1907), uses a subtler integration of gothic arch window and door openings, but does it, with absolute mastery, totally in sandstone, including the tracery mullions that divide the stained glass window elements. In terms of the stone mason's art, which often follows the architect's choice of fine-grained oolitic limestone (from Indiana) for such delicate work, this chapel, now primarily a music performing arts space with about 110 seats, makes beautiful stone-mountain music indeed.

The lovely Venetian Gothic pointed arch reaches its peak, so to say, in the gigantic Gailor Memorial (1952) entrance archway. Its size, which seems to dwarf any humans before it, seems to promise so much, yet delivers so little. The arch looks in fact rather like a gigantic white whale-maw for the new dining hall. Gailor is one of the more disappointing post-war

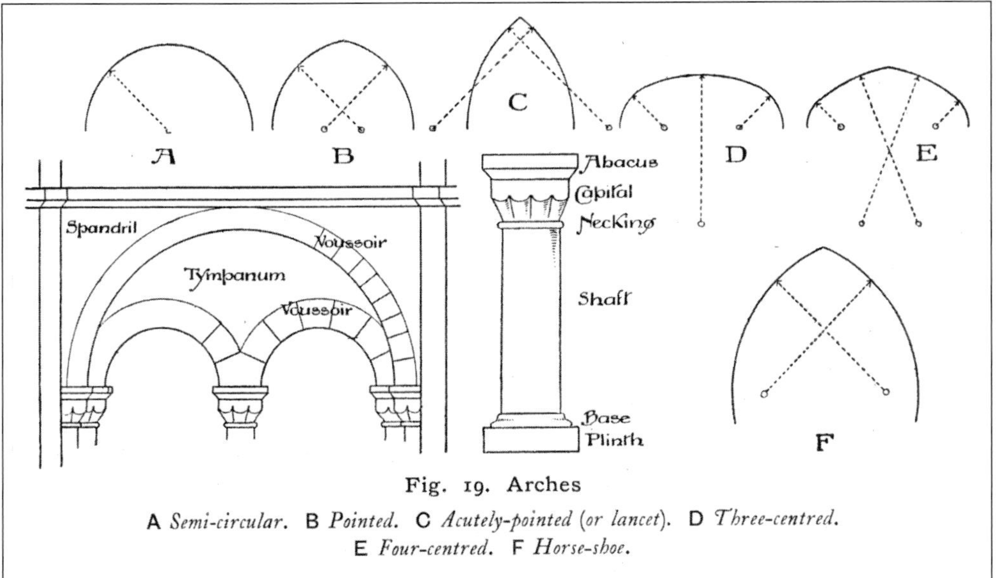

Fig. 19. Arches

A *Semi-circular.* B *Pointed.* C *Acutely-pointed* (*or lancet*). D *Three-centred.* E *Four-centred.* F *Horse-shoe.*

Some arch possibilities from Samuel Gardner's Guide (1922)

buildings, perhaps emblematic of Sewanee's post-war economic realities.

More happily, there are the arcades, that is, a series of stone arches hooked together in series, to form lovely covered walkways, particularly when the sun is at the right angle to punctuate the walk with light/shadow/light /shadow rhythms.

These are trickier to build, and frequently need buttressing, as with the arcade added to the south flank of Walsh Memorial Hall (1890) when it was completely gutted, re-fitted inside with reinforced concrete, and re-dedicated as Walsh-Ellett Hall (1958). Similar to these are the buttressed arcades of Guerry Hall (1961). Each of these segmented arches is slightly flattened, at their ten o'clock and two o'clock positions, a tudor-style compromise between the pointy gothic arch and the round-topped roman arch seen elsewhere on campus.

When we start taking the more detailed campus tour, building by building, we will see many other wonders of the stone mason's art. Bear with us. Writing goes a lot faster than stonework but won't last as long.

PERMANENT BUILDINGS & PRESTIGIOUS ARCHITECTS

One can hear the keen frustration welling up in George R. Fairbanks, Sewanee's commissioner of buildings and lands, as he reports to the University Board of Trustees in 1873:

> I most respectfully beg leave to again urge upon the Board of Trustees the importance of taking immediate action with reference to the construction of one at least of our permanent buildings. We have now carried on the school in temporary buildings, adding and enlarging from year to year, for five years past.
>
> The erection of the proposed building would relieve the pressure for Recitation and Lecture rooms, already inconveniently felt, and enable the Professors of the various Schools to fit up their Recitation and Lecture rooms with the appliances and apparatus especially requisite for their work.
>
> We are now without any hall of sufficient capacity to accommodate the whole body of students upon occasions of Public Lectures or Society Exhibitions. Our Library is in a temporary and unsuitable building, and the officers of the University are without offices.
>
> The proposed building would meet all these wants, and further the well-being of the University in all its departments, and it is certainly better economy to use in the construction of a permanent building the funds which must otherwise be expended in providing temporary structures, to be afterwards abandoned and become useless (Proceedings of the Trustees, 1873, p. 15).

There was an obvious deficiency in the University's finances, so soon after the disastrous Civil War, and plunging into the nation's economic distresses set off by the Panic of 1873. That kind of tension, perennially articulated by Fairbanks, between what the University needed, and what it could afford, dogged its leadership for much of the first century of Sewanee's institutional life.

Still, there has been that quest for quality, familiar to academics, who frequently have upper-class tastes and lower-class incomes.

Episcopalians in general, and Sewanee's leadership in particular, have always had a natural predilection for excellence. We want the best, they seem to keep saying, even if we cannot afford it.

So here is Fairbanks, no doubt enjoying at least intellectual agreement from the board of bishops and prominent laymen, pressing for a building that exists as an "elevation and plan furnished by Mr. Littel" that has been submitted to "the most reliable builders in Nashville," who have given a cost estimate of labor and materials. Besides, Fairbanks notes, the "timber can be cut at once upon our lands and prepared for use," while "our quarries are easily worked." He urges the board to approve work to start, "to excavate for the foundations and put up the basement walls on the solid rock" before the severity of winter sets in.

This building does not get built, immediately, though its general purposes get fulfilled when the Chemical & Philosophical Hall (1883), Convocation (1886) and Walsh (1890) buildings are completed.

What is built immediately is the Hodgson Library, because Telfair Hodgson offers to pay $10,000 for its design and construction. The joker in this gift is that the new library will sit where Hodgson wants it, up the hill towards Morgan's Steep, close to his holdings, but inconvenient to students and faculty alike.

Getting the best, for Hodgson, means getting the architectural services of Henry Hudson Holly (1834–1892). The Board of Trustees meet in New York City, on November 2, 1874, perhaps to thank Hodgson—who at that time had a parish in the fashionable suburb of Hoboken, New Jersey—and perhaps to enjoy a wee bit of New York's finest cultural bouquet after their business is done.

Now then, Holly, working out of his offices at 111 Broadway, is an architectural celebrity, thanks to his two popular books, *Holly's Picturesque Country Seats* (1863) and *Modern Dwellings in Town and Country* (1878). One of his best works would come after the two commissions at Sewanee, Rosemount (1893), a 37-room and 24,000 sq. ft. mansion of pink rhyolite stone in Pueblo, Colorado, built at a cost of $60,750. Rosemount is built for John A. Fletcher, one of those fabulous Gilded Age barons who made money as a merchant and banker, but also had extensive interests in cattle, mining, and agriculture.

The good news for Sewanee is that after the Hodgson Library is well underway, Holly will also furnish the plans for the new St. Luke's Hall for the University's school of theology. The bad news, sad to say, is that Holly submits claims for payment that are not honored, according to a sheaf of correspondence in the University Archives, until 1888.

From about 1930, up until the $18 million McClurg Dining Hall is completed two years ago, Sewanee stops indulging itself in the expensive habit of summoning Famous Architects.

Before that 1930 crash-landing—and particularly during its three earliest decades, when the University can least afford it—the let's-get-the-best school of doing things prevails. This includes securing the services of William Halsey Wood (1855–1897), Richard Howland Hunt (1862–1931), Charles Coolidge Haight (1841–1917), Ralph Adams Cram (1863–1942), Edward Lippincott Tilton (1861–1933), and Alfred Morton Githens (1876–1973). Holly and all these gentlemen are card-carrying members of the New York / Boston architectural establishment.

Cram, for example, formed a partnership with Bertrand Grosvenor Goodhue in 1901, dissolved in 1914 after a falling-out, but not until they had basically defined the terms of what would become the biggest American Gothic revival yet.

The big moment for Cram and Goodhue was winning the competition to design the campus of the American Military Academy at West Point in 1904. As the website (www.hdb.com) of the present-day successors to Cram, a Boston firm known as HDB / Cram & Ferguson, argues with considerable force, the 1904 win "epitomized the American turning away from the leadership of the Ecole des Beaux Arts and the beginning of the American Neo-Gothic movement."

This is precisely the moment that Sewanee chooses to enlist Cram as their architect. The man was prolific. He is credited with 500 to 600 buildings in his creative lifetime, including a whole herd of steel-skeleton Neo-Gothic churches, scattered all over the United States; collegiate campuses like Wellesley College and Rice Institute; and ecclesiastical buildings like the University Chapel (1924) at Princeton, weighing in at 249 feet long, the third largest university chapel in the world.

Cram is said to be the model for the foe-of-modernism, caricatured by Ayn Rand in *The Fountainhead* (1949), losing the argument to the uncompromising modernist architect-as-hero, Howard Roark, said to be modeled on Frank Lloyd Wright.

The fact that Sewanee starts its All Saints' Chapel, but runs out of funds for its completion, until 50 years later, puts it in good company with the Cathedral of St. John the Divine, Cram's humongous creation, still unfinished, more than a century after it was started with an architects' competition in 1889.

As we shall see, at Sewanee, Cram's dictates are not followed, so he essentially fires his own client. The underlying reality is that the work in Sewanee stops because of a financial crisis—University funds were lost with the Bank of Winchester failure in 1907—and when flush times return, Cram's successor firm still wants to finish the job. In the 1950s, the wonderful building is finished, but with another designer in charge.

The flip-side, of course, is that, despite its dreams of hiring fancy architects from far-off Boston, or New York City, Sewanee's architectural treasure may be at least 50 percent down-home talent, regionally based architects—often equally distinguished, from Birmingham, Atlanta, Jacksonville, and Nashville—working with competent local contractors, under stubborn on-campus managers. Sewanee may dream with its head in the clouds but it also builds with a down-to-bedrock reality.

SPECIFICATIONS FOR THE HODGSON LIBRARY

SEWANEE'S FIRST STONE BUILDING, HODGSON LIBRARY, was an elegant start for what turns into a 125-year tradition of architectural stonework; that's a long span for America, 125 years and still counting very much.

Unfortunately, for Sewanee lithophiles, this first building disappeared a century ago.

What we have left of it is a superb portrait, taken by Spencer Judd, with students, professors, librarians, and townspeople, artfully posed around it, as if for some high-fashion magazine (p. 32).

We also have some fascinating scraps of paper, squirreled away in the University Archives, that tell us about material costs, and most importantly, specifications for its construction. These handwritten pages are among the most valuable architectural artifacts in the University Archive.

We also have the building's footprint, because George Fairbanks drew it for the contractors interested in submitting proposals for excavating the building's basement. He asked that the work be completed by July 10, 1875. The excavation would be about four feet deep, on average, with trenches 30 inches wide to be sunk into the rock. The smaller of the two rooms would be 18 feet by 28 feet. The larger room would be 24 feet by 39 feet. Between the two foundations would be a six-foot-wide space leading to a back cellar stair up to ground level.

What follows is a virtual re-creation of Hodgson Library, minus its long-lost blueprints, built out of papier-mache specifications. **Nota bene**: Readers who have no patience for fine print can skip over these specs without hurting the author's or the architect's feelings:

Office of H. Hudson Holly, Architect

111 Broadway

New York, January 8, 1876

1. Specifications of the Masons Work and Materials required in Erecting and Finishing a Library Building to be built in Franklin Co. Tennessee for the University of the South agreeable to the drawings and specifications furnished by H. Hudson Holly, Architect.

2. DIMENSIONS. The plans, elevations and sections are to the scale indicated; but in every case where figures are shown, they are to be taken in preference to measurement by scale.

All figures are of the rough work, except door and window openings in stud walls, which are figured to joining side of stop bead.

3. DESCRIPTION OF THE WORKMANSHIP AND MATERIALS.

All the work throughout to be done in the best substantial and workmanlike manner, under the supervision and to the satisfaction of the Architect.

All furrings, centres, wooden lintles, girders and blocks to be furnished by the Carpenter. The blocks to be built in as required.

The entire building above basement will be finished.

4. EXCAVATION.

The Contractor is to do all necessary excavation for Basement, Areas, Cellar Steps, Foundations &c—the earth arising from same to be deposited near the building to be used for grading which will be done by the Owners.

5. MORTAR.

The mortar for masonry to be composed of the best quality lime and clean sharp sand mixed in proper proportions.

The mortar for Plastering to be the best quality lime—the finishing coat to be composed of the best quality white finishing lime, Plaster of Paris and White Sand or Marble dust.

The Cement to be of the 1st quality.

6. STONE WORK.

The Contractor is to furnish the stone and sand—the stone to be from approved quarry.

All the work colored blue on plans to be built of stone laid in mortar and carried up as shown.

All walls and piers to have large foundation stones where not resting on

Hodgson Library (Judd)

Rock or hard pan and in no case to be less than 3'6" below top of ground or area bottoms.

All walls to be built of stone with broken face laid in random courses or rubble work. Every stone to be laid over the joint underneath at least five inches.

That portion exposed to view to have joints perfectly horizontal and plumb and the joints to be tooled so as to fit square and close and all pointed with stone putty.

No discolored or imperfect stone to be used.

All stone to be laid on its natural bed.

Do all necessary cutting so that leader pipes and caps may set close to wall without scribing. Also cut grooves for all metal flashing where required.

Pointing will be done after the Carpenter work is finished and frosts are over.

The basement walls will be flush pointed on the inside.

To be foundations under cellar steps and outside platforms extending below frost and the area walls built as retaining walls battering on the outside 6" beyond 18" for every three feet in height.

7. BLUESTONE FLAGGING &c.

The sills to outside door and windows of basement to be of bluestone 4" thick.

Cellar steps to have bluestone treads 8" thick, the area coping 3½" to 4" thick—the chimney top to be capped with 4" bluestone.

The areas and steps made to suit the grade.

8. CUT STONE.

As shown by color on elevations to be of Freestone approved as to Quarry and light in color. All cut true with tooled faces.

This includes outside steps, copings, and platforms—the entire watertable around house, all sill lintles, and ornamental work above watertable.

The quoins to doors and windows on 1st story, the main cornices, frieze and neck mold and gables over the 2nd story windows including corbels.

The gutters to be made sufficiently large and have proper cant as shown by arrow on roof plans.

To be an iron strip ¼" x 1¼" mortised into stone and wood sill all as shown on detail Sheet No 14.

8. BRICK WORK.

The Chimney to be built of brick as shown and be of good quality hard burnt and no swelled or refuse brick to be used.

That portion above roof to be faced with first quality pressed brick laid in cement.

Turn Arch under hearth and over all openings.

Leave opening in large flue where shown on section and of the same area as flue—for the purpose of ventilation.

All flues to be close jointed. Fit up 7" earthen thimbles to all flues where stoves are required.

9. LATHING AND PLASTERING.

See Mortar Clause.

All the walls, ceilings, including that to underside of gallery, and furrings of every description throughout finished part of building to be lathed and then plastered. Two coats of well haired brown mortar and then hard finished.

The ceilings in basement to be lathed and then plastered one heavy coat of brown mortar.

The scratch coat to have 2½ bushels of goat hair properly whipped and soaked to one barrel of lime—the brown coat to have one bushel of cattle hair to one barrel of lime.

The hair not to be put in until the lime is thoroughly slacked.

The lath to be of good thickness and not over 12 lath on each heading.

The Reading Room and office will have a 5" x 10" cornice molded thus from molded arches over dormer windows as shown on section.

10. CONCRETE FLOORS.

The entire basement will have floors concreted in the best manner 3" deep of broken stone and cement with smooth and level surface—there to have sufficient slope to guide water to drain.

THE PROPRIETOR will furnish the furnace and appendages, marble mantels and hearths, grates, tiling, plumbing, bells, speaking tubes, gas pipes, and ornamental iron work; also, all grading, draining, wells, cesspools and cisterns.

THE MASON will furnish the fuel and stoves, to prevent the mortar from freezing; also, the mortar and brick for setting the mantels and grates, range and tiles.

THE CARPENTER will furnish temporary sashes, doors, &c. to protect the building from cold.

THE CONTRACTOR will tear away, patch and make good after the other trades, and render to the same all usual and necessary assistance, and have the whole premises clean and perfect, at the time mentioned in the Articles of Agreement, notwithstanding any omissions herein.

DETAIL DRAWINGS will be furnished by the Architect as the work progresses, and will in all cases supersede drawings of a smaller scale.

THE CONTRACTOR shall make no alterations from the drawings or specifications, without first consulting the Architect; but, should any error or inconsistency appear in these, during the progress of the work, it shall be the duty of the Contractor to duly notify the Architect, who will make proper adjustment.

Should the Contractor fail to have the work completed by the time mentioned in the Articles of Agreement, a forfeiture will be demanded by the Owner.

Henry Hudson Holly—one of those many 19th-century architects and artists ennobled with tripartite names—prepared another set of specifications detailing the carpentry, roofing, and plumbing to be done on the Library. Skipping the opening boiler plate of 1, 2, and 3, which is identical to that above, let us continue:

11. CARPENTRY.
All principal timbers to be of Pine. The Studs of Hemlock.
The joiners work to be close smooth and true and all work from the mill to be smoothed off before using.
The lumber for joiners work to be of the best clear well seasoned white Pine free from loose or black knots sap and shakes.
All the hardware to be subject to the approval of the Architect.
All the building to be warranted perfectly tight for one year.
The entire building above basement will be finished.
12. SIZE OF TIMBERS.
Floor beams 3 x 10 not exceeding 16 from centres.
Attic ceiling strips 2 x 6 " " 24 " "
Roof Rafters 2 x 8 " " 24 " "
Furring on outside walls 2 x 4 " " 16 " "
Studding 3 x 4 " " 16 " "
For size of truss timbers see detail sheet No. 13.
Plates 4 x 6 laid flat.
Floor trimmers and headers 4" thick.
Roof trimmers and headers 3" thick.
Hip Rafters 2" and depth equal to mitre.
Valley Rafters 3" and depth equal to mitre.
Ridge Pieces 2" and depth to suit the rafters.
It will be observed by referring to sections that the end slopes of roof run at steeper angles than side slopes.
13. FRAMING.
Floor beams resting on stone walls to be cut to a 3" bevel.
All that portion shown yellow on plans to be set with studding as before mentioned. The foot of which to extend to lower edge of floor beams wherever partition.
Main plates to be anchored to wall every 6 feet apart with good strong wrought iron anchors 4'6" long.
All rafters to be spiked to plate.

Frame four trusses as shown in details properly put together in the best manner as directed.

To be suitable wooden lintles over doors and windows back of stone lintles so as to trim square inside.

Build gallows frame over trusses for support of roof as shown in sections.

Fit up under gallery 5" turned posts with turned cap and base as shown in detail drawings.

14. BRIDGING.

All floors on 1st and 2nd stories to have two rows cross bridging 2 x 3 with two 10d nails at each end.

15. FURRING.

The contractor is to do all necessary furring and bracketing where required.

Provide all the necessary plugs to build into walls where furring is shown yellow on plans. Same to have furring strips 1 x 2" except those to outside walls which will be as before described.

All the above to be 16 from centres. The Contractor is to furnish all centres, blocks, girders, wooden lintles &c. where required and of suitable size.

Fit up rough grounds to all doors windows and wainscoting for the Mason to finish the plastering to.

16. ROOFS.

To be formed as shown on drawings and detail drawings and be covered with mill worked tongued and grooved pine plank.

Fit up Finials, Cresting, Dormers, &c. all as per detail drawings.

All the hips to have a 2¼ round on a ½" ground as directed.

17. TINNING.

Do all necessary flashing for chimney stack, Dormer windows, &c.—this to run at least 6" under slate.

The intersections of roofs with walls to have flashing work in with each course of slate.

All the above to be best quality charcoal tin lead plate.

The flashings on all brick work and stone work to be capped with zinc worked into the joints.

All gutters to have 2½" leaders to convey the water to ground.

The leaders will be fitted up with ornamental tops and be secured to building with ornamental iron straps as directed. The one nearest water closet will have leader run into tank.

The leaders will be made of galvanized iron except that portion above cap

which will be of lead and curve as directed.
The under saddle of roof cresting as per detail drawing.
Valleys to be lined with the best quality charcoal tin lead plate 14" wide.
All flashings and valleys to be thoroughly painted on both sides.
All the hips to be covered with No.10 Perfect Zinc and lap 2" on slate.
This to be made in order to fit smooth the wooden roll before described.

18. SLATING.

All roofs to be covered with the best quality Roofing slate dark in color and fastened with 1st quality tin nails of proper size, two in each slate.
Each slate to have a 3" lap, three thick at lap.
All broken and imperfect slate to be removed.
The roof boards to be covered with No. 16 waterproofing Manilla building paper before the slate is applied.
The whole when finished to be cleaned off and have one coat of saw oil and turpentine and warranted perfectly tight for one year.

19. FLOORS.

To be laid with 1 ¼" tongued grooved and mill worked Pine plank. Those to 1st and gallery floors to be not more than 5" wide. Those to covering room not over 9" wide. All to be blind nailed.
All the door saddles and hearth border to be of hard wood.
The floor joints to be thoroughly smoothed off after the plastering is done.

20. WINDOW FRAMES, SASHES, &c.

For number and size see drawings.
The upper sash to be arranged for stained glass and to swing inwards and be fastened with latches at top.
The lower sash to be hung with butts same as doors and fastened with 8" and 24" flush bolts and mortice latches with silver plated crank handles.
All sash to be 2" thick.
The two dormers will have 1½ double sliding sash hung on strong axle pullies with cotton slate-colored sash and have cast iron weights.
Basement windows will be made deeper than shown when the grade will admit not to exceed 3 feet above floors and have plank frames with ¼" swinging sash properly hinged and fastened.
All frames to be primed before setting.

21. GLASS.

All windows above basement will have lower sash glazed with 1st quality Double thick French sheet glass. Basement windows will have same single thick.

The windows above basement will have upper sash prepared for stained glass which will be furnished by the Owners.

Doors marked G will have figured glass to the satisfaction of the Architect.

22. DOORS.

All doors to swing as shown, panelled and molded on both sides as directed, and be hung with bolts of sufficient size to clear the trimmings and be of size as indicated by figures on the various floor plans.

Doors marked G on plans to be arranged for glass as directed.

23. BASEMENT DOORS.

External doors to be as shown 1¾" thick hung with 4 x 4 butts and fastened with 6" upright rim lock.

24. REMAINING DOORS.

The front and rear outside doors to be as shown 2" thick and fastened with 7" plain face mortise lock with bronzed face, knobs, and escutcheons and be hung with three butts.

The butts to be bronzed with Acorn tips steel bushed.

Other doors to be 1½" thick panelled same as outside door hung with two butts—these to be japanned with silver plated acorn tips and doors to be fastened with 5" mortise locks.

25. KNOBS, FURNITURE, &c.

The locks to be of approved quality and where not otherwise described to have brass faces and bolts with flat steel keys with white porcelain knobs and electroplated necks, bases, and escutcheons.

The Contractor is to provide all the necessary locks, fastenings, butts, knobs, furniture &c of every description throughout the building.

26. BASES.

All the walls to have a molded base as shown on detail drawings.

The walls to be protected from doors with walnut base knobs and elastic tips.

27. WAINSCOTING.

The reading room will have wainscot the height to be on line of window sill and made of matched and beaded boards.

The Library will be wainscoted where shown on sections. All as per detail drawings. All to have molded cap and base complete.

28. ARCHITRAVES, &c.

To be put up after the plastering is done.

Those to 1st story throughout and to windows in Library are to be 6" wide all as shown on detail drawings.

Library dormers will have backs made of narrow matched and beaded boards.

All outside plaster corners to have a ¾ wooden bead as directed.

29. STAIRS.

To be built as per drawings with ¾ risers and 1¼" treads.

Stairs to be enclosed and have doors where shown on plans.

30. LAVATORY.

The thin partition where shown will be made of matched and beaded boards and have capping on top. This to come within 3 feet of the ceiling.

Case up wash basin with door underneath and proper rack for towel as directed.

The water closet to be skirted 2 feet high above seat and be cased up with rising seat and lid complete and have proper paper box or drawer as directed.

Fit up water closet tank suspended to ceiling as required by the plumber. This to be about 2' deep.

31. VENTILATION.

Fit up all necessary ventilating flues where directed and as shown by green arrows on plans.

That shown in loft connecting Library ceiling with chimney to be of tin not less than 12" diameter. This to be covered with an iron grating with proper hole for the suspension of chandelier.

This flue to have proper damper over landing with cords attached for the purpose of working the same.

To be a tin pipe from water closet trap to leader pipe for the purpose of ventilation.

Fit up all ventilating registers of approved quality and size.

32. MISCELLANEOUS.

Fit up gallery cornice returning same across front of Library as per section.

Fit up balusters and hand rail to gallery.

All as shown on detail drawings.

Fit up Book shelves as shown on plans. Those on 1st floor to go from floor to ceiling and the one above to be 6" below truss and secured to tie beams with ⅜" iron rods.

All to have proper shelves as may be directed.

Fit up Cornice of wood around Library ceiling as shown.

All the above as per detail drawings.

33. PAINTING.

All the work that is usually painted both inside and out including all tin work, the fronts of all the shelves, stairs, &c. to have three good coats of white Lead and Linseed oil paint of such party colors as directed.

It's too bad the roll of plans seems not to have survived. Still, there are lots of moments when vivid details leap out from the technicalities. Best-quality workmanship is dictated in practically every sentence.

The Hodgson Memorial Library is given a benediction service on July 31, 1878, to celebrate its completion. Among the conventional words is this scriptural call and response:

V. The stone which the builders rejected
R. The same is become the Head of the corner.

One is tempted to see a small joke put into the otherwise conventional liturgy. Rev. Telfair Hodgson had offered to pay $10,000 for this new building, on two conditions, that he pick its location, and that he get a 99-year lease on 50 acres up between University Avenue and Morgan's Steep.

In a strongly worded letter of December 15, 1874, George Wesley Race urges his fellow trustees to reject Hodgson's offer by noting (1) that the new library would be too away from University Place buildings for the students to get books from it, and more importantly, (2) a 99-year lease on land so close to University Place would have "a value of at least $50,000."

Needless to say, the Board approves Hodgson's deal, deeding over a big chunk of land from University Avenue, what is now frontage on South Carolina Avenue, up past the Hodgson group of dormitories, and over to Morgan's Steep. Research on the subsequent history of that 50 acres would be fun to do.

Note, once again, the July 31, 1878, benediction date. This means that on July 31, 2003, a full 125-year tradition has arrived, like a gigantic certificate of deposit reaching its maturity date.

CROCKETS ET CETERA

SEWANEE'S MOST FAMOUS AND PHOTOGENIC LANDMARK, Breslin Tower, is High (very high) Victorian confection, rather like a tall stone birthday cake with knobby candles stuck out of its top.

The knobbiness on the tower's finials is caused by crockets, a decorative obsession of Gothic ecclesiastical buildings, going up all over Europe in the 12th to 15th centuries.

If you consult your dictionary, to sort things out, you will find the word *crocket* is derived from the French word for hook. It is obviously where we knitters get the word *crochet* too. If you use a pair of binoculars, to get your eyes close to the crockets on top of Breslin Tower, you will find that the leafy petal-like growth, so finely drawn in the dictionary's illustration, has melted away to a mere blobby knob of stone.

A neat set of crockets can be seen on the lovely white dormer window surrounds projecting from the roof of Breslin's architectural soulmate, Convocation Hall. Here, your architectural field kit should include a magnet, for it could be that these little dormer surrounds are of cast iron, though there is no way to reach that far without an enormous ladder, or without Spiderman's assistance. A reliable source says, however, they are not iron but wood.

Crockets make their debut on the stair tower finials of St. Luke's Hall. They continue to make their appearance on All Saints Chapel and Shapard Tower (1959), and on Guerry Hall (1961), the cleverly designed archaistic building set chummily up against the east end of Convocation Hall.

Crockets are also associated, etymologically speaking, with the word crotchety; that is, perhaps, a personality type that has hook-like projections, particularly as we get older and set in our ways.

What I'm getting to, in a periphrastic way, is to introduce the subject of playfulness in architecture.

Convocation Hall with gymnasts (Judd)

There is that kind of "form" which is supposed to "follow function" as the modernists decreed. There is also that form which is also just-for-fun.

In the 125-year evolution of Sewanee's architectural canon, the first "permanent buildings" (in George Fairbanks's insistent phrase) show a lot of deadpan seriousness. The two Henry Hudson Holly buildings, Hodgson Library and St. Luke's Hall, are very sober indeed.

We are not talking about chemical sobriety, though Fairbanks did manage to push through the Tennessee State Legislature a four-mile alcohol-sale exclusion zone—i.e., no saloons—to encourage student and community abstinence. One notable exception, praiseworthy or otherwise, the Ecce Quam Bonum faculty club continued to allow beer and wine on its premises. Behold, how good it is for brothers to dwell together in true fellowship; let's drink to that!

No, we are talking about a sober insistence on architectural orthodoxy, a dry academicism, not far in spirit from piety and cleanliness. It can be argued that the next four permanent buildings, while retaining this sobriety of form, show an interior playfulness.

Three wonderful photographs from the University Archives collection capture the new spirit:

■ One shows the interior of Convocation Hall's old east end being used as a gymnasium. Two young women in bloomers pose with a parallel bar. Behind them is a medicine ball and a set of rings suspended from the ceiling. We do not see them, unfortunately, work up a fine gymnastic frenzy.

There is a wonderful intimacy in this photo. Maybe it's the gym costumes contrasted with the hall's immense north-facing stained glass windows. Maybe these are poster girls for the new Muscular Christianity movement that is sweeping through civilization on both sides of the Atlantic at this moment.

■ The second photo, showing a student in his room, is apparently on the top floor in St. Luke's Hall. On the left half of the room, where the young man is curled up pretending to read something, there are sports paraphernalia (tennis rackets and flyers advertising baseball and football games). In the middle of the photo, behind his head, is a collection of oriental fans, and on the mantel is some rather fine-looking china. Both seem to be expressions of that late-Victorian estheticism reflected (albeit satirically) in Gilbert & Sullivan's operetta *The Mikado* (1885). Even the wallpaper, bedspread, and mantel shawl are of that excessive floridity evangelized by William Morris, James McNeill Whistler, and Walter Pater.

A top-floor room in St. Luke's (U. Archives)

■ The third photo (p. 44) shows a throng of young dandies, lolling about the entrance of Tremlett Hall, one of the old firetrap residence halls. Notice the two with giant sunflowers in their lapels. This is, of course, homage to Oscar Wilde, whose American lecture tour of 1882 was more than wildly successful for the High Priest of "Art for Art's Sake" (or as they would say, *ars gratia artis*, the motto of Metro Goldwyn Mayer). Gilbert & Sullivan, soon after this pop-culture efflorescence, satirized Wilde's followers in its wildly popular operetta *Patience* (1881). Richard D'Oyly Carte, producer of Gilbert & Sullivan musicals, actually proposed that Wilde do the tour and managed the bookings for him in about 200 U.S. venues.

Then, finally, there is the famous fin-de-siecle dinner party, on the roof of Breslin Tower, that somehow breaks many of the University's rules more or less at once:

> Breslin's best hour may have been at the turn of the century when a group of students known as the Anchovies staged a full-course, formal dinner on its top. All appeared in tuxedos, the moon was full, and service, including wines and cigars, was provided by a pulley and hoist from the ground a hundred feet below. A team of chefs and waiters insured that every plate was placed piping hot before the dozen cele-

Tremlett Hall gathering with two sunflowers (U. Archives)

brants. The esoteric repast was a natural consequence of a rule held inviolable by the club. Not one of its members was subject to error. Since there were no persons so nearly perfect as they, no new members were admitted, and when the last member graduated, the club disbanded forever. There has never been another formal dinner atop the tower (Arthur Ben Chitty, "Sewanee: Then and Now," *Tennessee Historical Quarterly,* XXXVIII, Winter, 1979, No. 4, pp. 12–13).

Thomas Nast cartoon from Harpers Bazaar, June 10, 1882

"WILDE ON *US*"

If there is ever a film, a period-piece evocation of the University of the South, around the time of its real coming of age at around 1899, it would be delightful to re-stage this scene, with all the Anchovies brandishing their sense of privilege, right up there among all the crockets.

GETTING CLOSER TO ST. LUKE'S

THE LINE DRAWING OF ST. LUKE'S MEMORIAL HALL appeared in the May 11, 1878 issue of *American Architect and Building News*. This indicates, if nothing else, that someone liked it —either the architect, or its client, or the trade magazine's editor—back in those days when self-promotional techniques were getting increasingly sophisticated. It also indicates some national exposure for the University of the South, whose institutional history, in terms of actual classroom experience, was barely 10 years old.

Study the essentials of this line drawing, because when you stand closer to the real building itself, you will be startled to know a whole lot has changed.

A Victorian view of St. Luke's Hall (Judd)

Back about 1957, St. Luke's was completely gutted inside and renovated, into four stories of classrooms and faculty offices. Happily, nearly all of the handsome exterior was left unmarred; less happily, the interior was carved up into rather soul-less utilitarian spaces that bear no resemblance to the building's original spirit.

The most notable change to the exterior is the fact that the four large tripartite windows, in the bays between the stair tow-

ers, have been replaced with double-decker sets of four much-smaller windows.

This was necessitated by taking the first floor, which had very high-ceilinged lecture halls, and splitting it horizontally into two low-ceilinged floors.

On the other hand, once the building "program" dictated the two-for-one split of this floor, it was done mighty well, with some handsome stone-cutting on the mullions (limestone) and spandrels (saw-slabbed sandstone) filling in around the smaller windows.

Up above, the two floors of dormitory suites were replaced by offices and classrooms; this meant a lot of plumbing, wainscoting, and fireplace hearths came out of the building; rather more sadly, it meant that the four corbeled brick chimney stacks came off the roof's ridgeline.

With the always-magnificent hindsight the present generation enjoys, looking back at the sins of a preceding generation, it does seem sad that we didn't retain this "mixed use" (lectures below, living above) spirit that is seen in all the "living over the shop" of today's New Urbanist and back-to-downtown loft developments. Happily, St. Luke's still has a few dormitory rooms on its top floor.

The single best interior space today, used as a seminar room, can be seen at the north end of the first floor. It is the old chapel, identified from the outside by its gothic-arched windows—one on the front (west), two on the side (north), and three on the chapel's altar end (east)—and inside by its barrel-vault ceiling. One can imagine how glorious it would be for the St. Luke's theologs—as the theology students are known—to celebrate a matins service with the rising sun streaming in through the diamond-pane windows.

In 1907, a new freestanding chapel was completed, about 100 feet south of St. Luke's Hall. This new chapel was paid for by Mrs. Telfair Hodgson and was capable of seating a much larger group of students and faculty. Though occasionally still used for services, since 1994 it has been renovated so as to provide a distinguished music and performing arts space seating about 110 people.

This former chapel is now used as a seminar room.

But let's continue our walk-around of St. Luke's Hall.

Notice that two gothic-arch windows have been blocked up immediately south of the altar triptych windows. The architect's decision to block up a window is always a risky one, inviting a damned-if-you-do and damned-if-you-don't quarrel from us sidewalk superintendents, though again it looks in hindsight like a mistake, like blocking up the windows on the second-floor tower stair landings.

Where the 1878 building meets what is obviously a later addition, there is a beautiful stone stack, about three feet square, rising from the basement all the way up over the roof, to serve the furnace when the building got central heating, perhaps around the turn of the century(?).

The lower floor of the back-wing addition is particularly infelicitous design. The windows, with their slashed horizontal schoolroom sash, bear no resemblance to any window in the original, while the slim cast-concrete cap makes its own rude gesture towards the original's more-ample limestone belt course. We learn a bit of what happened in *The Sewanee Alumni News* (August 1951), p. 9:

> St. Luke's seminary has a new addition which probably will be ready

for occupancy in the early fall. Designed by architect Hume Reeves, a theological student, the addition will house a bookstore, office for the dean, assembly room and social gathering place for 160. By means of the new addition, space will be released for the more efficient utilization of the seminary's facilities.

This flat-topped horizontal wing, one story-cum-basement, is Sewanee's first capitulation to the constant pressure to be contemporary. Fortunately, within a decade, an attempt is made to rectify the mistake. A subsequent floor added on top of the cast-concrete cap returns to dormer windows more contextually sympathetic to the original's fenestration.

An ornament on St. Luke's Hall doorway.

The best that can be said of this addition is that it does continue the stone-setting style of the original, which is a handsome "two against one" broken coursed ashlar. Up above the addition's cap, you may notice, the stone seems to be of a slightly different character. Much of the individual ashlar tends to be thinner, and correspondingly longer, resulting in ratios of up to 4:1, rather like the Crab Orchard stone that was wildly popular nationwide in the 1950s, quarried from the vicinity of Crossville, Tennessee. The ashlar up above also has a different face, with smaller bites particularly noticeable on the long thin blocks, the result of a lighter hammer technique than was used by the earlier masons, who seemed to favor a bold muscular cragginess in the face.

At least one other artifact is worth noting, when you walk around the back driveway, to reach the south flank of the addition. There is a steel fire stair, strapped to the exterior wall, that curves gracefully around the old projecting cornice. But imagine your panic, if you climbed out of that top-floor dormer window, to suddenly feel your legs dangling down into thin air, as you hang on for dear life, flailing your feet to reach the stair rungs, which hug the wall well set back from this curved handrail!

As we shall see, elsewhere, fires were a familiar fixture of Sewanee's history. So the fire stair was no joke.

Returning to the front of St. Luke's, it's important to note the old limestone sills on each of the stair tower entrances. They have been worn away, leaving a lovely sway, witness to many thousands of feet passing that way. Once you get inside, it is as if you've wiped your shoes on a mat, and left that history behind.

MONEY MATTERS

THIS LITTLE CHAPTER PROMISES TO DEAL with the unpleasant topic of money. If enough has been said, by its final sentence, the topic will not be brought up again. That's a promise.

The University of the South was still running a deficit in the early 1880s, as George Fairbanks's biographer reminds us, and that unhappy situation reflected itself in the tawdry look of the buildings. Fairbanks told the Board of Trustees that "there was a look of experiment and an advertisement of impecuniosity, and there was a lack of dignity" (Arthur Joseph Lynch, *George Rainsford Fairbanks: A Man of Many Facets* (1999), p. 149).

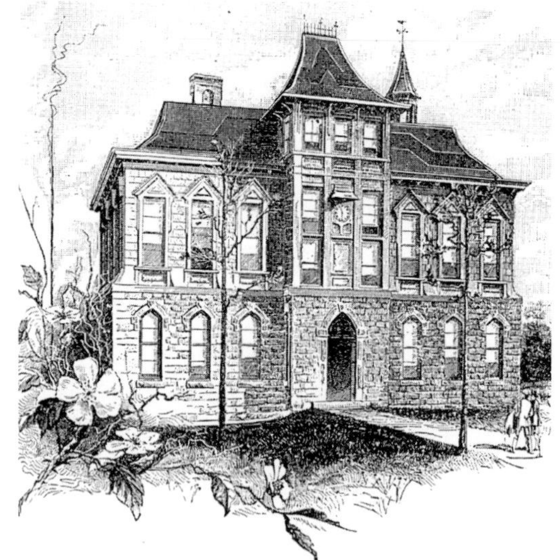

Chemical & Philosophical Hall (U. Archives)

Most of the Board would undoubtedly agree. After all, they were men of the world, widely traveled, and had seen what was the new look of architectural fashion, even if it was cunningly calculated to replicate classical antiquity.

At this point in the 1880s, there were two handsome permanent buildings completed, both by Henry Hudson Holly, a New York architect of great repute. Unfortunately, for whatever reason, the University refused to pay Holly what he was owed. In the proceedings of the Board of Trustees, for 1884, is this terse sentence: "The claim of Mr. H. H. Holly is again brought before us for $275" (p. 37).

This may or may not explain why the third permanent building, Chemical & Philosophical Hall (1883), has no named architect of record. Someone designed this rather unremarkable-looking building, because there is a ledger entry for May 19, 1883, saying "To Architects—Bill —$125." Perhaps with the unpaid sum owed to Holly, hanging in the air, no one (of re-

pute or otherwise) wanted to put their name on the new two-story scientific department building.

Telfair Hodgson's Plan for the Chapel by W. H. Wood (U. Archives)

On the other hand, when the fourth University building was on the drawing board, early in 1886, the architect of record was another distinguished easterner, William Halsey Wood (1855–1897). Wood did not live long enough to make the reputation of some of his peers, but his work was nationally respected, and ecclesiologically correct, something history-venerating Episcopalians prized highly. At the same time Wood was designing Convocation, his firm was one of four finalists in the design competition for the Cathedral of St. John the Divine in 1889 (Robert A. M. Stem, *New York 1880* p. 342). Closer to home, Wood did the original drawing for the Tennessee diocese's new St. Mary's Cathedral in Memphis. His death in 1897 led to other architects carrying St. Mary's to completion (John Henry Davis, *St. Mary's Cathedral 1858–1958*, [1958] pp. 92–94). Wood also did St. Paul's Church (1888) in Chattanooga.

Undoubtedly the prime mover of getting Wood involved was Telfair Hodgson, Vice Chancellor from 1879 to 1890, who also lived not far from Wood, in the newly fashionable part of New Jersey, part of each year.

Graphic evidence of this Wood & Hodgson duet is the fine pen-and-ink drawing, delineated by P. H. Ward in February 1886, showing what we know now as Convocation Hall and Breslin Tower; it is connected by a short cloister to what is clearly to be the University's new stone chapel. The lower left corner identifies the creator of this never-to-be contiguity as "William Halsey Wood, Architect: 764 Broad St: Newark N.J. / 226 5th Ave: New York N.Y."

Some comedy, of the Gilbert & Sullivan variety, enters at this point. There is a rival plan!

The chief exponent of this architectural fantasy is Silas McBee, an amateur architect who was principal of the Fairmount Academy in nearby Monteagle, Tennessee. He had joined the Board of Trustees about 1880, representing North Carolina, as a communicant from Lincolnton. His principal's aim, shared by others, was to create Fairmount as a church institution that might be "for girls what Sewanee was for young men" (www.duboseconf.com/history).

Anyway, McBee is a fascinating character, a man on the move. In 1890, he teams up with A. McC. Nixon, an Atlanta architect, and they draw a splendid Oxbridge-style quadrangle of buildings for Sewanee. Fairbanks, as the commissioner of buildings and lands, is caught in the middle of this controversial plan, as Arthur Lynch explains briefly (p. 157):

> The need for a comprehensive plan was brought to a head in January of 1890 when V. D. Walsh of New York gave a donation of $20,000 for a university building. Silas McBee, who was acting on behalf of the alumni association and board of trustees, and a Mr. Nixon of Atlanta proposed a plan that envisioned the Walsh building to be part of a quadrangle complex built in a Gothic style similar to that of Queen's College, Oxford. This was not what Fairbanks had seen as a comprehensive plan for sites and buildings.

If you look at the McBee-Nixon bird's eye view, preferably with a magnifying glass, you see that Walsh Memorial Hall has shoved the Telfair Hodgson chapel totally off the lot, and in fact, the 1890 plan remains virtually triumphant (minus a couple of spires and the front cloistering) as what got built here to this day!

Rev. Hodgson was so angry at the new academic building, Walsh, which he denounced as a "shoe factory," that he resigned as vice-chancellor.

Equally sweet honey for McBee, you need to know, in 1891, the Board of Trustees approved a resolution that "Silas McBee be engaged by the Board as a Commissioner of Endowment, for the term of three years, upon a guaranteed salary of $3,000" and in addition receive a 10 percent commission "on actual amount subscribed and collected in excess of $30,000

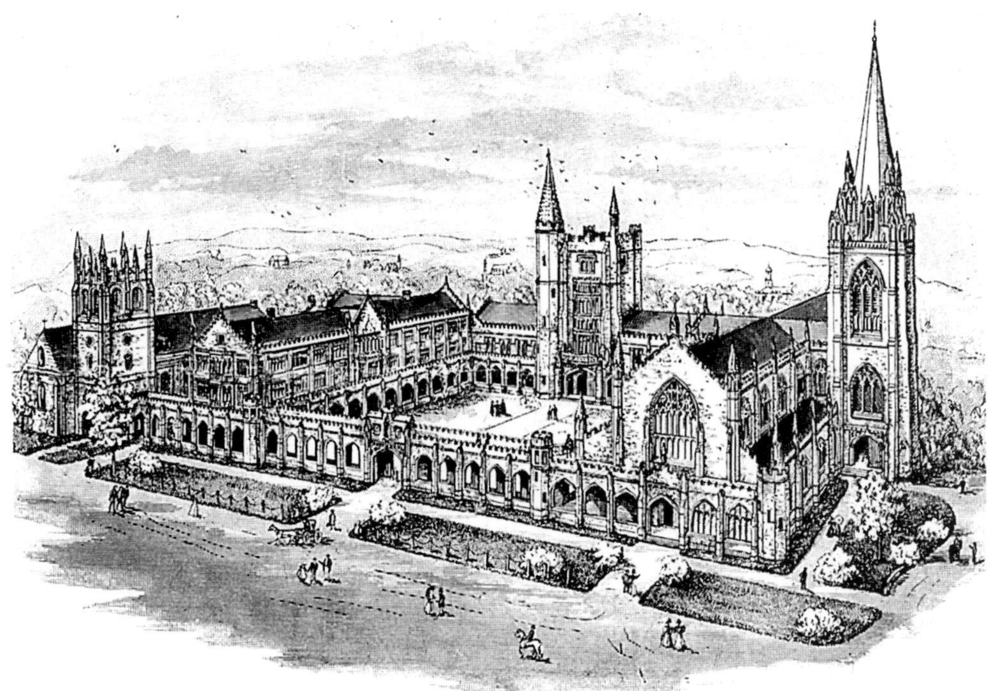

McBee & Nixon's plan (U. Archives)

per annum" (Trustee Proceedings, 1891, p. 54). In other words, once he had raised his $30,000 for the University, thereby earning his three grand, anything beyond that got him 10 percent more.

Now the sum of $3,000-plus does not sound like much, in these inflated days, until you pick up the ledger entries for the Chemical & Philosophical Hall expenses and see that about half of the workers on the payroll 1882–1884 received $1 per day. That, for nine-hour days, six days a week, may total out at about $300, annually, assuming there are no rain days, snow days, sickness, or layoff in the year to keep them off the job.

As to whether money matters, in Sewanee's history, of course it does. We need to go no farther than Arthur Ben Chitty's amiable essay, "Sewanee: Then and Now" (1979), to recall three instances, among many, of how critical money, or the lack of it, is to progress:

■ Some $500,000 is pledged to the new university, before the Civil War, and virtually none of those pledges can be called on after the war is over.

■ Charlotte Morris Manigault, living in exile in England, gives Bishop Quintard the money to build his new school of theology. "Mrs. Manigault not only paid the full cost of Saint Luke's Hall—$33,000—but gave substantial funds for the school's endowment and on her death left it her personal jewels, silver, and library" (Chitty, p. 8).

■ "In 1912 (Fulford Hall) passed into the hands of the new dean of the School of Theology, the Very Rev. Cleveland Keith Benedict, whose wife had been Olivia Procter of Cincinnati. Her (soapmaking family) fortune largely sustained the University through the very trying decade of the World War I years. She not only paved roads, installed water works, and built professorial homes but had enough to remodel and re-equip Fulford Hall" (p. 19).

One of my favorite acts of philanthropy, perhaps because it is the wellspring for one of my favorite campus buildings, is recorded on a brass plaque just over the door leading from Breslin Tower into Convocation Hall. It explains that this tower is erected in memory of Lucy, daughter of Thomas and Elizabeth Breslin, of Waterford, New York. Lucy's birth and death dates reveal her as eight years old. One can hear the clock bells chime for her every quarter hour.

More illustrious donors include Andrew Carnegie. His most famous quip is that "the man who dies rich dies disgraced," so he gave up his money into a charitable foundation that built hundreds of free public libraries and is still doing good today. In 1912, the Carnegie Foundation gave the Science Building that forms the bulk of the east side of the McBee-Nixon quadrangle.

There was also Mrs. duPont's family fortune that built Sewanee's fine little library, in 1965. Technically, it is said, Mrs. duPont's family fortune did not build the duPont Library, as she modestly and steadfastly refused to put her name on any gift. However, her anonymous gifts to Sewanee were so generous and so many that they put the University into a financial position to be able to to build the library with its own funds and name it after her.

Last but not least, in the honor roll of philanthropy, there is the Rockefeller family fortune, bankrolling the General Education Board, that helped with capital improvements for the University's previous library, housed inside Convocation Hall.

But the very best parable about why money matters involves the family of Jacob Thompson, whose generosity made possible the Chemical & Philosophical Hall.

As historiographer Chitty recalled—in a 1956 memoir based on discovering Thompson's memoirs in the archives at the University of Mississippi—when Thompson died, in 1883, there was a codicil in his will:

> I own $100,000 in the Bell Telephone Company stock, at Washington City. I request my wife to transfer this stock to the Trustees of the University of the South. . . . Should the stock not be valuable. . . . I request her to turn over to the University $10,000 (*Sewanee Alumni News*, Feb. 1956, p. 15).

The university officials, Chitty says, elected to take the $10,000, because they didn't believe in the future of that new technological creature, the telephone.

Here is Chitty's wry comment:

> Many realize that Sewanee is as great as Harvard but it is undeniably not as rich. This is why. It is the fate of some trustees—and boards thereof—to deviate from perfection. But when the Sewanee board of 1885 erred, it erred colossally.
>
> And if Jacob Thompson is not listed with such benefactors to education as John Harvard, John D. Rockefeller, Paul Tulane, and Leland Stanford, it is not his fault. He tried (SAN, p. 15).

That stock, valued at $100,000, less than a decade after the telephone's invention, would in succeeding decades have become a staggeringly large sum.

Money matters. Yes, indeed, money matters a whole lot. Particularly when good judgment goes with it.

SHALL WE GATHER AT THE GARTH?

CERTAINLY ONE OF THE BEST ARCHITECTURAL SPACES in Sewanee is not a building at all.

It's the cathedral-like close formed by the joinings of Convocation Hall's south side, the stone arcade and west wall of Guerry Auditorium, the north side of Walsh-Ellett Hall, the 1892 cloister and the 85-foot tall shaft of Breslin Tower, whose southeast corner makes a nip in the otherwise rectangular void known as the Guerry Garth.

There's a picture postcard prettiness about the Garth, but the real test of it as a *locus amoenus* ("place of delight") is how it performs when there are people present doing something of interest.

■ One sample, in the spring of 2002, comes with a student production of *Two Noble Kinsmen*, a rather obscure play said to be a collaboration of William Shakespeare (1564–1616) and John Fletcher (1579–1625), but probably the work of Fletcher alone. Anyway, the antiquity of the craggy sandstone walls, the surprisingly good acoustics, and the animation of young actors moving well together in the spring sunshine, make a big hit. Even the dogs, who wander freely among the audience lolling in the new-grass pit, seem to know their roles well. David Berry, directing in Tennessee after a year acting with the Globe Theatre in London, makes good use of the balcony, above the Guerry arcade, stretching the tiny stage so it is big enough for the great globe of Jacobean passions.

The "Atlas Pillar" on Walsh Hall

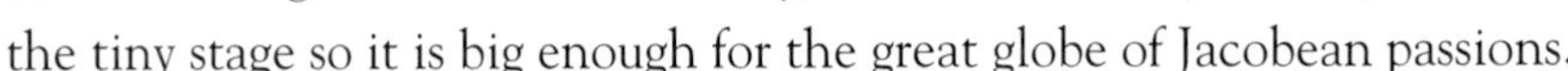

■ In mid-summer, 2002, the Garth becomes the venue for the Saturday afternoon chamber music recitals for about 200 students enrolled at the five-week Sewanee Summer Music Festival. Often the introductory voices of the performers, aged 12 to 18, are too soft for those of us in the very back to hear what is about to be played. But the ensembles project their

An early view of Convocation Hall and Breslin Tower (Judd)

strings, and woodwinds, and brass surprisingly well. It is not just that the young musicians are prodigiously good—they are—but that the Guerry Garth seems to enhance their work. So does the interplay of sun and shadows, from the buildings, the trees (pine, hemlock, walnut) and the flowering shrubs. Chairs are arranged to bear with the patterns of shade; this leaves irregular voids of grass, sunny spots for strolling between ensembles.

All in all, despite the executive crisis of 1890, when it is certain that the new neighbor will be that "shoe factory" (those words ascribed to the Rev. Dr. Hodgson), not the Vice-Chancellor's projected chapel, these buildings have achieved undoubtedly the best architectural (certainly the longest) marriage on campus.

Let's take a turn around this group of centennarians and see what we can see.

Let's take a stroll south under the 1892 arcade, donated by North Carolina trustee William A. Smith, glancing up at the wooden roof held up with a series of king-post beams.

At the southwest corner of Walsh-Ellett—currently administrative hierarchy on the first floor, and a mix of classrooms and faculty offices on the upper floors—there are several curiosities worth commentary.

One is a gigantic sandstone pillar; it is quietly doing the old Atlas-trick of holding up one corner of the building (see previous page).

There is no need to do that. It's just for fun, perhaps a test for the 1890 stone-carvers, remarkable nonetheless.

The other architectural curios are the two giant stone cylinders, containing a pair of spiral staircases, just wide enough for a single climber. That's why the cylinder on the left says UP on its threshold. The other threshold says OUT, rather than DOWN, which is the word reserved for the top. Woe to those climbers who cannot read.

My own theory is that this is a 1950s work-up of the Double Helix of

On a spring morning in 2003

genetic pioneers Watson & Crick. Supporting evidence is that the man behind these two architectural "follies," Dr. Edward McCrady, was himself a fine biologist before his Vice-Chancellor days (1951–1971).

These two staircases were added in the 1950s, and match up with two similar towers on the northwest corner of All Saints Chapel, because eventually (hope that never dies) there is supposed to be an arcade enclosing that would-be quadrangle too. Someone wisely decided, either for budgetary or esthetic reasons, not to complete that span. New blueprints were actually underway for this missing main arcade, as late as the mid-1980s, when unexpectedly the prospective donor died.

If you head east, after making the loop-the-loop climbs up and down, you will be under the arcade added to the building when funds for its modernization were donated by a wealthy Memphis eye-surgeon, Dr. Edward Ellett, who gave $250,000 to the renovating of the old Walsh Memorial Hall. If you glance up at the arcade roof here you will see reinforced concrete overhead.

At the southeast corner of Walsh-Ellett there is another surprise, probably another stone-setting experiment, Sewanee's one and only groin-vault constructed completely out of stone.

For about 70 years, this vaulted archway projected itself southeastwardly, like a great stone claw. It was also a favorite architectural frame for group photos, with six steps down to the ground on its north side, in the years before Guerry Hall was built there in 1961. One can imagine couples saying, saucily, meet me at the groin.

In the midpoint where all four archways meet, there is an acorn pendant (a "boss") of yellow sandstone, with the outline of oak leaves playfully carved on the acorn cap, and what looks like the remains of an old electric light fixture.

The boss, carved around 1890, remains Sewanee's most ambitious attempt at decorative carving in the local sandstone, a very difficult stone to work, not at all suited to such fine detail. Since sunlight never reaches it, it has suffered serious erosion from over a century of Jack Frost nibbling at it.

The missing light fixture, alas, was one of three finely wrought-iron lanterns, locally designed and crafted, that were heartlessly thrown away in the 1990s because their wiring was not "up to code."

Rub the yellow sandstone walls, on your right, and feel how soft the stone is here.

This groin vault, grabbing out since 1890 to connect itself with another building, was a kind of wish fulfillment, hoping that a new building would soon be erected there. The Cleveland Memorial Building did not attach itself until about 1964.

If you enter Cleveland through this door, as many University employees do most mornings a few minutes before 8 A.M., look immediately to your left and see (through the windowed and locked door) backstage at

Convocation Hall when it was the University Library (U. Archives)

Guerry Auditorium. Notice that the door opening has been tunneled through the immensely thick wall from the 1890s.

If you continue on north, with the backstage wall of Guerry Hall on your right, you will be in the Guerry Garth.

One of the many intriguing things about this ring around the Garth is that there is a great array of architectural circuitry programmed in here.

You can walk straight down the arcade, to the door at its end, and enter Guerry Hall's easternmost section.

Or you can step down into the Garth and walk back towards Breslin Tower.

For that matter, you can climb up any set of stairs, one floor, and step out onto the roof of the arcades, which themselves all have a multitude of decision-tree doors to choose.

Notice, if you're on top of the Walsh-Ellett arcade, built onto Walsh during the 1957 "evisceration" of the 1890 building that the new renovation allowed many of the classrooms to have doors opening directly onto this roofway.

Nowadays, most of these doors are locked, no doubt to accommodate the HVAC (heating ventilation air conditioning) bean counters dreaming of total energy efficiency rather than total freedom of random walk choices.

Let's say, for the sake of simplicity, you have not gone crazy testing the large numbers of alternate routes, but have simply rambled into the Garth.

To your south (Walsh-Ellett) are 12 bays of rectilinear windows. Each

bay is bounded by tall double-shouldered buttresses. The basement window cut-outs make a neat counterpoint to the crenellations on top of the wall. Like bass and alto. If it's a shoe factory, it's a damned fine one.

On your north (Convocation) is a handsome stone wall, pierced with round-topped windows.

There are two smaller round tops, on your left, and three larger round tops on your right.

The window grouping is interesting: the three big windows are divided as four parts, while the four (two visible and two virtual to match up with their four counterparts on the other wall of the hall) are in three parts.

More interesting, for detail pointers, is the fact that the west half of the wall is buttressed, while the east half is bayed with a row of billets (like short cylindrical logs) on top of the three bays.

Originally, back in 1886, this was a dual-purpose building. The gymnasium was in the east half and the ceremonial meeting hall was in the west half, with an open-woodwork dividing wall partitioning off the wildly divergent activities going on in both halves. So the architect ornamented his walls to reflect that divergence.

Note, also, while you're admiring the stonework, that all the vertical corners are "drafted" (sharpened with one-inch chisels) all the way up the buttresses and bay edges.

The Cavalier's marble bust or the "head between two heads"

If you look up at the top of Breslin, from the Garth, you can see an old iron pipe sticking out. This is probably not a gargoyle (downspout, literally a throat, like the word gargle) but something left over from when the old tower had a water tank inside it serving the campus buildings' plumbing system. When the tower was gutted, in the 1930s, that was one of the old elements that got heaved out. The four-faced clock was not implanted in the tower until about 1901.

Inside the Breslin Tower foyer, note that there is some fancy "two against one" stone-setting, in the wall behind which are small men's and women's restrooms. The outside walls, you may remember, are constructed of the simpler (and slightly cheaper) coursed ashlar. The brecciated marble bust of the periwigged cavalier speaks (probably in lisped French) for itself. This lovely *objet* is also known irreverently as "the head between two heads."

Adventurous souls may also wish to take the stone steps up into the tower, cunningly winding themselves up the walls, and may encounter a faculty member lucky enough to have his office quartered up there. Sewanee professor wannabes, like this author, undoubtedly covet one of these ivory-tower nooks above all.

Back in the tower lobby, enter Convocation Hall, if the door happens to be unlocked, as it (all too seldom) sometimes is. Unlike the old days of Sewanee, when you could enter this hall at most any times, to check out books on the Honor System, particularly the Fooshee Circulating Library novels and biographies, now somehow the place is kept locked tight 95 percent of the time, a damnable shame.

Anyway, if the door is unlocked, enter and steel yourself to be overwhelmed with the most beautiful hall on campus.

There's the dark wood, arrayed in beaded board panels, particularly the ceiling which has five-bead strips laid diagonally, nailed onto 3 x 4 purlins, which are mortised into 4 x 4 bigger purlins, which are mortised into enormous 12 x 12 beams, resting at each end on great stone corbels.

And there are the exquisite (running out of rave-words) stained glass windows, Tiffany-quality but done by the Geissler firm in New York City, depicting each of the dioceses that owned and controlled the University of the South at the time this magnificent hall was constructed.

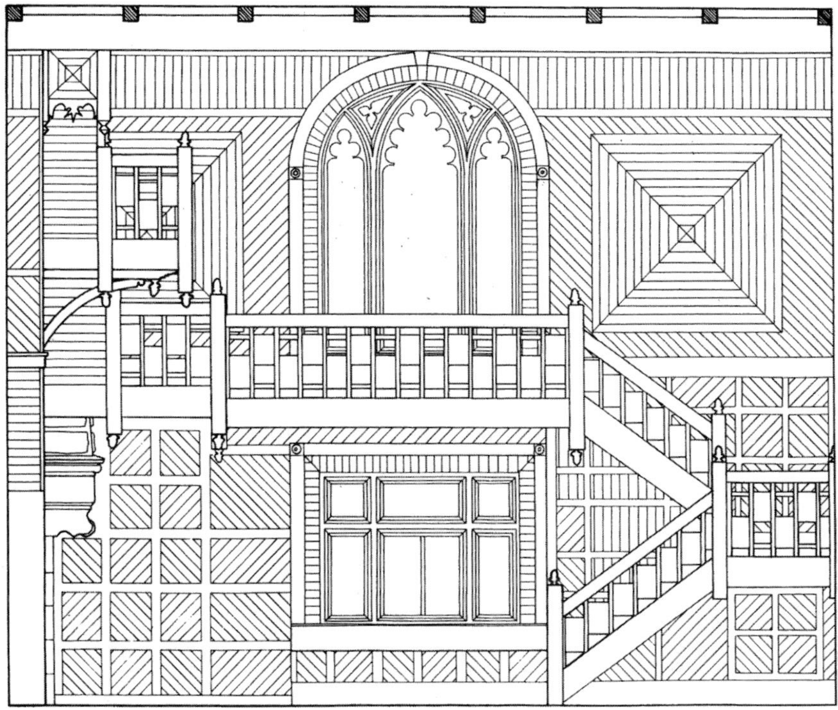

Convocation Hall's west wall as a 1987 measured drawing by Maggie Newlan (U. Archives)

And there are the two floor-to-ceiling stone fireplaces, one on the east wall, the other rather inexplicably stuck in the southwest corner, half-hidden behind the stairway, that wraps itself up under the west wall window (above), and then up to the access door into the Convocation Hall attic. Who knows what mysteries are up there, illuminated by the dormer windows, obscured by the dust of 115 years or so? Any of several campus ghosts, like the Headless Gownsman, may find this upper room just the best sort of lounging place, when off-duty.

(These two previous sentences are exploded, in November 2002, by getting a key to the door of Convocation's attic, which is entered by climbing up Breslin Tower's stairwell. Also discovered is the fact that the "access door" leads only into the north wall of the office of history professor Brown Patterson. The professor kindly notes that when Convocation was used as the University Library, this wonderful tower room served as the library director's office. As to the attic, that should be a chapter unto itself. The space is 30 feet tall, from floor to ridgeline, and its great wood trusses each have a wooden cross up in their apex! Regrettably, this fine interior space has been mucked about with, apparently to strengthen both its roof and its floor, and electrical conduit crawls around on its old wooden floor, higgledy-piggledy.)

There are also, in the great hall below, august oil portraits of the University founding fathers hanging on the dark wood walls.

The only really silly furnishings in the hall are the two faux suits of armor, still silly after perhaps being fabricated a century ago, the sort of venerable silliness that many Sewanee Old Boys still enjoy.

There is lots more to say about Convocation Hall, including the fact that on one occasion this past spring it was absolutely overcrowded, when too many University mountain community souls turned up for Wendell Berry's lecture, provoking a severe panic attack in claustrophobes like me. More typically, it serves for regular faculty meetings and as an amiable spot for other ceremonial occasions, like the annual meetings of Sewanee's 130-odd board of trustees, or the closing night reception for the Sewanee Summer Musical Festival students and their families.

At the very least, if you can't get inside this wonderful space any other way, you should sign up for a free campus tour. Your guide will get you inside and you will see all this Arabian Nights splendor for yourself.

THE RECYCLED HOTEL

THE MAY 13, 1898 EDITION OF THE NASHVILLE BANNER gave lavish coverage to the dedication of Hoffman Hall. This handsome five-story stone building marked a dramatic new era for the University of the South. Up until this point, the Sewanee undergraduates lived in rather ramshackle frame houses like Tremlett and Magnolia, or lived in small boarding houses scattered around town, or boarded with professors in their houses.

Hoffman Hall begins with a real oddity, the donation of a hotel that was dismantled, and shipped on board 82 railroad cars, from its North Alabama site to its recycled location in Sewanee.

> The gift took the form of a donation of a hotel at Bridgeport, which with its furnishings, had cost $90,000, and of $30,000 in cash. No sooner were the legal complications settled when workmen swarmed on the hotel like bees. Every portable thing was put on cars, even to the stone steps and the bricks. All was brought to Sewanee, and all has been used either in this building or in the five smaller structures that the indefatigable energy of the Vice-Chancellor has erected during the present year. It is almost the literal truth to say that there is little left unused today of the old Bridgeport Hotel that is bigger than a toothpick *(Nashville Banner)*.

The donor is Rev. Charles Frederick Hoffman, D.D., LL.D., D.C.L., of New York City. Don't let the string of degrees fool you into thinking he is an egghead. He is an enormously wealthy businessman, who subscribes to the late Victorian principles of the Christian socialists, and to the ideas of Andrew Carnegie's remarkable manifesto, "The Gospel of Wealth," published in *The North American Review* (June, 1889). This gospel says basically that the man who dies rich dies disgraced. In the next to last year of his life (1830–1897), Hoffman makes a trek to Sewanee and writes a travel

Hoffman Hall (U. Archives)

book entitled *A Ramble at Sewanee the Seat of the the University of the South*, privately printed in 1896.

At this point, it is good as usual to let Arthur Ben Chitty set the scene:

> In 1897 there died on Jekyll Island in Georgia a noble gentleman, the Rev. Dr. Charles Frederick Hoffman of New York. He had just visited Sewanee to preach the baccalaureate sermon and receive an honorary degree. He was so impressed that, before leaving, he told Vice-Chancellor Wiggins he would like to make a significant gift. Dr. Wiggins said the University needed a residence hall for junior students. Dr. Hoffman, on his deathbed, asked that such a gift be made from his estate. His son and other heirs were faithful to his wishes, and Hoffman Hall soon became a reality ... ("Sewanee: Then and Now," 1979, p. 13).

Jekyll Island is, of course, the home of the famous Millionaires Club, where the truly rich and famous of that day gathered to feel good about their blessings. The Jekyll Island Club was incorporated in 1886 in order to purchase the entire island and build a 60-room clubhouse hotel (www.jekyllclub.com). Incorporators included representatives of the Astor, Gould, Rockefeller, Morgan and Pulitzer families. Between 1888 and 1928 families built cottages, up to 8,000 square feet in size, as a winter hunting retreat, and undoubtedly as a marriage-game preserve, where socially eligible partners might be found in some abundance.

Hoffman's philanthropy was already well known. In 1893, for example, he was invited to give a sermon at Hobart College (Geneva, New York, another Episcopal-tradition college) on the occasion of the laying of the cornerstone for Hobart's new library, which was also being given by him. The sermon ended up being printed as a book entitled Christ, *The Patron of All True Education* (1893), with a copy given to Sewanee for its theological school library.

Here, again, is the Nashville account of the 1898 ceremonial moment:

> The Hoffman Memorial Hall represents a cash outlay of at least $50,000 if used with the utmost economy. Anyone who examines the interior is struck at once with the skillful use that is made of all available space, so that everything seems ample and yet no room is wasted.
>
> The plans were drawn by Mr. R. H. Hunt, of New York, who is recognized as one of the leading architects of this country, and who has been especially successful in designing some of the largest dormitories in the Eastern colleges.
>
> The contractors were Edgefield & Nashville Manufacturing Company, of Nashville, and this building is a monument to their careful and skillful construction (*Nashville Banner*, May 13, 1898).

The new dormitory was located across the street from where the Kirby-Smith Memorial is today, at what is now the intersection of Texas and University; at the turn of the century Hoffman was near what promised to be the center of a grand new campus. It was obviously a state-of-the-art building:

> The dormitory is of the beautiful Sewanee sandstone.
>
> The hall is 105 feet long, 50 feet wide, and, with its basement, five stories high.
>
> On three of the floors are eight suites of three rooms, each designed for two students. Another floor contains eight two-room suites designed for single occupants, to whom a higher rate is charged.
>
> Here, too, are rooms for the proctors who maintain order, and for the matrons who attend to the housekeeping.
>
> The dormitory thus affords accommodations for some 56 students, and such accommodations as are rare outside of the great and wealthy universities of the North.

Unfortunately, this building burned on April 7, 1919, so all we have of it is a photo of it, and the Nashville reporter's artful description of its essential features:

> The rooms are completely and handsomely furnished.
>
> There is hot and cold water on every floor, gas and electric lights in every room, steam heat and open grates in every study.
>
> The floors are double, and of hardwood, the trimmings also in hardwood, with natural finish. The roof is of slate.
>
> There are elevators for freight, and spacious stairways, with exterior ladders to provide against the remote contingency of fire.
>
> On the lower floors one finds that the inner court—that gave light and through drafts of air to sleeping rooms and closets—has been roofed with glass and affords a soft, diffused light to a large and handsomely furnished dining room and adjoining which are ample kitchens and sculleries, store-rooms and servants' hall.
>
> Here, too, are the engines, though the gas and electricity are manufactured elsewhere.
>
> There are also on this floor ample bathing arrangements, tub baths, shower baths, lavatories and dressing rooms, and the entire basement is so cemented that it would be possible to wash the whole with a hose as one would the deck of a ship.

Now the idea of recycling one building into another is certainly less strange than we might realize. Even 50 years ago, when we were embarking on the Age of Planned Obsolescence, Memphis entrepreneur Kemmons Wilson launched his first Holiday Inn, on Summer Avenue in Memphis, by furnishing its rooms with beds, chairs, and other items from a local hospital that was going out of business.

What makes the Bridgeport recycle interesting is that the hotel in question was known as the Hoffman House, built out of brick in 1891, close to the railroad station. As George Fairbanks reported to the Trustees, Hoffman's stone walls were lined with this brick (Trustees Proceedings, 1899, p. 95). Another detail, delicately omitted by the Nashville reporter, but explained by Fairbanks, was that the residence hall's urinals were in the basement.

Bridgeport itself was new, according to a historical write-up in the *Chattanooga Free Press* (October 18, 1981), written for the town's centennial year:

In 1880, Bridgeport Land & Improvement Company, with headquarters in New York, was formed.

It sought to industrialize this area and the period was a boom era populations expansion and full employment. Construction, both commercial and residential, was going full speed when the financial panic of 1893 forced the developers to withdraw.

New Hoffman Hall, built near the site of old Hoffman, which burned in 1919.

This was an era when Northern capitalists were busy exploiting the Southern states—mining and timbering, building railroads, port facilities, and heavy industries—and generally treating the region as if it was a Third World country. Charles Frederick Hoffman and his Jekyll Island kink undoubtedly viewed their efforts in the kindliest of lights. If Christ could be seen as the patron of all true education, He could surely also be seen as the patron of all true industrial development as well.

So new towns, company towns like Birmingham and Bridgeport, were springing up all over the South, bankrolled by large amounts of New York and Boston capital. Such efforts were encouraged by Southern politicians, who offered various inducements like tax abatements. Such inducements were not on the scale, let's say, of Alabama's half-billion-dollar package to lure the Mercedes manufacturing plant to Tuscaloosa, a decade ago, but were generous nonetheless.

Sewanee was one of the many beneficiaries of this new gospel of wealth.

FORT QUINTARD

THE SEGUE FROM HOFFMAN HALL (1898) to Quintard Hall (1901) is easy.

They were both designed by someone known as R. H. Hunt.

The clue, as usual, comes from George Fairbanks's always informative report to the Board of Trustees. Here is an entry for 1900:

> I submit, herewith, Exhibit "S", the plans, specifications, and contract for the building of the Quintard Memorial Hall, which is designed as a dormitory for the Grammar School students. The building is over 200 feet long by 40 deep, three stories and a basement. It will accommodate about 100 persons and will be our handsomest building. The architect is Mr. R. H. Hunt, of New York, and the contractors, the Edgefield & Nashville Manufacturing Company. The contract requires that the building shall be completed March 1, 1901, in time for the opening of the Lent term. The building, when completed, will cost about $50,000. The exercises for laying the corner-stone have been appointed for Saturday, the 28th inst., at five o'clock in the afternoon (p. 93).

Now it turns out that this is no ordinary architect, but Richard Howland Hunt (1862–1931), one of two architect sons of the hottest Gilded Age architect of all, Richard Morris Hunt (1827–1895). Both father and sons were trained at the Ecole des Beaux Arts, the Vatican of teaching architectural orthodoxy, and in fact Richard was born in Paris, a good place for the family to be during the American Civil War.

Richard Morris Hunt is best known for designing Biltmore (1895), a super-mansion in the mountains near Asheville, North Carolina; it has 250 rooms, sits on about 125,000 acres of forest, park, and gardens. Biltmore remains the quintessence of the Chateauesque style in America. Hunt's client was George Washington Vanderbilt.

Another work of Hunt's, one of many distinguished or at least famous works, was a mere 60-room wooden Tudor-style mansion for William K. Vanderbilt. Idle Hour, as it was called, was Vanderbilt's country estate, out on Long Island, in Suffolk County, on the banks of the Connetquot River. One of WKV's children, Consuelo, married the Duke of Marlborough. Idle Hour burned on April 12, 1899, when her brother, William Kissam Vanderbilt Jr., was on his honeymoon there with Virginia Fair.

Anyway, WKV senior decided to build another mansion in 1900, according to the architectural plans of Richard Howland Hunt.

RHH's plans were rather more grand than Dad's. The second mansion turned out to have 110 rooms and a final cost exceeding $9.5 million (www.dowling.edu/about/idlehour/history).

The only reason to rattle on at such length about the Vanderbilt edifice-complexes—the family did give small sums of their money to another notable Tennessee institution of higher learning—is to argue rather bluntly that Mr. R. H. Hunt had bigger fish to fry than Hoffman and Quintard.

After all, the budget for the two halls totaled a mere $100,000, a big sum for Sewanee, but a piffling amount compared to nearly $10 million for Idle Hour II. So one suspects that a correspondingly smaller scale of attentiveness might be devoted to the University projects. (Real architects are certain to pop up, at reading this, pointing out that smaller projects usually take MORE time, and trouble, almost inverse to the size of the commission. To paraphrase what Stanislavski, the great Russian theater director, once said about actors and roles, there are no small projects, only small fees.) Possible shortcuts would be (1) some off-the-shelf design for a building already completed, or (2) ripping off the design idea from another architect, or (3) something else.

So far, at least, research into Theory #1 has gone nowhere. By contrast, Theory #2 seems compelling.

Did the Virginia Military Institute's main building (1875) inspire Quintard's design?

Working by free association, we remember that Quintard is sometimes referred to as "a Bastille-like building" (Arthur Ben Chitty's phrase in "Sewanee: Then and Now," p. 13). The reference is mainly to Quintard's two best features, the twin towers with a battlement cresting, not seen until you come around to the old parade ground side of the building. They do bear a vague resemblance to the traditional iconography of the Bastille, long gone, always depicted as being a tall fortress with battlement cresting.

But the Bastille's two towers are always seen as sitting on its corners.

The next possibility is to think of some military institution like West Point. The campus of the U.S. Military Academy does have a parade ground, surrounded by buildings, but its essential collegiate gothic look dates from after 1904, when Ralph Adams Cram won the competition to give it a thoroughly new look.

We get much closer to the answer when we think closer to home, Virginia Military Institute, in Lexington.

If you go to their website (www.vmi.edu) and click on their archival campus views, you see some startlingly familiar images. The earliest is an 1857 lithograph. You see a square-ish building, with crenellated battlements, but in the middle, flanking the front entrance, are the two towers!

The next illustration, a grim photograph taken circa 1866, shows the building's shattered walls silhouetted in ruins. Such collateral damage would be inevitable: VMI's cadets and graduates, after all, did play major roles in the military campaigns of that war.

It is the next photo (p. 71) of VMI's main building, after being lovingly restored in 1875, that argues itself as the inspiration for R. H. Hunt's design for Quintard Hall.

With a quick sketch, taking the octagonal towers of VMI and rounding them off, in an ultra-swish Chateauesque style, good architects like Hunt & Hunt could knock out the design over lunchtime.

We may need to remember that Sewanee's founders originally had two divisions. The younger students went to the Junior Department, from 1868 on, a name soon changed to "Sewanee Grammar School," a preparatory school for the University.

The first headmaster of this school was Professor Robert Dabney, tellingly enough, from Virginia.

The military paradigm for the school arrived early. SGS students wore uniforms of "a grey sack coat" and "grey pants with black stripes."

The original Quintard Hall with SMA's cadet band (Judd)

Once the University and the School seemed secure about their distinct identities, there was a move to establish a separate campus, as a two-page typescript (of anonymous authorship) in the University Archives explains:

> In 1884, Dr. Hodgson, the Vice-Chancellor, proposed building a complete plant at Morgan's Steep, with accommodations for 80 students. These plans were never realized, but in 1892 the University bought the old wooden hotel building which occupied the site of the present Sewanee Inn (Elliott Hall). In August 18, 1908, the Board of Trustees changed the name of the grammar school to the Sewanee Military Academy in order more clearly to define its scholastic character and to emphasize the military feature of its organization. Also, a few years preceding this, the grammar school had occupied Quintard Hall completed in 1901.

As to the site for the new military school, which therefore dictated the site and parade-ground orientation of Quintard Hall, there is a typewritten note initialed by the University's first archivist, Sarah Hodgson Torian, explaining how the school campus began as a proposal to honor Bishop Polk with a park. Mrs. Torian quotes two brief items from Sewanee Life (Aug. 23, 1884):

■ Minutes of the Board of Trustees, University Papers, Ser. B, No. 35, p. 70: Resolved, that a committee of two bishops and two laymen be ap-

The north face of Quintard Hall as it looks today

pointed to select a portion of ground, at a suitable distance from our present college buildings for the purpose of its conversion into a park to be known by the name Polk Park (1884, p. 17).

■ Taking in Tomlinson Spring and the romantic glade leading to it, there will be almost unlimited opportunities for landscape gardening. Let all dwellers in the west end urge and help on the work. A little effort and aid from each will serve to secure a lasting pleasure to the neighborhood.

Among the actions of the board was a resolution to establish a park in honor of Bishop Polk. This move is one in the right direction. Parks and wide streets should be the first care of a new place.

Since no action grew out of these resolutions, and there is no sport or building in memory of our most illustrious founder Polk, I hereby petition that the parade grounds at the Academy be marked in his memory and hereafter known as Polk's Parade.

The next trick to getting the school a dormitory was finding someone to finance it. Here is Arthur Ben Chitty's charming anecdote about the genesis of Quintard Memorial Hall:

> When Bishop Quintard died in 1898, his son-in-law, Vice Chancellor Wiggins, called on the Bishop's brother George in New York. Would

> George give funds for a suitable memorial to the great Bishop at Sewanee. The answer was yes. But what form should the memorial take?
>
> For twenty years the Trustees had pondered the question of separating the boys in the Grammar School from the men in the college and seminary. Various solutions were suggested and some tried. Disciplinary and academic problems remained. Plans were drawn up for a Bastille-like building located in Polk Park, an undeveloped area a half mile from the chapel, in a place where the terrain permitted a full size parade ground.
>
> Although George Quintard is reported to have been less than pleased that his brother's memorial should be a prep school with military overtones, the practical needs of the institution won the day, and Quintard Hall, the largest building on the domain, rose in lonely splendor ("Sewanee: Then and Now," pp. 13–14).

The point, as Fairbanks reports to the Trustees in 1900 (p. 94), is that George Quintard had another idea entirely—that of building a chapel as a memorial to his brother, the late Bishop of Tennessee:

> Bishop Gailor had an interview with Mr. Quintard and urged him to build a Grammar School Dormitory, on the ground that Sewanee needed an endowment or additional source of income, and that such a dormitory would not only supply an educational need, but would also yield a large revenue to the University.

As a successful industrialist—head of the Quintard Iron Works in Brooklyn—George Quintard could easily see the dollars-and-sense point that Bishop Gailor was making.

Looking at Quintard Hall today, there are a couple of things that need to be explained.

What you see is a totally different building, fitted into the shell of the original hall that burned down on April 7, 1919, and was rebuilt a year later. The principal difference between the original exterior and its replacement comes on the roofline. A peaked roof gets replaced with a flattish roof.

One rather jarring problem outside is using the wrong color sandstone on the two front (Tennessee Avenue side) stairways. This mismatch dates from the extensive reworking of Quintard in the 1990s.

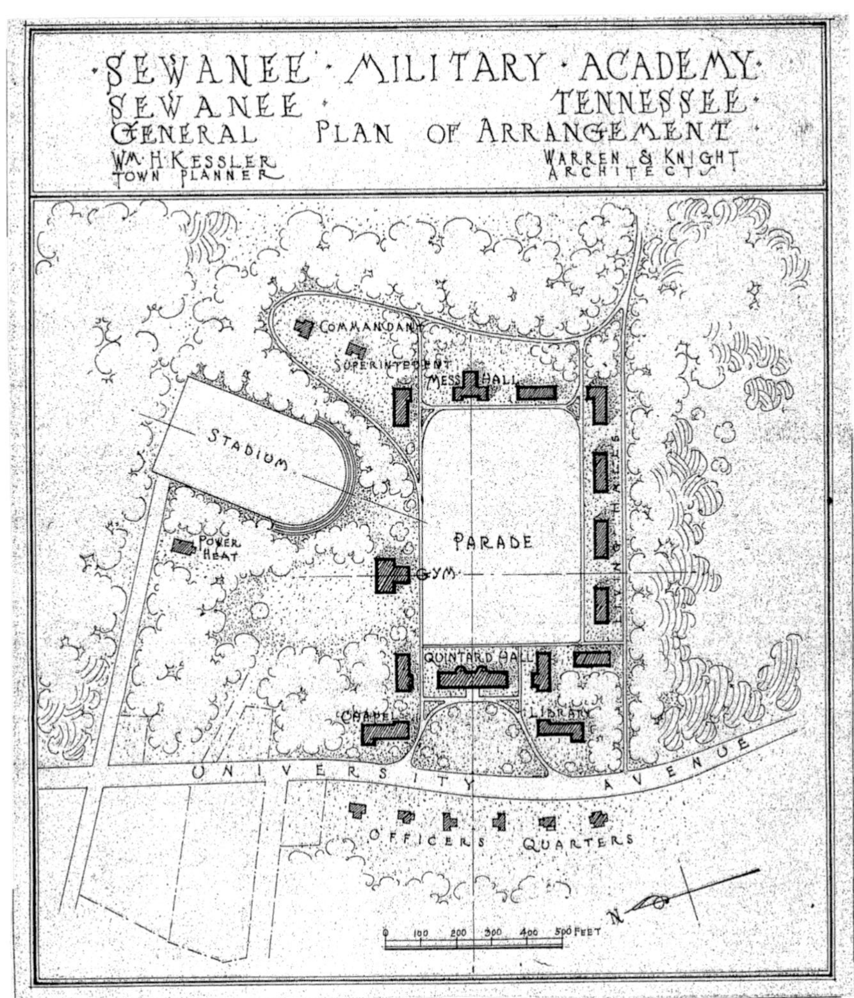

Site plan for SMA circa 1917 (U. Archives)

Perhaps self-obvious but worth stressing anyway, Quintard Hall was situated on the best ground of Polk Park, with a commanding view of everything that went on—military (then), athletic (now), or otherwise.

Its square-shouldered orientation in 1901 sets up the rest of the SMA campus, rather like the Wallace Stevens poem about placing the jar on a hilltop in Tennessee, which then imposes order on the wilderness around it.

A delightful surprise—for this researcher on July 16, 2002—is discovering a small blueprint site plan for the SMA campus (see above). Regrettably, it is undated, but from the two principals whose name appears responsible for this work, it would probably date from about 1915 or so, when Warren & Knight / Architects were just starting to do a lot of work for the University (as we will see in later chapters).

What is best about this blueprint is the presence of the name "Wm. H. Kessler / Town Planner."

Once again, as with the Hunts, we encounter the phenomenon of the son who follows his illustrious father:

> George Edward Kessler was born in Bad Frankenhausen, Germany, in 1862. His parents came to the United States where his father died in 1878. George's mother, Antonie, decided that George, with his creative interests, should be a landscape architect, and moved back to Europe, where George studied botany, forestry, landscape design, and civil engineering. He returned to the United States in 1892 to begin his career.... When Kessler died in 1923, he was nationally recognized as a landscape architect and city planner. His body of work included over 230 projects in 23 states and 100 cities. His portfolio included plans for cemeteries, communities, park and boulevard systems, estates and residences, fairgrounds, parks, and schools (www.georgekessler.org).

Kessler is best known as the chief landscape architect for the Louisiana Purchase Exhibition, also known as the St. Louis World's Fair of 1904, and the restoration of the site later as Forest Park. Others, like the author, know him as the man who created the Parkway system in Memphis, 1900–1901, connecting the city's much-loved Overton Park with a linear park through which a roadway ran, around the perimeter of the city, all the way to Riverside Park, on the Mississippi River bluffs. He and his firm also did an early campus plan for Vanderbilt University in 1905.

It is the view of the Kessler Society—their website provides the capsule biography above and includes a complete list of his projects—that George Kessler is virtually forgotten today. That may be partially true, though all city-lovers can point to their own favorite Kessler creations, even if they don't always know he did them.

Regrettably, his son's work is at this point not known, beyond the SMA site plan.

As to its details, they mostly speak for themselves, as not having been followed, like hundreds of other campus plans paid for and then permanently shelved.

Still, there is the eerie exception of the proposed location of a chapel; this is precisely where the University's school of theology will put its wonderful new Chapel of the Apostles!

ECCENTRIC SPACES

THE TITLE OF THIS CHAPTER IS STOLEN from Robert Harbison's *Eccentric Spaces* (1977), a wonderful and idiosyncratic book that explains the topographic relationships of art, literature, architecture, landscape gardening, and popular culture. Harbison's biography bears eerie parallels to mine—he was born in 1940, studied English at Amherst and Cornell (Ph.D. 1969), and lived in London from 1971 on, where he lectured at the Architectural Association—but the book suggests a mind brighter by several orders of magnitude.

Sewanee has a whole host of eccentric spaces. They are the outward and visible signs of an inward and spiritual idiosyncrasy. As some of the Old Boys of my generation used to say, in so many words, you don't have to be crazy to be up on the Mountain for four years, but it certainly helps.

Let's reel off just a few of its many institutional eccentricities:

■ Sewanee has quite possibly the biggest university campus in the world (10,000 acres more or less). It is known in simple feudal terms as the Domain.

■ Sewanee is the last university in the United States still owned and controlled by the Episcopal Church. Other institutions, like Kenyon College, have severed their church ties, in this increasingly secular world.

■ Sewanee celebrated its centennial in 1957, despite the fact that its first academic year didn't get underway until 1868, an act of rewriting history that seems to go utterly unexamined these days. (One commentator growls about this sentence: "Standard practice, old boy, standard practice! The year 1857 was the first meeting of the Board of Trustees. I don't know any school, even state schools, that count from the first day of classes. Look at the University of Georgia, one of several state universities that claim to be the 'oldest,' though its classes didn't start for years. Rhodes College, one of our archrivals, has a particularly bogus date.")

■ Sewanee operates itself as a company town, electing to give ground leases to faculty and others wishing to live in the community, even when it does not own the buildings that sit on these particular plots of ground. The all-powerful Lease Committee has the final word on all such leases, and leasehold improvements, though it passes on its recommendations to the Vice-Chancellor, who can by fiat override the decision if he chooses.

■ Sewanee's highest-ranking official is not its Chancellor, who elsewhere is top barking dog, but someone called the Vice-Chancellor. It takes newcomers (like me) many weeks to catch on to this nomenclatural oddity. Chancellors are nominal and ceremonial heads only, elected by the Board of Trustees, and are by definition a bishop from one of the (now 28) dioceses who own and control the University. The Vice-Chancellor runs every other show in town.

■ Most endearingly, perhaps, Sewanee professors still wear academic gowns when they teach, an archaic and anglophilic custom that has quite rightly been laughed off the stage nearly everywhere else.

Given such institutional eccentricities, it is not surprising that there should be topographical quirks too. Let's take a virtual ramble to visit some of my favorite places on this soi-disant Domain:

This lichen encrusted stone bench at University View is like an artifact of an ancient race.

■ First stop, in August 2002, is Manigault Park, a splendid greenspace with a shade canopy of towering oaks, tulip poplars, hemlocks, and white pines. At its south edge is a bronze plaque embedded in the ground, a few feet from the row of diagonally parked Faculty and Staff (designated by purple striping on the pavement) vehicles on Georgia Avenue. The plaque reads: "The Society of Sewanee Scholars / donates this tree in honor of Professor Thomas Spacarelli / April 11, 2000." The tree is a 12-foot-tall oak, absolutely stone-dead, what some of us phud-bearing types see as a fitting tribute to much of what passes for scholarship these days.

■ The Texas Avenue entrance to Abbo's Alley—the wonderful ravine garden which everyone should ramble through at all seasons of the year—is a set of iron gates attached to two tall stone portals. The only problem,

Abbo's Alley north entrance

each gate is only 4 feet 6 inches, so the pair total 9 feet, while the span between the two portals is 14 feet. The effect is rather like the narrow shutters hung on either side of a 1950s picture window. The finials for the two stone portals are cast iron burial urns. This rather-sad memorial (no names please) was added to the campus as recently as 1996.

■ One of the best bluff-edge vistas is Morgan's Steep. Assuming you drive there, along a road of that same name, there are a couple of spots to park your vehicle. Then you descend a flight of stone and cement steps, roughly the thickness of the Warren Point Sandstone bed there, down to an apse-like bluff shelter. There, of course, you can easily leap back about 10,000 years and imagine your hunter-gatherer friends and family camped out in that beautiful spot.

If you go north along the bluff-trail here, you can see the first of a series of sandstone quarries, where perhaps 10 to 15 feet of the old slab was quarried, 1876–1900, for the University's first stone buildings, including Hodgson Memorial Library, which occupied the spot where Hodgson Hall is now, about two blocks north of the bluff-edge.

■ There's a flagstone-paved courtyard within the north half of Woods Laboratories. This amiable space, wrapped on all four sides by a three-story building, has as its central feature a circular lily pond. The one and only person seen using this space, in nine months of random observations, was a young woman playing the violin, during the Sewanee Summer Music Festival. Signs taped in Woods Lab stairwells asked musicians not to practice there, because the sound carried up and down that space. So the violinist found a spot, without any restrictions imposed, that could reach far more unwilling ears than in any stairwell!

■ On that portion of the athletic field, just west of the football grandstands, are several indications on the ground where, in bygone days, events like the discus, shotput, and hammer-throw might have been held during spring track meets. During its annual Fourth of July orgy of events, this mostly-grassy spot gets utilized by the Dog & Mutt Show, a must-see fantasia for doglovers of all ages, and the Cat Show, more subdued, naturally, but also great for us pop-anthropologists.

The annual celebration actually begins with a pops concert on July 3, free, in Guerry Auditorium, but the emotional start of Independence Day is the 8 A.M. flag-raising ceremony at the Juhan Memorial Bridge (where the flagpole is naturally); it comes complete with old-timey wind band, Boy Scout color guards, prayer by the University chaplain, and of course singing those tear-wringing anthems like "America, the Beautiful."

The emotional fireworks of the day trails off into the night with a street dance, outside the Sewanee Market convenience store, on the east side of U.S. 41A, which is eerily devoid of all vehicles. The gathering is absolutely inter-generational, some people dancing to a very loud rock band, but most everyone else simply standing around, voyeur-like, waiting for something truly exciting to cap off their holiday.

■ A much better spot, for voyeur-types like me, is on the front porch of Shenanigans, with a mug of yummy brown ale. This modestly priced restaurant (sandwiches, quiche, lasagna, etc.) has been operating successfully for a good many years, where University Avenue intersects with 41A, in an old dry goods store that looks very much as if it will collapse any minute, like the House of Usher.

Shenanigans seems to be an exception to the come-and-go retail sector of Sewanee's "downtown," which has no supermarket (Piggly Wiggly is six miles away in Monteagle) and few other essentials generally assumed to be part of any small college town. It does have a health food store, a hairdresser salon, a bank, a gas station, two real estate brokerages, a law office, a coffee house, and a couple of nifty-gifty shops, but commercial prospects for a place with about 2,800 year-round residents, and about 1,300 students, seem perennially a bit shaky.

My theory about Sewanee's eccentricity, as a cultural landscape, is based on wildly inadequate samples.

Part of the explanation is that it is located on a mountaintop in Middle Tennessee, rather than in a much tonier locale like Cambridge, Massachusetts, or Palo Alto, California.

But part of the explanation, and big enough to merit this idiosyncratic chapter, is that Sewanee's built environment is laden with informality, particularly its campus buildings, which are a unique blend of Oxbridge anglophilia tempered by down-home and rock-solid Tennessee mountain culture.

All you have to do to test this gross generalization is to compare mental snapshots of this campus with that of its small-college archrival, Rhodes College, which underwent a surgical name-change from Southwestern at Memphis, about 15 years ago. The campus architecture at Rhodes is absolutely by-the-book Collegiate Gothic, no exceptions, none, no other way acceptable. The result is a buttoned-up absolutely too pretty to believe, rather like its Ivy League first-cousin Princeton, except that Rhodes has a tall iron perimeter fence that shouts to its Memphis neighbors: KEEP OUT! THIS MEANS YOU!

Architecturally, that fence says volumes, the college-as-gated-community.

Sewanee has only those two sets of stone portals, at opposite ends of U.S.41A highway, that announce you are now entering the Domain of the University of the South. No gatekeepers or guardhouse like Rhodes. Maybe that's why the two gates at Abbo's Alley have a five-foot gap between them.

Other than that, Sewanee is a virtually gate-free community. To that happy fact I take off my old floppy hat.

THE GREAT ARCH CONSPIRACY

SOME TIME AROUND 1900, AND LASTING UNTIL about 1920, there is the sudden and remarkable appearance of great arches in Sewanee's new buildings.

No conspiracy is involved, of course, only the conspiracy of fashion, which makes a certain look "hot" for a while, and then warmed-over, leading to the next new look.

In architectural terms, the latest Romanesque Revival look may hark back, like a pack of hounds that is picking up a lost scent, to some long bygone days, say the eighth century.

There is also the distinct possibility that Sewanee's sudden appetite for great round-top arches is a reflection of national icons like H. H. Richardson's Marshall Field Wholesale Store (1885–1887) or Louis Sullivan's Chicago Auditorium (1887–1889).

The great panjandrum of architectural historians, his royal highness Henry-Russell Hitchcock, calls them "cavernous entrance arches" (*The Pelican History of Art: Architecture: Nineteenth and Twentieth Centuries*, 1977, p. 314).

The University Press Building was vacant for some years before being reclaimed for Physical Plant Services' administration staff. (U. Archives)

We see two such notable examples on the Sewanee campus in the University Press Building (1904) and the Kappa Alpha House (1916).

What now houses operational headquarters for Physical Plant Services, on Alabama Avenue where it intersects with St. Augustine, was originally built to house the University of the South Press. Anyone in the copy-editing, typesetting, galley-proof reading, and printing business knows the necessity for good lighting, which may explain the larger than necessary entrance porch arches, as well as the array of large box-top windows all around the rather modest-sized square building. (You won't find "box top" in any architectural dictionary; it's just my jokey way of contrasting lintel-topped windows with "round top" windows.) Or the porch arches may be a simple but able expression of architectural fashion.

The Kappa Alpha House (p. 24), on University Avenue's north end (near Emerald-Hodgson Hospital) has an even showier stone entrance arch, fashionably battered (flared out) at its bases, though the weight of the front porch's two side openings is borne by gigantic stone lintels, also executed in bravura-style stone masonry.

On a more modest scale, but one of the handsomest buildings on campus, there is the University Supply Store (1904). It has nothing but round top windows—on its front, on its back, and on both its sides. Sorry, when you peek around back, rarely seen because it's below grade, the basement has box-top windows.

There is so much round-topping here, in fact, that what we see is an "arcaded masonry facade," in HRH's regal words; that is, a series of arches forming a wall, which is precisely what Richardson's Field Company masterpiece in Chicago does.

Richardson used great coursed ashlar blocks of rock-faced red Missouri granite, while the University Supply store used great coursed ashlar blocks of rock-faced Tennessee sandstone.

The buildings are equally amiable. With appalling criminality, however, Chicago tore down the Field building for a parking garage, 50 years ago. Sewanee committed only what might be architectural misdemeanors, some years ago, when it covered up the back windows of what is now the University Bookstore. Partial mitigation of this misdeed comes from the fact that you can still see these round tops outside on the back wall.

Also, mysteriously, there appears to be an original entrance, on the north wall, that has been blocked up, albeit quite well with matching sandstone ashlar. Research to date has failed to turn up any photos showing this was another entrance.

Unfortunately, the original plans for the University Supply Store have not survived, nor has (so far) any architect of record turned up. Blasphemous as it may sound, to the American Institute of Architects, this gem of a building could well have been built without any architect at all!

There are a few other notations to be made about this 1904 building.

It occupies a highly visible "front door" status for the University of the

University Supply Store with "Crow's Nest" pavilion on right (U. Archives)

South. It is often the very first University building visitors set foot in, to get directions, and perhaps to pick up a campus map. Regardless of its other functions—selling trade books, text books (in the basement), backpacks, sweatshirts, school supplies, and so on—the University Supply Store serves de-facto as an information kiosk, a welcome center, and ought to be treated with greater respect (such as unblocking the back windows on the upper and basement floors).

It's a handsome building at the roofline as well. Notice the exposed rafter tails, right under the slightly flared-up eaves, a popular roof profile in the Craftsman period, where such structural elements are made visible, rather than covered up, as architectural fashion dictated before and after this period.

Archival photos show that up through the 1950s the Supply Store functioned as a grocery store, drug store, soda fountain, and so on, what we would today call a "convenience store" and more. At the south end of the main building, where sweatshirts etc. are sold, notice the pyramidal shaped

Hodgson Memorial Infirmary in the 1920s (U. Archives)

ceiling. This was the old Crow's Nest, an open-air pavilion serving the soda fountain crowd of undergraduates and their (once in a blue moon) party-weekend dates.

What is now the lower addition, or annex, of the Supply Store, plus the Quid Nunc Cafe next door, dates from the late 1960s, when it was announced, in the *Sewanee Alumni News* (August 1967, p. 6) that there would be a new "pub and sidewalk cafe" added to the south end of the store. The handsome rendering, by architect Dan McGown Sr. (C'30), seems not to have been followed; a less-imaginative add-on was built instead. In recent years, a small deck was built on the Quid Nunc's south wall. The deck, overlooking the Elliott Park playground area, makes a pleasant place to eat and schmooze, about nine months of the year.

Maybe in years to come the "pub and sidewalk cafe" idea could be revived, particularly if the old Speakeasy Era notion of closeting beer-drinkers in dark enclosed spaces—like the grubby little pub in the basement of Bishops Common—is banished from campus facilities-planning mindsets.

Another major archy-textural artifact of this period is on the Hodgson Memorial Infirmary (1899). Its handsome triple arched entrance fronts on a deep-shady porch for convalescents. Above it, in the 1920s archival photo, behind a long ribbon of windows, is what looks like a sun-room, for patients and visitors. These two patient-friendly spaces make a strong contrast to the otherwise sober box-top-windowed wings.

Notice, of course, that the three arches are not round tops but more like the Tudor arches, slightly squashed at their 10 o'clock and 2 o'clock positions, a perennial favorite of Sewanee stone masons and those University officials who are nominally in charge of their construction.

Behind the infirmary, and bearing on its parapet its own identifying name tag, is the Emery Addition (1916). Here again is the cavernous entrance arch; this time it overpowers the rather nondescript building behind it.

If this was the nurses' residence—until they were moved west to the rock-and-brick residence called Phillips Hall in the 1950s—perhaps the rather intimidating and well-lighted porch served to remind its young women that at this point they would have to take their leave of their gentlemen friends and retire for the night.

Emery is one of those many buildings that cry out for solid anthropological documention to confirm what seems implied in its architectural expression. As my two aunts used to remember—they were both registered nurses trained in the starched-white uniform days of the 1940s—their personal lives were expected to be as straight as the seams on their white stockings. Emery's four-square vestibule seems to demand vestal virgins inside.

One more 1916 building and then we're done with arches.

This is the building originally built for Oscar N. Torian, on South Carolina immediately west of the Union Theatre. It may well be the handsomest residence in a town rather replete with handsome houses.

The Torian House on South Carolina Avenue

University Cemetery's west entrance

There is a lot to be said about this one—perhaps in a later chapter called "Three or Four Professors' Houses"—but what is immediately striking, for our purposes here, is its ample stone-arch entrance. The intrados (inner-arch) stones are smooth-dressed, offering a strong contrast to the extrados (outer-arch) stones, which are of the same rough face as the rest of the random rubble (12" thick) walls. For an understated house, chock full of dignity and reserve, the entrance makes a rather dramatic opening statement.

It should be explained, for those who like to know such things, that Mrs. Torian enjoyed a triple-threat celebrity status. She was the University's first and fabled archivist, given the vital role of determining what gets remembered and what gets consigned to oblivion, an awesome power to wield or withhold; she was the wife of the Hodgson Infirmary's immensely popular pediatrician, Dr. Torian; and she was the daughter of Rev. Telfair Hodgson, whose house was (and still is) immediately to the south, the lovely old carpenter gothic residence just north of the Vice-Chancellor's house (Chen Hall). The Torians' house sat on the equally fabled 50-acres, already written about above, that Hodgson obtained for 99 years in exchange for bankrolling the Hodgson Memorial Library in 1876.

Oops, one more stone gem, the winsome arched west entrance to the University Cemetery, also dated 1916, according to a memorial stone underneath the ivy.

So there you have it, the great arch conspiracy, knocked into a cocked hat.

Readers are asked to forgive the author's occasional silliness. The problem, if that is what it is, is that I have an immense fondness for this odd collection of stone buildings. Writing about them cheers me up immeasurably.

I might have almost as much fun writing about them if I loathed them. But the fact is that the more I get to know them, the more amiable they become, and the giddier my prose can sometimes be. So help me HRH.

ECCLESIOLOGY'S LAST STAND

It may not increase your appreciation of the myriad architectural virtues of St. Luke's Chapel (1907) to know that it is absolutely, certifiably, ecclesiologically correct. But you may really, really, really want to know the theological subtleties of terribly earnest Victorians as to what a perfectly acceptable ecclesiastical building ought to be.

For this delicate metaphysical issue, let's defer to HRH, Henry-Russell Hitchcock (b. 1903 and presumed dead by now), to fill in the background of what was called with an utterly straight-face the Ecclesiological Society.

The movement seems to start with a book by a British architect named A. W. N. Pugin (1812–1852) called *Contrasts* (1836). Pugin, and his father, also an architect, rather fancied castellated buildings. The contrast at issue is between the "Romantic Classicism" of the Greco-Roman tradition of building style, which had been dominant through England and most of the rest of 18th-century Europe, and the "Picturesque" viewpoint that touted such exotic styles as the Gothic, Egyptian, Moorish, and other architectural exuberance existing outside the pale of the Roman Empire. Here is HRH's take:

> Pugin's Contrasts marks a turning point even more than does the acceptance of (Sir Charles) Barry's Gothic design for the Houses of Parliament (1840–1865). Newly converted to Catholicism, Pugin believed the building of Gothic churches to be a religious necessity. His programme of Gothic Revival was far more stringent than any existing programme of Greek Revival, or a fortiori, of Renaissance Revival.
>
> If the Gothic were really to be revived, Pugin saw that its basic principles must be understood and accepted.
>
> Merely to copy Gothic forms was as futile, and to him as immoral, as merely to copy Grecian or cinquecento ones. The methods of building of the Middle Ages must be revived; architecture must again derive its character, in what he considered to have been the true medieval way,

Magdalen Tower, *Oxford, England*

from the direct expression of structure; and at the same time it must serve the complicated ritual-functional needs of revived medieval church practices (*Hitchcock's 19th and 20th Century Architecture*, 1977, p. 148).

Thus, in 1839, was formed the Ecclesiological Society, at Cambridge University. Etymologically, this coinage meant the science of churches, particularly the building, furnishing, and ornamenting of churches in a true and accurate way. With historical inevitability, and perhaps a sense of pious infallibility, this group started in 1841 to publish a journal called *The Ecclesiologist*. Ditto, in 1848, the New York Ecclesiological Society was formed, and soon began to publish *The New York Ecclesiologist*, which happily or otherwise happened to be the first periodical in America to devote itself exclusively to architecture and design issues.

Early leaders in this movement—all English-born architects—were Richard Upjohn, Frank Wills, and Henry Dudley. They imposed their principles rather firmly on American church design. Upjohn designed the immensely influential Trinity Church (1844–1846), a short walk from Wall Street, literally and figuratively, while Henry Dudley designed a whole host of churches across America, including The Church of the Holy Trinity (1852) and The Church of the Holy Advent (1856), both in Nashville, in partnership with Frank Wills, and the Church of the Nativity (1859), in Huntsville, Alabama.

The ecclesiologists's influence percolated through American circles—architectural, social, religious, and financial—for the remainder of the century. Individually, and collectively, such architects as were certifiably "ecclesiologically correct," to use a term not then in vogue, tended to get the commissions in wealthy urban parishes, particularly of the Episcopalian flavor, but also in the social-rival camps of Presbyterians and upwardly-mobile Methodists.

It should come as no surprise that all of Sewanee's early architects-of-choice were certifiably EC.

Silas McBee went on from his $3,000 a year post, as Sewanee's Commissioner of Endowment, to running *The New York Churchman*, after his smashing success promoting the Oxbridge quadrangle plan for the University of the South to implement in 1890 and beyond.

Just about the time that the EC-movement seemed to be running its course, Sewanee approved a new chapel for its school of theology, St. Luke's, as a memorial to Rev. Telfair Hodgson, with his widow standing good for the cost of its completion.

Very likely she and her family gave the nod to Charles Coolidge Haight (1841–1917), because his name had often been bandied about by her husband, at dinner parties and elsewhere.

Here is Haight's resume from the Society of Architectural Historians website (www.sah.org):

> F.A.I.A.—An architect, died February 9, 1917, at his home at Garrison-on- Hudson, New York. He was born in New York City in 1841, the son of Rev. Benjamin L. Haight, assistant rector of Trinity Church. He graduated from Columbia in 1861 and served as a Lieutenant and Captain of the Thirty-ninth New York Volunteers. Before taking up work as an architect, he studied at the Columbia Law School. He designed the brick buildings of Columbia College on Madison Avenue, now removed, and those of the General Theological Seminary in Chelsea Square. For Yale University he designed Vanderbilt and Phelps Halls, the University library, and the Mason, Sloane and Osborn laboratories, as well as new dormitories for the Sheffield School. Other buildings designed by Mr. Haight were the New York Cancer Hospital, St, Ignatius's Church, the Havemeyer House, the Second Field Artillery Armory in the Bronx, the Garrison Chapel of St. Cornelius on Governor's Island, and the Keney Memorial Tower at Hartford, Connecticut. He was a member of the Loyal Legion and the University, Century and Church Clubs of New York, and the St. Nicholas Society. He was elected an Associate of the American Institute of Architects in 1867 and a Fellow in 1869, a member of the Architectural League of New York in 1890, and of the National Sculpture Society. XIV—1917.

In the interest of full disclosure of totally-trivial matters, I was a member of the Society of Architectural Historians, 20 years ago. I found their journal dreary reading indeed; they, in turn, found out somehow I wasn't worthy of their heady fellowship, so they made no effort to get me to renew my membership.

Here are a couple of other crown jewels in Haight's rather long resume:

- In 1892 he was one of three distinguished architects solicited to submit plans for the new Morningside Heights campus of Columbia University. The other two were Richard Morris Hunt and Charles Follen McKim (possibly better known as the principal of McKim, Mead, & White).

According to the Columbia University website, Haight had designed several buildings for Columbia's midtown campus, at 49th Street between Madison and Park, before the momentous decision to move the entire university to a "surburban" site, a $2 million parcel occupied by the Morningside Asylum, from 116th to 120th streets, between Broadway and Amsterdam Avenue. So most people assumed that Haight had the inside track to get this plum of a job. He didn't get all of the commission; the lion's share went to McKim and his firm. The story of this competition, emblematic of a university on the make under an ambitious president, Seth Low, deserves a separate reading (www.columbia.edu).

- Haight also designed America's first cancer hospital, a Chateauesque-style castle at 455 Central Park West, back in the 1880s. It was in the news of a construction management trade magazine, GRID, in March 2001, because it sits on the same site as a $120 million and 26-story residential tower, that is slated for completion in November 2002, between 105th and 106th streets in New York City (www.gridsite.com).

- Besides his General Theological Seminary buildings, Haight's two major church commissions in New York City included Christ Church, at West 71st Street and Broadway; and St. Ignatius Episcopal Church (1902), at West End Avenue and West 87th Street. Elsewhere, he did up-scale churches like Old Holy Comforter Episcopal Church, on South Boulevard, in Charlotte, North Carolina; this was Charlotte's first suburban Episcopal church, with Tiffany glass windows and other finery. Haight's father, by the way, was Bishop of Massachusetts, according to the Charlotte Mecklenberg historic preservation site (www.cmfph.org).

This last credential, having a bishop for a father, may have outweighed all else. That's just a very rude guess. Those who delve into University Archives correspondence might find other truths to tell.

ST. LUKE'S CHAPEL

Recall the words of Henry-Russell Hitchcock, in the previous chapter, pleading that the "methods of building of the Middle Ages must be revived." If you look closely at St. Luke's Chapel, spending an hour or more gazing at this beautiful century-old structure, you would undoubtedly agree that the high ideals of the Gothic Revival ecclesiologists had been carried out with absolutely triumphal workmanship.

What follows is not meant as an architectural history lecture, but is intended merely to help you start seeing it for yourself, so you can gaze lovingly as you would on the first great love of your life. (I used to tell my sophomore literature students to read poetry carefully, and repeatedly, as if they were reading love-letters addressed to them. That dates me, dreadfully, since nobody writes love-letters any more.) One viewing is not enough. You are urged to come back, at different times of the day, and different seasons of the year, when the light is different.

This is being written on August 23, 2002, shortly after another viewing of the chapel, starting at 7:30 A.M.

We have to begin our tour somewhere, so let's start with an approach towards the front door, which happens to be on the south side.

Even before getting to the door, you see that the chapel sits up on a nice shoulder of the knoll occupied by St. Luke's Hall. Also, you see that the chapel is small, or at least small relative to All Saints Chapel. (At 233 feet long, 63 feet wide, and 61 feet high, All Saints is a "chapel" in the same sense that Gilded Age mansions in Newport are "cottages". All Saints, truth in packaging, is extra large; one size fits in all the saints rather comfortably.) St. Luke's, the one-saint alternative, is of about the same scale as a medieval parish church in a small provincial town.

If you choose one saint, St. Luke is an excellent pick. Some of us consider Luke the most intellectual of the gospelers, the chronicler of St. Paul's adventures, and a physician. Bishop Quintard, a medical doctor

St. Luke's Chapel was a memorial to Telfair Hodgson

himself before being called to the mountaintop, obviously had a great affection for Luke, and made him the spiritual head of the University's new school of theology. Mrs. Manigault, the donor for the building, is said to have wanted to name the building for the bishop, but when he objected, she suggested that earlier physician.

Unlike many churches, whose entrance door is unimaginatively placed right down the aisle from the altar, St. Luke's uses the sensible device of a side door, whose opening by latecomers distracts only a few people.

The arched entrance is simplicity itself. There is no stupid roof stoop, to detract from the beautifully beveled and notched "reveal" around the doorway. There is a raised moulding, around the arch top, to deflect any rain that might be dripping down the stone walls, keeping the water outside where it belongs.

On top of the entrance there is a stone cross; this particular design is called a "cross botonee," because it has three bud-like tips on each arm. There are two other such crosses on the ridge crest, one at the narthex (west) end and one at the altar (east) end. The word derives from the same word for bud that produced "botany".

Don't think you're reading too much into any of this.

Ecclesiologically correct churches are laden with iconograhic and numerological symbolism—lots of threes for trinitarians in particular—that enrich the spiritual experience.

The stone masonry on St. Luke's Chapel is generally conceded to be the best in the Sewanee neighborhood. Master stone masons like Carl Reid and Houston King invariably point to its traceries—the delicate stone mullions tracing intricate scalloped patterns around the stained glass window shapes—as all being done in Sewanee sandstone, rather than using fine-grained Indiana limestone for such tricky trim work, as 99 percent of such churches tend to do. St. Luke's is a sandstone lithophile's delight.

If you step closer to any one of these windows, you can see the delicate pointed finish on the reveals. It is difficult to imagine how many tiny mallet taps went in to dressing each one of the reveals. Each one has a "drafted" margin that subtly delineates it as a stone separate from its neighbors.

The stone-setting style used on St. Luke's is "two against one," that is, establishing a pattern of setting one big ashlar in a course, then setting two smaller blocks whose sum (plus mortar joint thickness!) equals the one. But these are laid not in a single horizontal course, but in "broken" stepped courses, which start and stop the courses in a beautiful and complex visual rhythm.

The two-shouldered buttresses, by contrast, are laid up coursed, with the joints of every other course at the midpoint of the block beneath and above. Those blocks turned into the wall as headers help make a better "bond" for the wall.

Unifying the various wall segments are two horizontal bands. The lower one, the water table, has the practical task of turning the rainwater out and over the foundation courses, which are thicker than those above.

The band underlying the window sills, called variously a belt course or a drip course, is more decorative, though it may also help protect mortar joints on the more exposed lower wall sections beneath it.

In many buildings, these horizontal bands are of a different stone, usually oolitic limestone, offering a contrasting color. In the case of St. Luke's, a glorious limestone-free zone, the contrast is achieved more subtly by different chisel groovings, what some aging mountain hippies might call grooviness.

Seriously, folks, let's remember that medieval stone masons worked with locally quarried stone; they didn't pick up the telephone and order a few hundred perch—a perch is about 24 cubic feet—of Indiana limestone.

St. Luke's Chapel offers the warm-fuzzy side of ecclesiological correctness.

The chapel windows are fun to admire for their considerable variety.

The west end, for example, has an arched opening, divided into two pointed openings, with two subdivisions in each arch produced by the stone mullions. Smaller arches sit on the bigger arches' shoulders. An asterisk-shaped piercing fills in the very top.

Again, nobody is policing your verbiage, to throw out a word like asterisk, just because it isn't in the medievalists's lexicon. Call it all whatever you want to, or better still, take a snapshot of it and simply trace its intricate patterns with your index finger, without saying anything at all.

One of St. Luke's beautiful stone-mullioned windows

The windows of the north side of the sacristy—the little square bump-out at the chapel's northeast corner—are a pretty trio of lancet windows, one in the middle tall and skinny, flanked by two small guys.

On the sacristy's east side are two small lancets. Also visible here is a tall and handsome chimney stack, rising skyward straight as a string, presumably serving an old furnace in the basement.

On the altar's north side is one cusped lancet window with a pierced top.

Suddenly, at this spot, you see the chapel's cornerstone, a lovely surprise.

Inside a deep-carved circle is a cross dividing the circle into four quadrants; inside of each quadrant is one digit of the date 1904.

As usual, with such great labors involved, the completion date will be a number of years later, probably 1907 or 1908.

Moving around to the octagonal tower provides another great moment, one of many such moments, in the frankest admiration of such a beautiful building. Octagons, besides offering a pleasing shape, are the geometry favored for such ecclesiastical furnishings as baptismal fonts, therefore perhaps an eight-sided symbol of holy innocence for the tower as well.

The first question, really basic, is why should we have one at all?

Early in the morning, however, the answer is visible; you can see (through the tower window screen-wire) the top of a bell, and part of an old wooden wheel. Pulling the bell rope, at the bottom of the tower, rotates the pulley wheel, attached to the bell, which tips, and causes its clapper to go clang and clang again.

Another answer to why-a-tower would probably be answered, in medieval times, by its also being used as a watch tower, just in case there were any marauding Vikings or any other foes known to be coming to the neighborhood. That may, or may not, explain the crenellated battlements on the very top of the tower. No doubt the bell would be useful sounding the alarm as well to folks many miles away.

(The climactic moment of one of my all-time favorite films, *Witness*, summons the members of the Amish community, to stand in witness against further bloodshed, by ringing an old bell. The community's timely response saves the day, in modern-day Pennsylvania, as it did countless times in antiquity.)

Oh, if only someone would open that slim little belfry door, to ring the bell and save us all again!

Sad to say, St. Luke's Chapel remains locked nearly all the time, these days. Occasionally it is opened for chamber music concerts, and it is the distinguished home for the St. Luke's Trio.

So today we don't get inside, to enjoy the stained glass windows, and admire the marvelous wooden roof, and the equally marvelous wooden rood screen, that was re-positioned rather too far back, when the whole interior was renovated in 1994 to accommodate a 110-seat performing arts space.

Instead, let's fall back on secondhand smokey experience, provided by that other demigod of architectural historians, Nikolaus Pevsner. Here is what he has to say, in *An Outline of European Architecture* (1970), about such English parish churches of the 15th century:

> Where the fantasy of the Late Gothic designer shows itself in the English parish church is in wooden screens and wooden roofs.... But the greatest glory of the English parish churches is their timber roofs, roofs constructed as boldly by the carpenter as any Gothic stone vaults by masons, and looking as intricate and technically thrilling as any configuration of flying buttresses around the east end of a cathedral. There is a variety of types: the tie-beam roof, the arch-braced roof, the hammerbeam roof.... The Conti-

St. Luke's roof beam trusses

nent has nothing to emulate these achievements of a ship-building nation. They are, in fact, strongly reminiscent of ships' keels upside down (pp. 163, 165).

Tomorrow is another day, as we still say in the Shallow South, August 26 to be exact. A key has been obtained from a key-keeper inside the Sewanee Summer Music Festival office in Guerry Hall.

It is near mid-day. Less sun-light is coming through the big chapel windows, so it takes a while for the irises to open up, in order to see the structural details of the splendid wooden roof. The electric lights are left off to sustain the late-medieval illusion. Pevsner's idea of seeing a ship's keel upside down makes a lot of sense, but only if you happen to know what the bottom of a very large, and very old, wooden boat looks like. Otherwise, let's try to simplify what we're looking at. A local ecclesiologist notes the idea is ancient (pre-NP) if you grasp the kinship of "nave" and "naval."

Okay, there are six very large and identical wooden trusses holding up the roof, in the basic shape of a great big A.

Each truss has a long horizontal beam that "ties" two diagonal roof-beams together; this tie-beam essentially prevents the two "principal' beams from collapsing outward over the stone walls under the weight of the roof above them.

The resulting triangle of the three beams is further secured to the tops of the stone walls by "wall posts," a pair of thick curved wooden braces, like a pair of parentheses, that rest on projecting stone feet.

Above the tie-beam is a "king post" rising up to tie into the ridge piece. Smaller horizontals further tie the king post to the two principals. This junction, happily, creates a cross at the center of each wooden truss.

Between each truss there are also, obviously, pairs of rafters, that help support the roof decking beneath the great weight of slates above.

The altar end of the chapel has a central stained glass window, divided as a three-panel triptych, within which are (left to right) a handsome young gowned Sewanee scholar, a compassionate Christ, and St. Luke.

Beneath the window is a 13-panel depiction of a crucified Christ, in the center, flanked by his 12 disciples, all painted on wood panels, identifiable in the conventional iconography of that day.

In the right hand corner, as you face the altar wall, is the small notation, carved into the oak paneling, that these altar panels are a memorial to Frances Glen Potter Hodgson (1845–1907), who apparently died about the time the memorial to her husband was being completed.

At the narthex end of the chapel is the rood screen, a work of art composed of a lattice of wooden arches. (The word "rood" is simply an Old English word meaning pole or rod; by extension, it was the cross on which Christ was crucified.) The rood screen's lower arcade of arches has a 6 + 1 + 6 composition, just like the altar-panel arrangement, or an architectural echo of it. The center of the screen is a large archway, as if to say to those who approach, "I am the way, the truth, and the light." Reinforcing this symbolic notion, perhaps, is the wooden cross sitting directly above the rood archway on top of the rood beam.

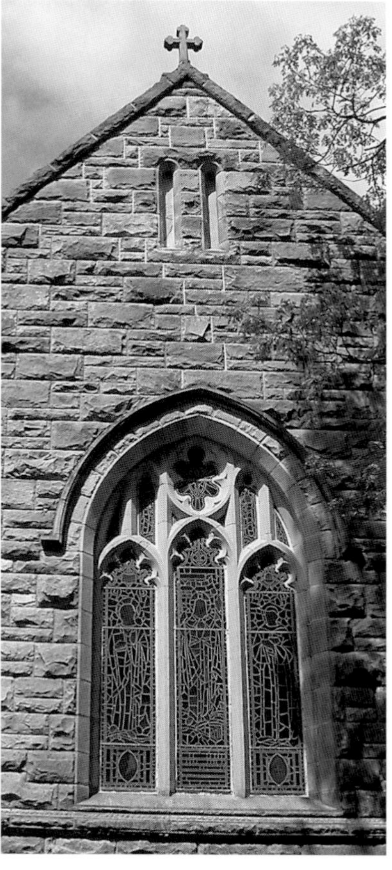

St. Luke's Chapel east-facing window

More can be said, obviously, within this old sacred space. We could talk about the simplicity of the plaster walls; the black iron electric light wall sconces with the faceted and frosted globes; the old art-glass windows, with amber-colored panes around the borders, and colorless but frosted-over diamond panes within; and the handsome joinery of the wooden choir stall seats along the walls.

But my favorite way of saying goodbye, or (with affection) see-you-again, is to pause on the way out through the vestibule, to see one last time its interior stone walls, its pair of twinned arch windows, its octagonal font, and the lovely vine-scrolled ironwork hinges on the arched pair of big wood doors you are leaving behind you.

The best example so far of the surety that we can

always learn more about buildings like St. Luke's Chapel comes with a trip to the University Archives near closing time on August 26. There, in Map File drawer 12, is discovered an eight-sheet set of plans for the chapel dated 18 June to 23 June 1903!

This is the oldest-surviving set of plans for any building on the University campus.

These beautifully hand-colored plans bear the stamp of Charles Haight's office in New York and give additional documentation of value, including:

- the precise dimensions of various elements of the 74'7" long and 23'2" wide chapel;
- the notation for the bell tower—"turret to be carried up to top of water table"—indicating that it will be designed and constructed some time in the future;
- the floor joists will sit on centered piers (colored brick red) 11'11" from the side walls.

These eight blueprints also represent the high-technology of that day. According to our googly-eyed researcher (www.google.com), the National Blue Print Company was founded in 1898, in New York City, while the Makepeace Company was founded in Boston, in 1895, with the help of Frank Brunner, another reprographics pioneer, owner of the Keystone Blue Paper Company, of Philadelphia. Our unabridged dictionary says that the verb "to blue-print," was first used in the 1885 to 1890 period.

Here is a bit of the Makepeace Company's website-based history (www.makepeace.com) of the fledgling blueprint industry:

> Prints were made by placing tracings atop sensitized paper, clamping them in a flat frame under glass, and rolling the whole business out the window on rails—hence the early preference among blueprinters for the upper stories of buildings. When the sun didn't shine, printing stopped. . . . Exposure times were very slow, and each print had to be

individually exposed and developed by hand in a bath of water and chemicals that turned the exposed image areas a rich Prussian blue.

A few years later, Makepeace invented the first electric blueprint machines. They used "carbon arc illumination, rich in the ultraviolet light necessary for exposing the emulsion of blueprint papers." Exposures took about 25 minutes while the lamp traveled along the paper to deliver uniform exposures. Later machines used gas-fired dryers, but typically the developed blue prints were hung up on clotheslines to dry.

One final word to our University friends-in-power: Please remove the ivy from the walls of St. Luke's Chapel!

As any botanist, or geologist for that matter, will surely tell you, this ghastly creeper is doing nasty things to these stone walls, insinuating its way into the mortar joints, and otherwise up to no good there at all. Even when it gets stripped off, it leaves its whiskers, which mottle the walls rather like adolescent acne. Vines on the doors inside are quite enough botanical ornamentation.

Fear not to strip off the ivy. It is not an endangered species. Nor is Sewanee in the Ivy League. It is, as some other liberal arts college markets itself, in a league of its own.

St. Luke's Chapel west-facing window

COGNITIVE MAPPING

JUST WHEN I START FEELING SMART, SOMEBODY THROWS a book at me; it's by Mary K. Rossi, and is a 142-page master's thesis she did, at Western Washington University. The title gives no clue as to her field—"Spatial perception, memory, and meaning: utilizing cognitive maps to understand the gothic elements of All Saints' Chapel in Sewanee, Tennessee" (1998)—but her opening sentence drops in the word anthropology.

Anyway, cognitive mapping has a nifty ring. Let's go do it.

Here are a few helpful sentences from her introduction:

> Addressing architectural spaces as meaningful narratives and texts constitutes a useful paradigm for understanding spatial perception and its effects on behavior. . . . Texts, both visual (what people see) and verbal (what people are told or read), convey these narratives in a recognizable manner allowing individuals to formulate an understanding of the meanings embodied in architectural spaces. In other words, socially-constructed narratives in our memories mix with individual interpretations of visual and verbal texts resulting in a sense of understanding (Rossi, p. 4).

Despite a certain circularity to these sentences, we can pull out, with Rossi's help, about three key equational propositions: 1) narrative = the "what" of meaning; text = the "how" of meaning; and 3) memory = producing and reproducing meanings.

If you don't get our meaning, just yet, let's slice off one more hunk:

> Cognitive mapping, then, involves the mental activity of comprehending the world and can be extended to include the organized representation, in map form, of that understanding (Downs and Shea 1977). Cognitive maps serve as a valuable methodological tool for linking

human perceptions and actual behavior; they create an important connection useful in examining the predilection for a particular architectural style over many centuries (p. 59).

The authorities cited, by the way, are Roger M. Downs and David Shea's wildly influential book, *Maps in Minds: Reflections on Cognitive Mapping* (Harper & Row, 1977). Let's hope you read it soon, along with Peter Gould and Rodney White's *Mental Maps* (Penguin, 1974), and that old geezer Claude Levi-Strauss's *Myth and Meaning* (Schocken Books, 1979).

The afternoon spent ambling, possibly shambling, through All Saints Chapel on August 27 is exceedingly pleasant. That is, few other souls are around, except for a couple of workmen, apparently underneath the floor; their voices issue forth from the ventilating system, softly and indistinctly, like happily haunted spirits.

Someone has left behind a single-sheet folded program headed "Induction of New Students into the University of the South" with an August 27 date on it (but no clock time on it).

How very thoughtful! Here is a text! From which we can extract meanings!

Here, reduced to its skeletal essentials, is how new students are induced:

WELCOME / *Dean of Students*

COMMENTS AND INTRODUCTION OF VICE CHANCELLOR / *Dean of the College*

REMARKS OF THE VICE CHANCELLOR / "Honor at Sewanee" / *Vice Chancellor*

THE HONOR CODE / *Chair of the Honor Council*

SIGNING OF THE HONOR CODE / *Each student, as directed by the Proctors, shall come forward and sign the Honor Code.*

INDUCTION OF NEW STUDENTS INTO THE UNIVERSITY / *The Vice Chancellor / All new students will rise.*

"By virtue of the authority granted me as Vice Chancellor I declare you fully enrolled students of the University of the South. I welcome you into all the benefits, opportunities, challenges, and privileges of your role as students, and I charge you with all the obligations and responsibilities pertaining to your life among us. Go now in peace and seek the light of wisdom in this place."

THE UNIVERSITY PRAYER / *Associate University Chaplain*

"Almighty God, the Father of our Lord Jesus Christ, we Thy servants, implore Thy blessing upon this University. Give the Spirit of Wisdom to all those to whom Thou has given the authority of teaching and government.

"Let the students grow in grace day by day; enlighten their minds, purify their hearts, and sanctify their wills.

"Bless all who have contributed to this institution; and raise up to the University, we humbly pray Thee, a never-failing succession of benefactors; through our Lord and Savior, Jesus Christ. Amen."

Memorial Chapel window in south wing of All Saints' Chapel

Though it is difficult to top the "never-failing succession of benefactors" phrase, in the power of prayer, there are actually four other texts folded in, like a handful of walnuts, into this ceremonial cake: (1) the honor code, (2) the university motto, (3) statement of purpose, and (4) alma mater.

High-level theorization seems to impel us to get at least the kernel of each one:

■ "An adequate conception of Honor demands that one shall not lie or cheat or steal" and "a peculiar responsibility for punctilious observance of those standards of conduct." Have you been punctilious lately?

■ "Behold how very good and pleasant it is when kindred live together in unity!" Sewanee's Old Boys, graduating before 1969, may recall that Psalm 133's older latinate version uses fratres (brothers), but the new more gender-neutral language seems more PC. See Daphne Spain's *Gendered Spaces* (1992).

■ The statement of purpose is quite laudable—"to develop the whole person through a liberal arts education of high quality", etc.—though it also notes that this purpose will be "pursued in close community," which some longtimers may feel as a descriptor of Sewanee is rather too close to the mark.

■ The Alma Mater is rather conventional—fitting right in with 500 other institutional hymns whose words cannot be remembered—and apotheosizes Sewanee as "Our Glorious Mother." See Spain's *Gendered Spaces* once again.

Missing from the printed program is a sense of the pageantry of such ceremonial moments, with faculty in full academic regalia, sitting up in the oak-carved choir stalls, and the most senior faculty sitting with their backs to the wall, on what is called affectionately "Death Row" (Rossi, p. 90).

The 30 questionnaires that the young researcher sent out to do cognitive mapping yielded 15 responses, from recent graduates, older alumni, faculty, parents, and others tied to Sewanee.

One graduate (p. 80) recalled the "sensory experiences" of the Chapel including the choral and instrumental music, the candles, the incense, the processions, in an architecturally lively space.

Another graduate commented on the removal of state flags, a decade ago, several of which had vestiges of the Confederate flag in them, most assuredly non-PC, and recalled the superstition of not stepping on the University Seal, embedded in the chapel floor, until you graduate (p. 87).

One parent of a graduate said this: "All Saints is like a history book. The building integrates via its structure the Christian beliefs, symbols, and events" (p. 99).

University seal at entrance of All Saints' Chapel

Another parent particularly liked how the music and voices "soar up high and surround the people" (p. 98).

Yes, Virginia, there is a Santa-like methodology to all this scholarly madness. But somehow the theoretical buttresses seem at times to overpower what they are propping up.

It is not your fault that you—and your fellow graduate students—talk funny.

The idiolects (anthropology, semiology, whateverology) you learn from your professors and their mentors don't always illumine—to borrow Oxford's latin motto, DOMINUS ILLUMINATIO MEA, on a stained glass window in the chapel's Treasury Room, right above the book of benefactors—the topic sweating under the glare of your high-wattage worklights.

You do occasionally learn groovy buzzwords, like the word "emic," a linguistics term which Rossi explains now means insider, though perhaps that makes all us outsiders "anemic" as well.

Above all, Virginia, there was life before deconstruction, meaningful life, just as there was life before television.

We probably ought to think of cognitive mapping as a cartoon diagram of the inside of our skulls. There we find the little cogs that go round, and round, and make us think.

CALLING ALL SAINTS TO ACCOUNT

All Saints Chapel is remembered by visitors to campus in its "finished" form, circa 1959, with some modifications since then, like the installation of additional clerestory-level stained glass windows.

Oldtimers like me remember it in its more humble form, from about 1911 when the "temporary" wooden roof was put on it, until it ceased having daily services for the academic year 1958–1959.

Photos help give an accounting, of the paid-in architectural balance circa 1907, and what was left that it owed.

Sewanee's master photographer Spencer Judd took this candid portrait (below) around the time of the 1914–1918 war. It shows that the narthex was not built, on the west end, and its vertical progress stopped about four to five feet up into the clerestory window openings.

These openings were glazed, with what would be 50-year-old temporary sash, and a rather low-pitched composition roof was put on over its wooden decking, rafters, and double-crossed trusses.

The interior photo (p. 108), shot by Spencer Judd as well, shows that

All Saints' Chapel circa 1917 (Judd)

All Saints' Chapel circa 1917 (Judd)

the criscross trusses are rather handsome in themselves. The carpenters perhaps had a hunch that their workmanship would be looked at for a good many years. Notice also the lower rood beam, on which the cross is sitting, exactly above the three steps from the nave up into the chancel.

There were two arched bays spanned with choir stalls, then, instead of the three bays there today.

Behind the 1907 altar was a temporary wall, stopping three bays short of where the east wall is today, which means that two bays and the entire apse-shaped sanctuary was left unbuilt until the late 1950s.

The ecclesiastical look of 1907 was rather markedly plain; possible exceptions to this sweeping generalization would be the choir's ecclesiologically correct gothic joinery, with wood-carved finials, and the splendidly carved pulpit, with five saints, one on each of its paneled corners.

There was also the large oil painting—by Sewanee's distinguished artist in residence, Dr. Johannes Oertels, who had a studio out on the edge of Morgan's Steep—hung above the rather simple draperied altar.

No organ console is in evidence, because no benefactors, either singly or in succession, had offered to bankroll one. There was presumably an organ of some kind, installed in subsequent years. (The author's attitude towards music is that of the spotted dog sitting in front of the RCA Victrola: he listens with dumb pleasure to what music comes forth from the master's voice.) One longtime resident recalls playing "a real tracker pipe organ with a parallel pedal board that pre-dated the chapel; its pipes are now absorbed into the St. Luke's organ."

The electric lighting seems to be minimalist, probably because the clerestory windows, even in their unfinished form, provided lots of daylighting, as the single shaft of sunlight says so well. There are said to be gas lamps on the piers, since most buildings in Sewanee did not get electricity until 1916.

This long exposure (gauging from the over-exposed nimbus around the two windows flanking the altar) managed to light the interior sufficiently well to pick up even the darkest ceiling details. The photograph's superb lighting and composition also argue it is a work of the masterful Spencer Judd.

Notice also the worn-thin battle flags hanging on stanchions above the arches. These were joined, at some point, by state flags, which were then, as mentioned before, replaced by the (now 28) diocesan banners.

There is also—one final detail indicating the low financial balance circa 1907—single thickness pine flooring without any subflooring. The beautiful marble parquet floor that is in All Saints today owes its existence to a contractor's mistake, as related in a letter (25 September 1981) by James Waring McCrady, written when he donated a set of his father's All Saints Chapel blueprints to the University Archives:

> At first Dr. McCrady did not seriously think Sewanee could afford marble floors, and he supposed that the work would have to be done in local sandstone. However, he mailed blueprints to several stone companies to get estimates for the job in marble.
>
> All of the estimates were prohibitively high, as expected, save one—and that one asked approximately half the amount suggested by the others.
>
> Dr. McCrady was as delighted as he was astonished at this unlikely bargain and immediately signed a legal contract to proceed with the installation of the marble.
>
> The chapel is essentially ten and one-half bays long; the blueprints sent out showed the three and one-half choir and chancel bays in detail, but for the nave they showed only the first and last bays along with an indication that there were five identical ones in between.
>
> The winning company had failed to note this indication. You can imagine how staggered they were when they arrived on the spot and found a space twice as large as what they had in mind when they made their bid and signed their binding contract.
>
> They would, of course, have lost a very large amount of money had they been held to the contract; however, the University in its charity

> agreed to split the difference between what they should have charged and what they legally did charge. Thus they did not lose so badly as they might have.
>
> It is much to the credit of the embarrassed stone company that in spite of their working at a loss they did an absolutely perfect job. The floor is of impeccable quality and workmanship, its joints so smooth that the fingertip cannot find them without the aid of the eye.

That kind of happy ending must have made at least some of the saints smile.

PUTTING A WOOD ROOF ON AMBITIONS

THE YEAR 1907 MUST HAVE BEEN AWKWARD for Sewanee's leadership.

On the one hand, the University is celebrating its 50th year of existence; on the other, it is facing a financial crisis that has put a stop to construction on All Saints Chapel.

Putting a wooden roof on the partially built chapel is undoubtedly a sobering visualization of the University's straitened circumstances. It must have been a daily rebuke for having grand heaven-reaching aspirations.

During the next few years, as a result, there is a dramatic scaling back on University programs.

Following the still-semi-fashionable methodology of our social-science colleagues, and their neo-literary collaborators, we can pluck a few "texts" from the University Archives to extract the deeper meaning of this financial distress.

One set of "texts" are the annual Bulletins—what we would today call catalogues—providing lots of information about the various course offerings, students enrolled, and requirements for completing a degree.

The other "texts" are the *Cap and Gown* yearbooks from that era.

The Bulletin bearing the date of February 1907—since the academic year began in early spring—lists the names of students enrolled in each department: Theological Department (31 students), Law Department (22), Medical Department (146), and Academic Department (120), for a total of 319 students.

Following the vagaries of British usage from Sewanee's inception, the word "department" corresponded to large units we would call a "school" or "college"; and just to make things really confusing, what today would be called a department was in 1907 called a "school," as in the School of Greek, School of Mathematics, School of Physics, and so on.

Anyway, what is startling about the 1907 numbers is that the Medical Department is the biggest academic game on the mountain. We also need to know that the 1907 bulletin lists 39 faculty and 10 administrators.

In 1911, by contrast, there are only 96 students enrolled at the University of the South.

What in the world has happened?

The answer is easy to point out. In the 1911 Bulletin there is only "Theology" and the "College of Arts and Sciences." There is no Medical Department anymore; it was discontinued in 1909. There is no Law Department anymore, it was discontinued in 1910. It would appear that the students voted with their feet.

In 1911 there is some attrition among faculty (30 still in service) and a small bump-up of administrators (12) to carry on the "business of learning" to a student body one-third the size it was just four years before.

A full explanation of this metamorphosis will undoubtedly be forthcoming when a full-length history of the University is written. The University's first historian, George Fairbanks, died in 1906, just before all those

Cap and Gown *illustration 1907* *(U. Archives)*

PRIZES

The Kentucky Medal for Greek:
HENRY MARKLEY GASS . . . . Tennessee

The Master's Medal for Latin:
HENRY MARKLEY GASS . . . . Tennessee

Ruggles-Wright Medal for French:
PAUL JONES, Jr. . . . . New York

Van Hoose Medal for German:
DAVID ROSS DUNHAM . . . . Florida

E. G. Richmond Prize in Political Science:
GEORGE VICTOR PEAK . . . . Texas

The Columbus, Georgia, Graduate Scholarship:
GEORGE VICTOR PEAK . . . . Texas

The Bishop Knight Medal for Declamation:
JAMES FERGUSON FINLAY . . . . South Carolina

The Louisiana Medal for Oratory:
JAMES FERGUSON FINLAY . . . . South Carolina

The South Carolina Medal for Essay:
MARCELLUS SEABROOK WHALEY . . . . . South Carolina

First Honor, Medical Department:
JOSEPH LEE KIRBY-SMITH . . . . Tennessee

Cecil Rhodes Scholarship for Tennessee:
HENRY MARKLEY GASS . . . . Tennessee

[93]

calamitous events occurred. Later historiographers like Arthur Ben Chitty seem to be uninterested in such matters. Anyway, there is a surmise that arch-rival Vanderbilt University may have offered the right urban setting for both programs; also, the Academic (AKA "Arts & Sciences") students were known to look down on the meds as lesser mortals.

What seems certain is that, in a few short years, there is something like a revolution at Sewanee, overthrowing "professional" type educational programs, in favor of a whole-hearted devotion to "liberal arts" and sciences.

It is almost as if Cardinal Newman, in his classic *Idea of a University* (1852), had come to Sewanee and had driven out the professional money-changers, that is, pitching out everything of a practical wage-earning nature. The degree program in civil engineering had to go. Even the typing and stenography course had to go.

Perhaps the young gentlemen who came to Sewanee already had the promise of a secure future income?

That may have been true for a large portion of the students, but certainly it was not true for all. Some students came here despite a struggle to get the $300 or more it cost a year for tuition, board, lodging, laundry, fuel, lighting, and janitor fees.

The other set of "texts" for understanding a long-gone Sewanee are the *Cap and Gown* yearbooks.

They paint a happy-go-lucky Smart Set, confident of their futures, witty in their wordplay, capable of slipping into Latin or Greek with an offhanded ease.

There are still the founders' churchly trappings—such as dividing the year into Lent Term, or more happily, Easter Term (spring), Trinity Term (summer), and Advent Term (fall)—and there are still the Gownsmen wearing the Oxford cap and gown.

But there are also touches of real worldliness. The lovely gowned Greek goddess (p. 112) offering the laurel wreath to those listed as winning University prizes also has a Gibson Girl hairdo—a look made fashionable by Charles Dana Gibson's magazine illustrations of that era.

And there are heavy weightings towards the athletic (football, basketball, baseball, track, and gymnastics) and the social (fraternities, clubs, and debating societies) that tend to argue that our business here is too important to be distracted by lectures.

Or maybe that is just a yearbook editor's pose. A friend of mine who did postgraduate study at Cambridge, 40 years ago, recalls that it was considered poor form to be seen coming out of the library, because that indicated he was something like a grind or a bookworm. It was far better, he said, to be seen coming off the tennis court, or stepping off a train from London, or be in the company of a lovely young woman.

Above all, nothing in *Cap and Gown* yearbooks mentions "hard times" or anything like the fiscal realities that the University's leadership are grappling with in those days.

In 1912, the University falls back on its old ways, still praying for a never-failing succession of benefactors, and in facts lands one of the biggest philanthropists of all time, Andrew Carnegie. The steelmaker tycoon, or at least one of his foundation agents, agrees to bankroll the money for a new Science building.

In the 1911 Bulletin we learn that this Science Hall will be "100 feet by 40 feet, fireproof, being built of Sewanee sandstone and having reinforced concrete floors, stairways, and roof" (p. 20).

Over the main entrance, of this decidedly secular-looking building, there is carved in gothic script the single word SCIENTIA. The old latinophilous professoriat have struck again.

THOUGHTS ON LABOR DAY

It is September 2, 2002, Labor Day, a modern holiday recognized all over the United States, but not at Sewanee. Students here labor in their own way. So do all the professors, administrators, and campus staff. This is not an anti-labor sentiment. The University grinds its way through most other holidays as well.

Labor Day seems a fitting moment to memorialize all who worked on Sewanee's marvelous stone buildings.

The best tribute so far is a one-page chapter, "Stone Masons, Carpenters, and Manual Laborers," in Patricia Short Makris's book, *The Other Side of Sewanee* (1997). She is writing about family members, and the townspeople she grew up with, mostly on the other side of the tracks from the University campus:

> The first known stone masons at Sewanee were listed in the 1880 census records. They were: Frank and Reuben Short, their brother-in-law William "Buck" Thomas, P. Tate Statem, and R. J. Gillespie. Frank Short was the master stone mason in charge of the others. One of his first projects was constructing the first freight sandstone depot.... The earliest carpenters listed in the 1870 census records were: W. McCoy, Frank Marquet, Frank and John Pratt. Elick Johnson, Peter Foster, and Claiborne Rose were the manual laborers, and R. J. Gillespie was listed as a plasterer.... My father, Reece Short, told me that Mr. James "White" Campbell was one of the master stone masons while he was working at the University of the South quarry. Later on Will Campbell, son of White, was the master stone mason at the University of the South. Carl Reid was the master stone mason for the construction of All Saints Chapel.... There are many more stone masons, carpenters, and manual laborers unknown to the public, but their work is well documented in the stones (Makris p. 87).

Regrettably, no masons' marks seem to have survived, on Sewanee buildings. (In another distinguished collection of sandstone buildings I studied in 1999—constructed a century ago in Batesville and Mountain View, Arkansas—I was pleased to discover some buildings with the initials of the master builder involved.) The closest thing we have to a "signature" is on a stone retaining wall, about one-tenth of a mile long, below the Domain portals on the squiggly highway to Cowan, constructed by a Civilian Conservation Corps crew. At the wall's midpoint are a number of fieldstone pieces, projecting forward from the wall enough to say 19, on the up-side of a T inside an outlined triangle (the Tennessee state highway symbol), and 36 on the down-side.

There is also a bronze plaque set into the wall of the All Saints Chapel ambulatory—a beautiful daylighted white plaster wall passageway wrapped around the outside of the altar wall—listing all of the University officials, architects, and contractors working on the Chapel, plus the names of 93 "artisans and helpers" involved. The honor roll shows strong family traditions—there are five McBees, four Kings, four Gilliams, three Reids, three Greens, and so on—that have labored on Sewanee's buildings for four generations now.

Singled out for special mention are Carl F. Reid, master mason, and Will Campbell Sr., quarry master. Campbell is the only mason who worked both during All Saints' opening stages and during its completion. He is depicted in stained glass in one of the history panels at the west (narthex) window of All Saints.

Those of us who are certain we will never get our names on a bronze plaque—perhaps until we die—may feel envious of this public mention.

The best documentation of work on a single Sewanee sandstone building comes in Alfred Louis Warriner's privately printed memoir, *The Way It Was* (1975). Warriner devotes a whole chapter (pp. 102–118) to describing the big stone house his family built in 1915, "The Cliffs," a large two-story random ashlar house which still sits about 200 feet from the cliff edge overlooking Lost Cove, immediately west of Natural Bridge. Besides his remarkably vivid recollections of the labors involved, Warriner includes in the chapter 18 half-page photographs that follow the construction step-by-step towards completion. The crew of 12 included Warriner, his brother, and his father; six laborers, all from the area, a master stone mason, Tom Hamilton, and two other masons, Lee and Matt Finney:

All of the stones were hauled up 400 feet to the top of the mountain site from the huge boulders which had fallen from the cliff centuries ago. We blasted these rocks, some of which were as large as box cars, into various sizes from ten pounds to not over 200 pounds. They were placed on a flat bed with small iron wheels and pulled up by a steel cable, which wound around a rotating axle by a pair of mules.

Lee Finney, Matt Finney, and Frank Short, circa 1912 (Tennessee State Library and Archives)

The rocks were unloaded on to the ground, and then placed on a Tennessee wagon bed and hauled to the site. They were thrown off onto the ground and the masons then squared off the edges and fitted them into the walls. Each and every stone was of a different size and of many different shades of brown, pink, light blue, and rusty streaks, making it a most beautiful color and pattern on each wall.

The excavations for walls, basement, etc., were made by pick and shovel down to solid rock. The foundation walls are 18 inches to 20 inches thick. The first floor walls up to second floor are about 12 inches thick and top floor 8 inches. All the interior walls are backed up with a 5 inch hollow tile. This provides great strength as well as insulation. All wall finish is plaster (pp. 103–104).

The photo of Lee and Matt Finney, and Frank Short (above), was copied by the Tennessee State Library and Archives (TSLA), during its 1986 effort, "Looking Back at Tennessee," going county-by-county to round up a collection of memorable photographs for the Tennessee Homecoming celebration.

Another wonderful men-at-work photo (opposite page) shows Sewanee's masons repairing the pinnacles on Breslin Tower some time in the

1960s. Damage had been done many years before, with the tower possibly struck by a meteorite, according to Professor Lorenz (an astronomer). No other verifiable details survive on the back of the archival photo. The close-up also fails to convey the essential fact that the masons are working on scaffolds 100 feet off the ground.

The TSLA photo is file-dated as 1912, so perhaps the three masons are working on the Carnegie (Science Hall) building at the time. Andrew Carnegie's money, among other things, pays for some unbelievably thick walls, which can still be seen in cross-section as you climb the stairs from the basement passageway between it and Cleveland.

Given the anti-labor sentiments of Carnegie, and his executive henchman, Henry Clay Frick, it seems like a fitting tribute for Labor Day to recall what happened in 1892 during the Homestead strike:

> Carnegie's mighty steel industry was not immune to the economic downturn. In 1890, the price of rolled-steel products started to decline, dropping from $35 a gross ton to $22 early in 1892. In the face of depressed steel prices, Henry C. Frick, general manager of the Homestead plant that Carnegie largely owned, was determined to cut wages and break the Amalgamated Association of Iron and Steel Workers, one of the strongest craft unions in the country.
>
> Behind the scenes, Carnegie supported Frick's plans . . . If the union failed to support Frick's terms, Carnegie instructed him to shut down the plant and wait until the workers buckled. "We . . . approve of anything you do," Carnegie wrote from England in words he would later come to regret. "We are with you to the end." (www.pbs.org/wgbh/amex/carnegie).

Masons repairing Breslin Tower pinnacle (U. Archives)

This backgrounder for the PBS "American Experience" documentary on Carnegie continues with the actions that led to a bitter and violent strike.

It resulted in the lockout of the steel workers from the Pittsburgh-area plant. There were gun battles between the Pinkerton detectives and the strikers, for 14 hours, leaving three detectives and nine workers dead. Pennsylvania state militia took over the plant, armed with Gatling guns and other firepower, and let strikebreakers enter the plants to run it:

> Authorities charged the strike leaders with murder and 160 other strikers with lesser crimes. The workers' entire Strike Committee also was arrested for treason. However, sympathetic juries would convict none of the men.
>
> All the strike leaders were blacklisted. The Carnegie Company successfully swept unions out of Homestead and reduced it to a negligible factor in the steel mills throughout the Pittsburgh area (PBS backgrounder).

The Homestead Strike haunts Andrew Carnegie (1835–1919) for the rest of his life. He returns to Homestead in 1898 to dedicate a building that would house a library, concert hall, swimming pool, bowling alleys and a gymnasium.

In 1901 he sells out Carnegie Steel to J. P. Morgan for $480 million; this becomes the basis for America's first billion-dollar corporation, U.S. Steel, and makes Carnegie the richest man in the world. In 1902, he creates the Carnegie Institution of Washington, a national scientific research institution that would be a resource for all universities. After establishing a number of other philanthropic trust funds, Carnegie establishes the Carnegie Corporation, in New York, in 1911, with $150 million, to "promote the advance of knowledge and understanding by aiding college, university, technical and scientific research" (www.carnegie.org).

Carnegie's generosity, unparalleled in the history of U.S. philanthropy, is a matter of architectural record, in the form of libraries, schools, and university buildings, all over America. Sewanee's Carnegie Hall (1912) is a worthy sample of that philanthropy.

DESIGNING A NEW SCIENCE BUILDING

Readers will by now not be surprised to learn that there is yet another prestigious New York architect hired to design the new Science Hall. He is Edward Lippincott Tilton (1861–1933).

Tilton's architecture career begins in the firm of McKim, Meade & White, then he goes to Paris for three years of study at the Ecole des Beaux-Arts. In partnership with William A. Boring, their firm wins the competition to design the Main Immigration Building at Ellis Island (1900). This landmark Beaux Arts building is one of the famous icons of American public architecture.

According to a sketch on the National Building Museum's website, coinciding with their travelling exhibition on Ellis Island buildings, Boring & Tilton also did new medical facilities for Ellis Island:

> In designing this new medical complex, the architects cloaked the latest technology in sharply differing styles. For the hospital buildings fronting on the Ferry Slip, Boring & Tilton chose a French Renaissance expression. They took care to mimic, but not upstage, their picturesque Main Immigration Building with its huge copper finials (www.nbm.org/blue-prints/fall98).

The idea of cloaking the "latest technology" in a traditional style seems also to have been adopted in the case of the Science Hall—which despite its sandstone's contextual similarity to its quadrangle neighbors, Walsh and All Saints, is remarkably secular in its style—plainly non-sectarian, more or less as Andrew Carnegie wanted such educational buildings to be (according to Arthur Ben Chitty's "Sewanee: Then and Now" sketch).

It seems likely that at some time Tilton's work attracts the notice of the Carnegie charitable trusts, judging from the large number of libraries, museums, and art galleries he does, up to and through World War One; it

seems probable that this connection leads him to be given the Science Hall commission.

Andrew Carnegie's money endowed the University's "Science Hall"

More importantly, for Sewanee, forming a new partnership in 1916, known as Tilton & Githens, his firm will design three dormitories—Johnson Hall (1925), Cannon Hall (1925), and Tuckaway Inn (1930)—as well as at least one professor's residence near the campus.

Tilton's long career includes winning one of two American gold medals at the Paris Exposition of 1890, being a co-founder of the Society of Beaux-Arts Architects and serving on its Paris Prize Committee for 25 years, then later serving a year as president of the American Institute of Architects (www.sah.org).

In his report to the Board of Trustees, Vice Chancellor W. B. Hall notes that Hodgson Memorial Infirmary was destroyed by fire, on February 11, 1911; when rebuilt, with $16,000 in insurance money, the new infirmary will be totally fire-proof (p. 56). So will the new Science Hall:

> The Infirmary fire forcibly recalled to our mind the increased fire risk to Walsh and All Saints by a building connecting the above at the rear of the Quadrangle. The proposal was made to the architect to place the building 50 or 75 feet further back, making it more fire-proof and connecting by an arcade with the other buildings. At first Mr. Tilton objected. The lowest bids we have had exceed $60,000, so Mr. Tilton

> accepts our suggestion and is working over the plans. I am of the opinion that a shorter, wider, fire-proof building as far as is possible, connected as above outlined, would be more serviceable, of less fire risk and still maintain the architectural effect (p. 56).

From still another source, the weekly student newspaper, *The Sewanee Purple*, for February 29, 1912, we get a series of details about what the new Science Hall will be like, inside, floor by floor:

> In the basement will be located the boiler room, coal bin, cement testing laboratory, water analysis laboratory, storage room, vault, etc.
>
> The first floor will be devoted to the School of Physics. The plans include a class room, dark room, supply room, preparation room, offices, physical laboratory, optics and electricity....
>
> The second floor will be taken up with the Chemistry Department and will include: lecture room, laboratories for general, organic and analytical chemistry; balance room, office, private laboratory, museum.
>
> The third floor section of the building will be devoted to the Department of Engineering and the Biological Sciences. It will contain office, lecture room, library drafting room, biological laboratory, anatomical laboratory, and pathological laboratory....
>
> The length of the building will be 100 feet and the breadth 68 and the height, exclusive of the tower, 50 feet.

The tower, first featured in the 1890 McBee-Nixon quadrangle plan, does not materialize at their heady height, only at the more modest 14 feet in Tilton's plans. On top there would eventually be a domed astronomical observatory, mentioned from the beginning, as a suitably scientific crown for the Science Hall, but not actually bankrolled until the 1940s.

The "secularity" of the building, mentioned earlier, manifests itself in the box-top windows, arrayed as triplets, on all levels. Only on the first floor front are two pairs of triplets given a "segmental" arch top, echoing the massive segmental arch entrance between them.

This entrance is one impressive piece of work. It is cut as a deep reveal, 9 feet across and 9 feet high on each side, but most impressively, it is 5 feet 4 inches thick!

The building's uncommon massivity can be sampled elsewhere. For example, because the building's north end was pierced, at each floor, to connect its corridors with the new Cleveland Memorial Building (1967), you can pass through a 38 inch thick round-top arch in Carnegie's basement; through a 29-inch-thick pointy-top arch on the first floor, and another pointed arch, 25 inches thick, on the second-floor landing.

This landing opens, through a lovely little bayed-out space, onto the roof walkway that connects with upper story doors on Walsh-Ellett and Guerry Hall. Here, please notice, two straight stone stacks, 3' x 5', flanking the bayed-out opening. It seems likely that while one stack would have vented the furnace, the other stack very possibly was for venting one or more scientific laboratories. (Not exactly, recalls a longtime professor: "The eastern stack is a chimney which for half a century belched huge clouds of soot and coal smoke, severely staining the surrounding buildings. The labs were all vented through roof pipes concealed by the battlement wall.") Now that Carnegie has been thoroughly de-scientized—for Printing Services (basement), Treasurers Office and Housing Office (first floor), and the Art History Department (top two floors)—it is difficult to know precisely what was originally where.

The same *Sewanee Purple* story also provides another significant chapter to our ongoing coverage of "how to pay for it all" without undue compromise:

> The history of our new Science Hall embraces several years of struggle unknown to most of us. It had its beginnings six or seven years back in the conditioned donation of Mr. Carnegie, who, it will be remembered, promised us the $60,000 provided we would raise $100,000 from among our own ranks.
>
> The campaign for this $100,000 was marked by many reverses and seemed at several points to be a hopeless undertaking.
>
> In Mr. C. A. Coffin of New York, who took a deep interest in this campaign, as well as in several others, the University found its friends in need, and in 1909 was able to announce the successful completion of the campaign and the safe deposit of the "Special Endowment Fund" with a neighboring trust company.

Whatever the University's financial situation actually was, or became, there would be no more academic buildings constructed at Sewanee for the next 50 years.

THE DIXIE HIGHWAY COMES TO TOWN AND BRINGS PROSPERITY WITH IT

JUDGING FROM THE BOARD OF TRUSTEES PROCEEDINGS, and other documentary sources, Sewanee goes through some rough times in the decade from 1907 to 1917.

Here at one end is Vice Chancellor Wiggins's comment on the Bank of Winchester disaster:

> The failure of the Bank of Winchester, which was operating a branch here at Sewanee, came as a heavy blow to our community. It happened at a most opportune time for the University—January 31—when we were in vacation.
>
> The funds on deposit to the credit of the All Saints' Memorial Chapel were allowed to offset an overdraft of the Corporation, and by that arrangement the University lost nothing.
>
> The people of the community had on deposit at the time about $40,000, but it is now thought that the depositors will be paid nearly, if not quite, in full. The few who owned stock in the bank will suffer a total loss.
>
> At the urgent request of our residents, I co-operated in the movement to organize a local bank with a capital stock of $10,000, which has resulted in relieving the people of their depression and embarrassment.
>
> In closing this review, I must again call your attention to the fact that the income from all sources does not nearly meet the immediate needs of the University; that the deficit for each of the past four years averages $7,000, notwithstanding the low standard of salaries which we maintain, and which we are unable to increase without adequate public help (Proceedings, 1907, p. 85).

The new bank, known as the Bank of Sewanee, operated in the north end of the Supply Store; this probably explains why there is a fine old bank vault in the basement's northeast corner behind the store's textbooks counter. Ads appearing in *The Sewanee Purple* say that the Bank of Sewanee is the "depository for the University of the South" and identify the bank's president as Telfair Hodgson, son of the former V-C, who served as the University's treasurer for about 30 years.

In the particular issue of the Purple (May 20, 1916) where the bank ad appears, the front-page story uses bold-print headlines saying "$186,000 Raised on Sewanee's Debt." The story explains that this sum has been raised from funds and negotiable pledges in the various Episcopal dioceses of the South "towards the dissolvement of the $300,000 debt now overhanging the University."

This sum looms rather large, when contrasted with the University's "total endowment and scholarship funds" of $395,190.73, precisely $1,908.13 more than that balance-sheet category for 1915.

The $300,000 debt can also be compared to that year's operating expenses total of $96,522.64, of which $55,117.18 is the year's total for salaries.

A few years later, with three disastrous fires, destroying the Sewanee Inn (1918), Hoffman Hall (1919), and Quintard Hall (1919), Sewanee's fortunes seem to be at their nadir. Indicative of the incredible buffet of shrinking course offerings, the University's Bulletin for 1918 announces that there will be no more engineering courses offered for the 1918–1919 academic year. A good number of students also went off to the war.

Ironically, it is at this same moment that several really good things happen. One is the creation of the Million Dollar Endowment Fund.

The other is the coming to town of the Dixie Highway.

The nation's first big highway-building effort, codified as the Federal Aid Road Act of 1916, gets stalled by America entering Europe's war in 1917. But shortly after the armistice, in November 1918, the need for good roads reasserts itself as a national priority.

Two of the earliest national efforts are the Lincoln Highway Association, creating a national route connecting New York and San Francisco, and the Dixie Highway Association, creating a comparable north-south route between Chicago and Miami.

The organizational meeting for DHA is held on April 3, 1915, in Chattanooga. After the war, momentum picks up again, according to a major article in *The Sewanee Purple* (Nov. 7, 1919), saying that "The Dixie Highway Nears Completion." Two parallel or braided routes are developed, with counties agreeing to bankroll the cost of construction by bond issues. The "eastern" route will link Knoxville and Chattanooga; the "western" route links Nashville and Chattanooga, and of necessity passes through Sewanee, on its way up the mountain from Cowan to Monteagle. (Until the association disbands in 1927, DHA headquarters remain in the Patten Hotel, a 12-story fireproof hotel in Chattanooga's downtown; this luxury hotel advertises in the Purple as well.) Unlike today's U.S. 41A route, however, the original Dixie Highway comes up the mountain, with a 24-foot-wide right of way—a 12 feet strip of macadamized paving and 6 feet unpaved on its sides—to level out on the mountaintop along what is today Maple Avenue. It then follows the R.O.W. of the U.S. 41A bypass before veering north around the curve past Shenanigans and runs into Sewanee's mini-business district on University Avenue. The highway traffic then flows into the grand curvature, past the Supply Store, All Saints Chapel, and the original Sewanee campus, then on past the newest Sewanee Inn, nearest to the golf course's ninth hole, then across the present highway and bypass to the airport and Midway, where the old highway can still be seen, then on to Monteagle.

The north wing of Tuckaway Inn

This re-routing may have stimulated, in part, the rebuilding of the Sewanee Inn (1922), in stone and fireproofed concrete, and the location of its new fireproof neighbor, Tuckaway Inn (1930), at the significant juncture of Tennessee and University, plus that other major commercial destination, the Supply Store.

None of this sounds precisely like the aggressive follow-the-highway strip development of today, but in the automobile-mad 1920s, this is a Miracle Mile corridor for what has been a sleepy little college town. Earlier mountain-slope roads were said to be so bad that cars used to be brought to the mountaintop by train.

This highway, and its 1937–1938 concrete paving improvement, 32 feet from curb to curb, determine the landscaping of University Avenue, as can be seen from the semi-circular stone tree wells (in front of the ATO House) and the retaining walls (both the ones below grade on University Avenue's west curb and the ones above its grade in front of All Saints Chapel) that now look as if they have been there forever.

Symbolically, at least, the Dixie Highway seems to arrive just in time to bring an era of Jazz Age prosperity along with it. Some of the most amiable new buildings on campus arrive at this time. There is the Sewanee Inn (1923), designed by Warren & Knight, plus Cannon Hall (1924), Johnson Hall (1926), and Tuckaway Inn (1930), three architectural graces designed by the New York firm of Tilton & Githens.

This handsome threesome blend New York urbanity and craggy Tennessee stonework. They are relaxed, unlike their staid predecessors; they seem to be enjoying themselves, like Tuckaway's cylindrical porch columns of stacked-up stone, and having architectural fun, like Johnson's just-for-the-halibut stone buttresses.

SOUTHERN ARCHITECTS GET THE NOD

SUDDENLY, AROUND 1916, THERE'S A DRAMATIC SHIFT in the architects Sewanee selects for its new buildings.

Up until this moment, all of the major campus buildings (except Walsh Hall) are the work of prestigious Eastern Establishment architects.

But in 1916 a firm from Birmingham, Alabama, named Warren & Knight, gets the nod for doing a package called "three professors houses." The original specifications, dated and signed on September 20, 1916, actually call for four such houses, but one of them is scratched, with an ink pen, without further explanation.

Eugene H. Knight—who draws two of the three sets of five-sheet house plans—is a cousin of Albion Williamson Knight, University Vice-Chancellor from 1914 to 1922.

When the *Sewanee Alumni News* (May 1950) does a four-page answer to "Why Does Sewanee Need Gailor Memorial?" one of those photographed in the burned-out ruins of Thompson Union, planning its rebuilding, is identified as "architect Albion Knight of Birmingham" (p. 7). He looks young enough to be a grandson of his illustrious namesake. Bishop Albion Williamson Knight was the first missionary bishop to Cuba (1904–1913), bishop in charge of the Panama Canal Zone (1908–1920), seventh Vice Chancellor of the University of the South (1913–1922), then bishop coadjutor of New Jersey (1923–1935).

Two of the three houses in the package are famous today—Alumni House, on University Avenue, and Mrs. Oscar N. Torian's House, on South Carolina Avenue. The third house, noted in pencil on the outside of the blueprint roll as the McDonald House, has not yet been sleuthed out as to whether it survives and where it is.

Warren & Knight's name, and their successor firm of Warren Knight & Davis, also appear on five major projects subsequent to 1916:

- They figure into the quadrangle plan for Sewanee Military Academy,

Gorgas Hall's main entrance

with their name appearing opposite Wm. H. Kessler, Town Planner, on an undated sheet in the University Archives.

▪ More significantly, in 1920, they are responsible for a plan, also mostly unbuilt, to do three new small dormitories close to where Hoffman Hall used to be, before it burns down in 1919. Only one of these three units, simply known as New Hoffman, gets built, immediately north of St. Luke's Hall. According to a couple of presentation boards for the new dormitory, in the blueprints room of Physical Plant Services, Warren & Knight have a "branch office" in Sewanee, in 1920, an indication they have lots of work to do and expectations of more to come.

▪ They design the new Sewanee Inn, completed in 1923, for the intersection of University and Tennessee.

▪ A generation later, they do Gorgas Hall, the L-shaped SMA residence hall, built in 1951, immediately west of Quintard Hall.

▪ Their final work for Sewanee is Hunter Hall, dating from 1953, but it looks a bit like a 1920s building, according to its vergeboard ornament and big stone lintels. It might reflect old plans left over from Warren & Knight's 1920 design for Cannon Hall which wasn't built with their plans. A memorial to Chaplain Cannon was originally part of the Hoffman units, getting an announcement as a construction start in 1920, but doesn't get built. Cannon's second start, in 1924, a different building on a different lot, is re-allocated to the more prestigious New York firm of Tilton &

Githens. Cannon, on a South Carolina Avenue site, will be discussed in a subsequent chapter.

The official lifespan of the Warren Knight & Davis architectural firm is 1906–1961, according to a really nice website (www.skyscrapers.com), and they do at least three fine Art Deco / Art Moderne beauties for the Birmingham skyline—the 16-story Alabama Power Building (1925), the 16-story Watts Building (1928), and the 14-story Protective Life Building (1928). Among their university buildings are nine dormitories for Auburn University, 1938–1952, the last finished about the same time as Gorgas and Hunter.

The firm's home-state achievement is memorialized in a 151-page catalogue authored by John Schnorrenberg; it is titled *Remembered Past Discovered Future: The Alabama Architecture of Warren Knight & Davis, 1906–1961*, and published by the Birmingham Museum of Art for its 1998 retrospective show.

Schnorrenberg acknowledges Eugene Knight as the Vice-Chancellor's cousin.

Regardless of the circumstances of their entree to Sewanee, based either on intrinsic merit or on benign nepotism, Warren & Knight's three professors' residences introduce a new look into the campus.

The houses are handsome combinations of stone, brick, and half-timbering, designed for the new auto-mobilized suburbia. They are dignified, but casual, bearing an amiable informality that seems to anticipate the post-war age. At the same time, they are sited quite close to the University's more formal academic and ecclesiological buildings. It seems possible that their unabashed secularity may have baffled traditionalists. Today, in the 21st century, these two very different architectural styles seem to co-exist quite happily together, just possibly because of the common palette of materials, principally sandstone and heavy timbered expressions.

Remarkably, according to the 1916 specifications, the houses were built for a total of $8,738.50. This breaks out as $2,467.50 (House No. 1), $3,060 (House No. 2), and $3,211 (House No. 3).

These three houses also seem to pre-figure the design of the Sewanee Inn, particularly in its half-timbered front gabled entrance, though the Inn's arcaded porch also pays homage to the academic buildings a couple of blocks away. The Inn's square stair tower is quirky, *sui generis*, and may have been drawn so as to say that Warren & Knight can do the high-falutin' collegiate gothic stuff as well.

The most interesting aspect of the new Sewanee Inn is its dual-use role. It opens as a "summer resort" for the July 1 to September 9 season, in 1923, and then becomes a student dormitory for the academic year.

In the 1924 season, the Sewanee Inn begins advertising itself around the South, as open from June 17 to September 12, complete with "modern conveniences, chalybeate water, high-class service, cool nights, golf, tennis." Only those who know what chalybeate water is—a mineral spring water containing salts of iron and imagined medicinal properties—need be impressed that it is part of the Sewanee Inn's amenities package. This particular ad appeared in the *Sunday News*, Charleston, South Carolina, on June 1, 1924.

The Sewanee Inn became Elliott Hall in 1953 (U. Archives)

Undoubtedly some guests would continue to arrive by train, in the 1920s, but more and more arrivals would be by automobile. This accounts for the odd jut-out on the Inn's northwest corner. It is a single-bay porte cochere. This gives the Inn one more innovation—the first University building to acknowledge the automobile.

Once you arrive, in the 1920s, perhaps with one person parking your car for you, and another toting your bags down the arcaded porchway to the lobby entrance, you come into a large and well-lighted lobby.

The lobby is, by eyeball measurements, about 30 feet wide, 40 feet deep, and 20 feet high. The east and north sides are a mezzanine floor with well-turned balusters. The west side of the lobby is mostly glass, small panes with tall french doors, leading into the ballroom / dining room. These tall doors are topped by tudor-arched "lights" which echo in glass the same arch-tops as the porch arcade outside. The south wall is dominated by an enormous sandstone fireplace, with a massive stone mantel, supported on four cube-like corbels. An equally fine fireplace, it is said, got levitated out of the dining room to be installed in the new Vice-Chancellor's residence.

My guide for the September 9 inspection tour, head resident Annie Smith, takes me down through what was first the ballroom, then carved-up and drop-ceilinged into offices, and then in recent years re-converted to a batch of "loft" rooms. The one I see has a rugged steel ladder, rather like a fire-escape ladder, mounted vertically on the wall, providing access to the upper deck of the loft. It also has some stone interior walls, still as lovely as they were in 1923, highly prized by the students who apply to live in one of them.

Elliott Hall, as the Sewanee Inn has been known since 1953, is undoubtedly one of the more popular dormitories, probably as much for its quirks and eccentricities—like the square stair tower with the tall slotted windows, arrayed in cascades of threes, and its funny little pyramidal tower cap—as for any other factor like convenient location.

This is an uncommonly good building, per se, but it also deserves remembrance as a kind of "Stonewall's Last Stand," the last of the solid 18-inch-thick sandstone carried through to interior walls, a generosity of material dimensions that we don't get to see much anymore.

STOCKBROKER'S TUDOR

IN THE 1925 REPORT OF TO THE BOARD OF TRUSTEES comes the happy news that the enrollment of the student-body has reached "the high water mark in the history of the University." Drum roll, please. The big number is 306.

Still, this does put pressure on the residence halls, which are few in number and of decidedly mixed quality. Sewanee cannot hope to compete with splendid new campuses like Southwestern Presbyterian University, relocated from Clarksville to Memphis in the mid-1920s; Southwestern's architectural look seems to have been cloned from Princeton University. With a life-cycle of eight names so far, most recently Rhodes College, the most permanent thing about it is the unwavering faith in upper-case Collegiate Gothic.

Looking at Cannon Hall (1925) and Johnson Hall (1926), both of whom were started and stopped a bit before completion, it is clear that

Architect's rendering of Cannon Hall (U. Archives)

their architect, Alfred Morton Githens (1876–1973), has moved on beyond a slavish adherence to ecclesiologically correct design. His two amiable works aim somewhere more towards what might be called "Stockbroker's Tudor," looking like manor houses, for the affluent smart-set of the financially roaring 1920s.

This style change may be ascribed, perhaps, to Githens feeling so thoroughly comfortable in this design milieu at Sewanee. He breaks with tradition with what seems like total self-assurance.

After a first-rate academic preparation—getting a B.S. degree at the University of Pennsylvania (1896), attending the Ecole Nationale Superieure des Beaux Arts, in Paris, the Pennsylvania Academy of the Fine Arts (1898), and the American Academy in Rome (1901)—Githens works as a draftsman for Cope & Stewardson, Philadelphia, and for the U.S. government in the Restoration of the L'Enfant Plan Committee, appointed by President Theodore Roosevelt.

Githens works for Lord & Hewlett in New York (1903); then for Cass Gilbert (1904), whose firm does the Woolworth Building, the U.S. Supreme Court Building, and a half-dozen sandstone buildings at Oberlin College (1908–1931); then he forms a partnership with Charles Coolidge Haight, who we remember is the designer of record on the superb St.

Cannon Hall

Luke's Chapel at Sewanee. This firm of Haight & Githens lasts until about 1916, when he forms another partnership with Edward Lippincott Tilton, who does Sewanee's sturdy new Science Hall (1912) with Andrew Carnegie's pocket change.

So when Githens arrives in Sewanee, in the 1920s, it is obvious he has already been there, not only working alongside Haight on St. Luke's Chapel (1907) but also designing the original plan for the Phi Delta Theta house, a drawing of which is included in the Cap and Gown yearbook for 1907.

Johnson Hall

One more absolutely pertinent fact—popped from the *National Cyclopedia of American Biography*, Volume 58, p. 319—is that Githens is teaching architecture at Columbia University (1917–1921) and at Princeton University (1925–1926). He not only knows the brightest and best, of the coming generation of university architects, he is on the campus of both institutions absorbing what works and what doesn't, every week.

So here is the glowing description of Cannon Hall sketched for the Trustees in 1925 (p. 54):

> The new dormitory for college students, to be known as Cannon Hall, in memory of our beloved former Chaplain, the Rev. John Brown Cannon, and the gift of the Rev. and Mrs. C. K. Benedict, is rapidly approaching completion.
>
> This building was designed by the firm of E. L. Tilton and A. M. Githens, associated architects, of New York City.
>
> It will accommodate 50 students, and it is to be the most modern and splendidly equipped of all our dormitories. The bathrooms will be of marble and tile, with the latest sanitary fixtures, and the water pipes throughout the building are to be of brass.
>
> The building is to be two stories, over a basement, with space under

a high pitched roof for a common-room 25 feet wide by 60 feet long, with a large open fireplace at one end.

There will also be four rooms for storage of trunks, etc., and a trunk lift will run from the basement to this attic floor.

Cannon starts what Johnson finishes rather better.

Both have big stone lintels, really Craftsman Style or Adirondack Style in spirit, not squared off in ashlar form but irregularly shaped, typically like big pot-pies in profile. Both have brick trim-outs around the windows, again a nice expression of materials, providing a bit of polychrome contrast to the craggy randomly-set fieldstone walls. Both have stone buttresses, seemingly placed at random, almost for fun, though some civil engineers might provide some rationale for their placement, as between the largest arch windows on Johnson's southeast corner, or on Cannon's east end, where there are six windows randomly sized and placed.

Johnson Hall from the west, rear view

If you want to see what fun it is to do Stockbroker's Tudor, come to Cannon's exuberant east end, even though it is now mostly obscured by mature foliage. The 1925 sketch, done in pastel crayon, apparently for *Cap and Gown*, expresses this look so confidently it may be the architect's own rendering (p. 143).

There is the merest nod to Collegiate Gothic, so slight you might not notice it, notably in the deep-reveal Tudor arch entryway for Cannon, featuring the curious devices of two blank escutcheons, flanking what looks like a little stone caret, typographically speaking, as if the window above is to be inserted in the line of windows already there.

Johnson's entranceway is post-gothic, totally of this world, really quite lovely. Instead of the dressed-stone reveals done for Cannon, there are rough-ashlared voussoirs forming the archway, but this arch is supported by the wall's quite-undressed fieldstone rounding its way towards the jambs.

Johnson does have six large gothic-arch windows on the projecting wing, which illuminate a commons room on the southeast corner. The recent-replacement windows are stupidly ill-sized and darken the otherwise amiable commons room excessively. Frankly speaking, with a few exceptions, too many of the "alterations and additions" work done on buildings like Johnson can be characterized as "mutilations."

Johnson Hall window

Johnson Hall was built before a donor was secured, as part of the University's optimistic plans to add a new dormitory for each new academic year, to relieve the overcrowding in its older halls. Then the new donor appears; she is Mrs. Crawford Johnson, of Birmingham. Everyone smiles. The stock market stays up until the next residence hall, Tuckaway Inn, is finished in the 1929–1930 academic year.

Johnson has the same amenities as its sister, according to *The Sewanee Purple* (Dec. 9, 1925), with a couple of differences:

> Instead of the cement floors that have been used in the more recent buildings, the floors will be of hardwood over concrete. The floors of the numerous bathrooms will be of the same marble tile that was used in those of Cannon Hall. . . . It will temporarily care for 58 students, but as soon as the halls become less crowded, the number will be more limited, and the dining room will be installed.

Johnson gets even better, when University Avenue is raised, during the 1937–1938 highway paving; this creates the necessity for stone steps and a fine low stone retaining wall, which adds a lovely garden-type enclosure between the dormitory and University Avenue.

THE AWESOME PHI DELTA THETA HOUSE

ANYONE WHO HAS LIVED IN SEWANEE for a fortnight or more knows what a small and fascinating world it can be. You keep running into the same cast of characters, performing several different comedies at once, with all concerned convinced it's just delightful coincidence. No more need be said about this, because a hilarious novel could be written, or a murder mystery for that matter, set in this remarkably close-knit community.

Architectually, it often seems, we see "small world" coincidence in abundance.

My favorite example is the relationship between St. Luke's Chapel and the Phi Delta Theta House.

About the same time the chapel is under construction, the fraternity is gathered for a cornerstone-laying ceremony, on a chapter house directly across Georgia Avenue from the chapel. If you want to see the distinguished cast of characters at the cornerstone laying, it is well covered in *The Sewanee Purple* (July 2, 1907).

Superficially, of course, there is dramatic contrast between the two buildings, one sacred, one secular. But looking at them on September 12, 2002, there is the tantalizing clue of the two octagonal towers; one is tall, for St. Luke's belfry, and one is short, for Phi Delta Theta's three-story spiral staircase.

But the fraternity runs out of money, and caps off the house at the top of its first story, a bit like what happened to All Saints, but on a much more modest scale. During the flush 1920s, the brothers raise enough money to complete what is absolutely the most astonishing fraternity house on Sewanee's campus.

Here, with a handsome rendering of the new chapter house, is a front-page story in *The Sewanee Purple* (October 3, 1928), announcing that the Phi Delt house will be ready for the brothers on November 3:

The Phi Delta Theta House, during Sewanee's V-12 Navy officer training days, circa 1943 (U. Archives)

> When all is finished the house will have, in addition to the one large room and bath-room above this, a wing on each side and another room in the rear.
>
> One of the outstanding features of the house will be the beautiful and costly oriel window above the front door. The window, overlooking the walk, will add much to the beauty of the building.
>
> The large room upstairs, which will be reached by a spiral staircase in the tower to the left of the front door, will be used as a meeting room.
>
> A large fireplace similar to the one downstairs will be in this room, on the opposite side from the oriel window.
>
> In the left wing will be a pool room and in the right wing will probably be put a kitchenette. The room in the rear is to be a sort of living-room with a sun-parlor effect.

The rendering seems to bear the same artistic hand as the rendering of Cannon Hall, and the rendering of Johnson Hall (*The Sewanee Purple*, June 26, 1926) with a cameo of Mrs. Cameron Johnson beside it.

No one will gasp at learning the common denominator of all three is Alfred Morton Githens.

He undoubtedly does the design around 1907, when he is in partnership with Charles Coolidge Haight, who is credited with the St. Luke's Chapel design. He is also on Sewanee's campus when the fraternity house is completed, sandwiched in between the Tilton & Githens' firm's Cannon, Johnson, and Tuckaway jobs.

(The Tilton & Githens partnership, by the way, lasts from 1917 to 1932, according to the usual semi-reliable sources. The Great Depression undoubtedly wipes out that business as it does thousands of others.)

Rear view rendering of 1907 (U. Archives

My official inspection tour of the house takes place at 2:30 P.M. on September 12, 2002.

Let the record reflect that there is no one on the premises.

The scene in the great hall, about 30 feet by 30 feet, with a horizontal beam-and-purlin ceiling 20 feet tall, looks rather like the morning-after-an-orgy scene in *Animal House*, a trashy movie dear to my heart since its screenplay was written by my Dartmouth classmate, J. Christian Miller III.

There are chairs and sofas overturned, beer cans and plastic beer cups strewn artfully over the floor, and assortments of stains no one wants to look at too closely nearly everywhere.

Over the great stone fireplace (south) is a gigantic moose head. Over the entrance door is a gigantic buffalo head (north). High on the west wall is a gigantic elk head. Along the east wall is a mezzanine floor. This narrow balcony is a good spot to stand above the hoi polloi and watch all the animals (quick or dead) at play.

In more heroic, avowedly literary terms, the scene could also be Heorot Hall, a few days after Grendel has been there dining on Beowulf's warrior kinsmen.

The problem, according to the usual unreliable sources, is that the Phi Delta Theta chapter is suffering a two-year suspension of activities, or possibly suspended animation, meaning that it cannot do the normal fraternity things like rush or pledge new members. Morale seems visibly low.

This is too bad, terrible in fact, for the Phi Delta Theta house is by far the most interesting fraternal building on campus.

Central Hall of Phi Delt House, sporting trophies of Bison, Elk, and Moose

In addition to the great mead hall—with its heavy oak beam ceiling, oak wainscot, white stuccoed walls, and combinations of thin slotted windows (north), and large gothic arch windows (east and west) mullioned in triplet—the Phi Delt house has a small west wing once used for TV watching and music listening; a larger east wing dominated by a pool room, with oak benches on the east wall arrayed rather like chancel choir stalls, and a plaque saying the room was bankrolled in memory of Telfair Hodgson Torian, perhaps to commemorate his many happy hours there circa 1928. On each side of the fireplace are arched openings leading to a long (45 feet by 18 feet) exposed rafter (AKA "cathedral ceiling") room. The space beneath the turret on this room's east end seems to have been designed as a kitchenette, or at least as a wet bar, given the quarry tile on the floor.

Spiraling up the triangular wooden cheese-wedge steps in the octagonal tower leads to a number of doors, mostly padlocked off, but ends up on a still-open roof deck, that offers a splendid tree-top view of the Sewanee campus. Unfortunately, the cement-bonded rectangular deck panels look as if they will leak, sometime soon, if they do not already, reminding us all that this landmark campus building may be in imminent peril.

The only disappointment of my unauthorized tour is not getting into the second floor room with its glorious oriel window. Sorry to say, this is said to be the secret "mystic" room, which we uninitiated will never see!

Outside, on the east wall of the Telfair Hodgson Torian pool room of the Phi Delt house, is a small gunmetal plaque with a jarringly significant statement to make:

> The first house built by any fraternity in the South, and the first owned by any chapter of Phi Delta Theta, was erected on this site by Tenn. Beta 1884.

Wow.

The statement shakes me personally, too, because the old rental house I am living in happens to be this very same 1884 house.

It was moved once after the stone chapter house was begun, about 50 yards east, across Alabama Avenue. That site was picked for the duPont Library, so the house was moved again, about 200 yards south, to its current location, at 283 Alabama, where it is now and hopefully will be long after I'm gone.

Now I will make no claims for its National Register of Historic Places significance other than if the plaque's statement is verifiably true, then 283 Alabama is REALLY important, despite its movement (twice) tending to disqualify it by traditional nomination criteria.

Some kind of claim should also be made, based on its Eastlake Cottage architectural merits, which include a fine wood truss ceiling, with four collar-brace beams and one king post (with crucks on either side), and more victorian gingerbread than any fastidious restorationist might dream of. The floor is also highly unusual, in being an intricately patterned parquet composed of alternating darker and lighter woods; its short strips are also a great way to use every scrap of good wood coming out of the sawmill.

The window sash around the checkerboard pane windows needs work, as well, but surely there is enough Old South fraternity-derived cash—where the venture capitalist brothers learned all their best moves!—to pay for a winsome restoration and then some.

Original Phi Delt house (283 Alabama)

Anyway, to have either Phi Delta Theta house on campus is remarkable; to have both these architectural gems is altogether awesome, as the young swells would so well say it.

A BUMPY STRETCH OF ROAD FOR SEWANEE

TUCKAWAY INN (P. 145) IS FINISHED IN 1930 and adds a touch of real class to the campus. It is designed to be another "dual use" facility, like the Sewanee Inn across the street, serving guests in the summertime and then housing students during the academic year.

The Sewanee Purple takes an admiring look in its October 8, 1930 issue:

> Admittance into the building is gained through three French doors. The foyer is paved with a modern type of imported broken tile while the walls are wood paneled to a height of about six feet. The wall is finished in light tan.
>
> At one end of the room is a wide fireplace quite in keeping with Sewanee.
>
> The chandeliers and wall lights are made of especially designed wrought iron.
>
> Miss Johnnie Tucker's suite and a guest suite are immediately behind the foyer.
>
> The dining room is one of the most beautiful on the Mountain. Like the lobby it is paneled and paved with tile. The most distinguishing feature however is the row of arched windows looking out to the south.
>
> Only the most modern equipment has gone into the kitchen. This includes a large electric Frigidaire, copper electric dishwasher, and a large modern coal range. . . .
>
> On the second floor are the nine guest rooms. Each has a bath.
>
> On the same floor, but on a different level, are the rooms for the students.
>
> The third floor is designed solely for the use of visiting athletic teams who come to the Mountain to play Sewanee.
>
> Miss Johnnie Tucker, who owned the old Tuckaway, will have charge of the new building and complete charge of its operation.

By the time Tuckaway Inn is finished, as the last of the three Stockbroker's Tudor residence halls by Tilton & Githens, an uneasy silence falls over the campus. It is a somnolence worthy of Rip Van Winkle, a 20-year nap, wherein nothing much happens construction-wise except the Miracle Mile of University Avenue.

You can see where the urban-like highway starts, by the unprecedented presence of concrete curbing, and where it ends, by the curbing's sudden stop, a mile later, close to where the new Sewanee Inn is now.

Obviously the 32-foot-wide concrete paving job would not have happened without the fiscal generosity of New Dealers in Washington, who apply the Keynesian principle of government as the employer of last resort, and even let the work crew apply their collective personality to it, in the "19 (T inside a triangle) 36" writ large in stone on the retaining wall built part way down the mountain towards Cowan.

Similarly beautiful rockwork dating from this Civilian Conservation Corps era can be seen along University Avenue, particularly in the stone steps and retaining wall creating a garden-like enclosure in front of Johnson Hall; the downslope retaining wall in front of the Gailor House (where Chen Center is now) and its next-door carpenter gothic neighbor, Hodgson House, on the northwest corner of University at North Carolina; the semicircular tree wells in front of the ATO House; and the upslope retaining wall around the trees in front of All Saints Chapel.

The only building recorded during this era—possibly the work of the CCC boys as well—is the 1937 movie theater built on the downsloping west side of the Thompson Union.

The Sewanee Purple notes in its February 1937 issues that the French Movie series brings a sell-out crowd of about 175 patrons to its first-ever foreign movie offering, *Madame Bovary*. Other entertainment options are tuning in to network radio programs, dances in the gymnasium (like the Mid-Winter featuring Kay Kyser's Orchestra), dining and dancing at Clara's in Monteagle, fraternity house orgies, or more recklessly, making a long road trip to Chattanooga or Nashville. Given these options, providing a state-of-the-art movie house would seem heavenly.

The dream comes true, according to the Purple's front-page story of September 30, 1937, headlined "New Theatre Building May Be Ready Before Holidays":

Tuckaway Inn (U. Archives)

The latest development of the Western Electric laboratories, Mirrophonic sound, is being placed in the theatre, and two Motiograph projects will be installed in the project booth.

None of the apparatus from the old auditorium is being used.

Thus fitted out, the Sewanee Union Theatre will have the best equipment of any motion picture house between Nashville and Chattanooga. . . .

The main entrance in the new theatre will be through the present (Thompson Union) lobby whose interior will be remodeled. There will be two exits by the main entrance and two more exits on each side of the building, making seven in all.

One of the two exits which open into the main entrance, by the ticket booth, will be for colored people, and the other, for the convenience of those patrons who park their cars in the parking lot planned on the site of Dr. Kirby-Smith's present office.

There will be a four-foot slope from the back of the theatre to the front. The wall finish on the inside will be rough stone, and the back and ceiling will be plastered.

Walter Dakin, Tennessee Williams's grandfather, on the Tuckaway lawn (U. Archives)

> The lighting will be indirect from the ceiling and floor lamps will be placed at every fourth row. The aisles and inside foyer will be carpeted.
>
> Twelve earphones for the deaf will be installed according to the latest plans.

During the Great Depression, and after, the leading indicators of economic distress are the enrollment figures tabulated annually in the Bulletin.

In the 1929–1930 academic year, 307 students are enrolled; then from 1930 to 1933, 281, 242, and 219; then holding on, bumpy to steady, from 1934 to 1939, 223, 239, 221, 237, 225 and 257; then a slight upturn, 1940 to 1942, with 296, 322, and 324.

But as America enters the war, something remarkable happens to Sewanee. After a 1942–1943 enrollment of 268 students, the University begins a 30-month participation in the Navy's V-12 unit program:

> The University of the South is the site for a Naval Training School for prospective deck or ship officers and pre-aviation Trainees as a unit in the V-12 College Training Program of the United States Navy. The Navy V-12 Unit was established at Sewanee on July 1st, 1943 (Bulletin, 1943, p. 4).

So for the 1943–1944 academic year the enrollment summary says there are "72 civilian students" and 483 in the V-12 unit; the following year, there are 366 V-12 students and 62 civilian students.

Company A is billeted in Sewanee Inn, Company B in Johnson Hall, Company C in Cannon Hall, and Company D in Hoffman Hall.

The Navy program takes over the campus so completely that instead of *Cap and Gown*, as its annual has always been named, Sewanee calls its yearbooks for 1944 and 1945 *Gown and Anchor.*

After VJ Day, 1945, the new academic year posts what is close to an all-time low enrollment, 37 students.

But a return to happier times is on the way. There are 218 summer session students, in 1946, 157 of them veterans, while the new 1946–1947 academic year sees 511 students, 359 of them veterans, the biggest enrollment in Sewanee's history. What a difference a year makes!

Similar fine numbers come in for 1948–1951: 557 (296 veterans, 259 civilians), 576 (224 and 352), 513 (no breakdown), and 524.

There is no construction of significance from 1937—when the 400-seat movie theater is built—to roughly 1950—when Thompson Union is rebuilt rather quickly after a fire guts the 1883 building—but there is a bit of memorializing in this no-build era.

A small tombstone-like marker—at the corner where Texas Avenue leaves University and lopes along the north side of the Kirby-Smith Memorial parklet—says simply "May 5 / 1939."

What's going on here?

The question is presented on September 18, 2002, to Waring McCrady, the person most knowledgeable about Sewanee (and lots of other interesting stuff like heraldry). He says the date marks the day the Kirby-Smith Memorial is dedicated.

So here is another built artifact of the no-build period.

The Kirby-Smith Memorial is a staid hemicycle of stone, wrapping itself around a square stump-like monumental column with the General's visage and dates (1824–1893) affixed, as a large medallion of eternal bronze.

There are also two memorial-type books on Sewanee in this period.

One is Moultrie Guerry's *Men Who Made Sewanee* (1932). It uses the approach of traditional hagiography, providing concise saints' lives of James Hervey Otey, Leonidas Polk, Stephen Elliott, Charles Todd Quintard, George Rainsford Fairbanks, Telfair Hodgson, General Edmund Kirby-Smith, William Porcher DuBose, plus a final chapter of "others of that company, men and women."

Also published in 1932 is *Sewanee,* a "collection of history, tradition, gossip, character sketches and ghost stories" compiled and edited by four formidably talented women, Lily Baker, Charlotte Gailor, Rose Duncan Lovell, and Sarah Hodgson Torian.

The simultaneity of the two books gives rise to the unconfirmable suspicion that the ladies cooked up a spicy dish to clear the intellectual palates of anyone reading Guerry's solemnly worshipful tome. *Sewanee* had a purple binding, and was immediately dubbed "Purple Sewanee," in jokey contrast to the student newspaper *(Sewanee Purple);* it was re-issued in 1961 as *Purple Sewanee,* and remains eminently readable to this day.

THE 1946 OLMSTED BROTHERS PLAN

SUDDENLY THE UNIVERSITY SEEMS BULLISH ON GROWTH.

Perhaps it is part of the national euphoria of winning a great world war in 1945.

Perhaps it is the local satisfaction in getting 511 students enrolled, for the 1946–1947 academic year, at that time the highest enrollment in Sewanee's history.

Whatever the cause, the Board of Trustees approve three rather significant contracts, as reported in these Proceedings minutes for 1946, p. 42:

> Contract was signed with Olmsted Brothers, Landscape Architects, of Brookline, Massachusetts, for a study of the present University campus and for their suggestions for future development and expansion.
>
> Contract was signed with Warren, Knight, and Davis, Architects, of Birmingham, Alabama, for their advice and suggestions in the over-all plan, and for the final working plans for such buildings as may be ready for construction.
>
> Finally, contracts were signed with the firm of Cram and Ferguson, as Consulting Architects, for completing All Saints' Chapel.
>
> A great deal of work has already been done by these three firms, and for the first time in her history the University is now in a position to adopt a specific pattern of development to guide her future expansion.

Now it should be conceded that the Olmsted firm, stretching from 1857 to 1950, worked on approximately 5,500 projects, according to Witbold Rybcynski's *A Clearing in the Distance: Frederick Law Olmsted and America in the Nineteenth Century* (1999). So the work for Sewanee was an admittedly small deal. The firm was trading off the immense prestige of its founder (1822–1903) and that of his two sons, Frederick Jr. and John Charles. In nearly a century of landscape architecture, the firm designed remarkable numbers of famous parks, landscaping for wealthy clients' new mansions,

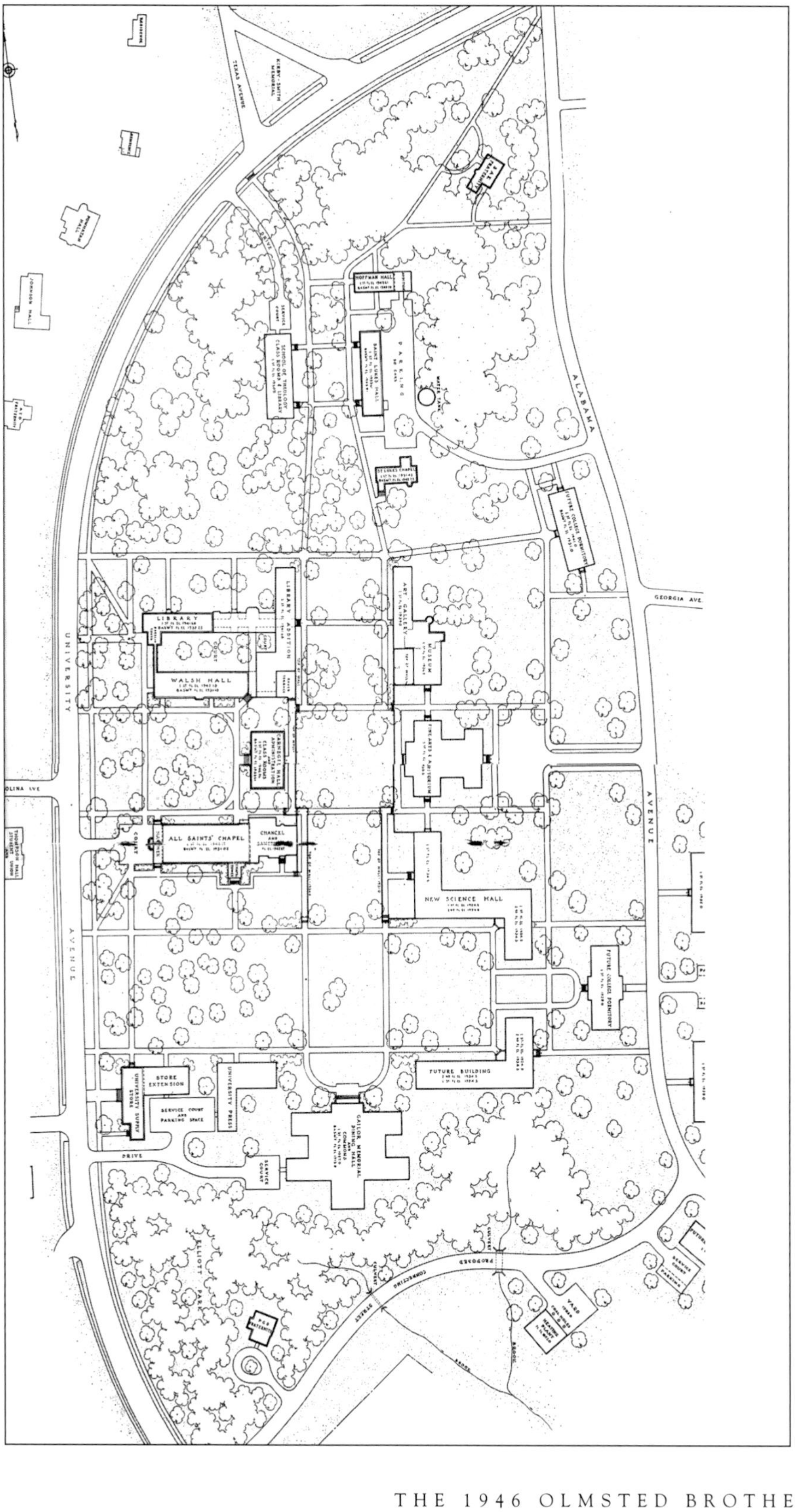

Olmsted Brothers plan of 1946 (U. Archives)

and a surprisingly large number of prestigious college or university campuses, including Yale, Stanford, Smith, Oberlin, Bryn Mawr, Duke, Johns Hopkins, Vassar, and Notre Dame, to mention only a snooty few. Obviously, then, the FLO cartouche on a set of plans certified it as the very best. But let's see the Sewanee plans for ourselves and pretend it has been drawn up by Mr. X.

The Olmsted Brothers plan (p. 149) is dated Sept. 3, 1946, and looks like a slab of unchopped beef liver, if we see only the shape delineated by University Avenue's gracious curve (west and north), a gently undulating Alabama Avenue (east), and a much shorter curving "Proposed Connector Street" (south rather like Mitchell Avenue today).

The central principle, obviously, is the six-block-long mall, rather like Thomas Jefferson's plan for the University of Virginia campus, replicated on countless campuses like Peabody College in Nashville.

The difference is that instead of the wonderful Palladian library building seated at the head of the table, so to say, we get the proposed "Gailor Memorial Dining Hall and Commons." Perhaps it is someone's joke that the important thing for Sewanee undergraduates is to fill up their stomachs instead of their heads.

Also seated around the greensward table, beginning in the northwest corner, and moving clockwise, are a library addition, an art gallery and museum, a large fine arts and auditorium building, and a new secondary quadrangle, defined by the new zig-and-zag science hall, a future dormitory, a future building, and Gailor.

Not to get too literal about it, but see for yourself, Olmsted Brothers seems to be devising a cruciform space.

Balancing the secondary quad to the east, like a cathedral transept, is a large wooded quadrangle between All Saints' Chapel (north), University Avenue (west), and a clump of business-related buildings of the University Supply Store, Store Addition (where the telephone exchange is located), and the University Press (unhappily dormant now) making a mass counterbalancing the future splendid massing of the chapel.

Actually, this cross shape is the old Beaux-Arts plan, the mall with wings, popular all across America, from Berkeley to Chapel Hill. In the case of Sewanee, however, the Beaux-Arts layout totally ignored the topography of the space, which pitches and rolls dramatically as it will. Happily the malling of this crucial space never materialized.

There are other nice features to the 1946 plan worth pointing out, notably, the absolute relegation of automobile traffic to outside the campus, with the exception of the delivery truck service courts for Gailor and the Supply Store, a small parking lot for the Fine Arts & Auditorium, and a 50-car lot for the St. Luke's School of Theology. Everything else is accessible only on foot or by bicycle.

Unfortunately, or otherwise, very little of the 1946 plan is followed. When a coffee-table-sized illustrated brochure, titled *The Fullness of Opportunity* (1947), is circulated to raise big bucks for the University's centennial era, the 1946 plan is planted in the heart of that campaign. A boxed statement accompanying the Olmsted Brothers plan makes the following declaration:

> The architects for all University and Academy buildings except All Saints' Chapel are the firm of Warren, Knight, and Davis of Birmingham, Alabama.
> The architects for All Saints' Chapel are Cram and Ferguson of Boston, Massachusetts.
> The landscape architects are the firm of Olmsted Brothers of Brookline, Massachusetts.
> The plans and sketches, as excellent as they are, are subject, of course, to change or modification before construction is begun if any change seems wise in the light of further study.

That last statement proves to be colossal understatement. WKD does only two more buildings, Gorgas and Hunter, while Cram and Ferguson are removed, and virtually nothing in the Olmsted plan gets followed.

Still, if you thumb through this 24-page brochure, beautifully illustrated with architectural renderings and a half-dozen site plans for the hospital, library, gymnasium, and Sewanee Military Academy grounds, you get the distinct impression that this Christmas Wish List is as real and realizable as anything the University has ever done.

After all, did not Sewanee launch, in 1947, a capital campaign to raise $5,000,000?

A CHRISTMAS WISH-LIST

On March 1, 1950, a fire devastates the old Student Union (aka Thompson Hall).

There is a hair-raising description of a series of fires of unexplained origin appearing in the *Sewanee Alumni News* (May 1950) issue. But the most devastating fire fully involves the Union:

> The costliest fire in recent Sewanee history started in the attic of the McKellar Little Theatre on the second floor of Thompson Hall about nine o'clock in the evening of March 1. Although each of a dangerously long list of recent fires had been extinguished promptly, Sewanee luck ran out in the Union blaze. Two fire hoses in the auditorium could not be used. Discovery of the fire minutes earlier might have saved the building. Only courageous work of staff, faculty, and students saved the movie theatre, built in 1937 and protected by fire doors from the older part of the building, which dated back to the early 80s.

Fires have always been a plague on Sewanee's campus, during its early years, owing to the fact that most of the buildings are of wood, often using antiquated heating and cooking units, and the town has no adequate firefighter force or reliable fire hydrant system. But the rash of fires of "unexplained origin" include one in the attic of St. Luke's Hall, two days before the Union fire; on the intervening day, between those two fires, a fire starts in the frame bus station in Monteagle and spreads to the hotel building next door, burning its interior completely. Then on April 20 there is a fire in the attic of the Sewanee Inn which is quickly extinguished. Other mysterious fires, two or three years before, include one in Rebels Rest; one in a Walsh Hall office, "originating on a bookshelf containing some modern novels, a fire in the library storage stacks of Breslin Tower, another on the bookshelf of the athletic office in Ormond-Simkins gym, and an early morning blaze in the basement of old Virginia Cottage."

But in the case of the Union fire, the University uses the old strategy of taking a lemon and squeezing it for lemonade. This local disaster becomes a rallying cry to raise money for a big new campus building. A double-truck institutional ad in the *Sewanee Alumni News's* May 1950 issue asks "Why Does Sewanee Need the Gailor Memorial?"

Three of the five illustrations for the appeal to raise $300,000 for the new Gailor building are photos showing the Union fire and its aftermath. It is a powerful and undoubtedly effective emotional appeal to Sewanee's alumni.

The ad's fourth photo shows the exterior of Magnolia Hall (1873) and explains that it "is the oldest building now in use by the University" and "houses the dining facilities for over two-thirds of the students."

The ad's fifth visual element is an elegant architectural rendering of what Gailor might have looked like, but as we will see, the best laid plans of mice and men oft gang aglay (as Robbie Burns may have sooth-sayed it). Gailor as built looks NOTHING like Warren, Knight, & Davis's dream centerpiece for the new Olmsted Brothers malled campus. Explanations why this happened will be forthcoming in a later chapter (that's a promise!).

The ad program-budgets Gailor as follows: Dining Hall and Kitchen ($100,000); Lounges, Faculty and Student ($20,000); Recreation Room and Coffee Shop ($40,000); Six Student Activity Offices ($60,000); and Dormitory Rooms for Students ($80,000).

Actually, the 1950 ad about Gailor Memorial is a follow-on to a coffee-table-type brochure called *The Fullness of Opportunity*, printed up in 1947, to launch the University's ambitious Five Million Dollar Campaign. This ivory-covered brochure opens with some purple prose worthy of the Sewanee school color (royal purple, chosen back in 1891):

> For the fullness of opportunity there should be a grand design, a plan by which the fullness of opportunity can be realized. If there is no design, the fullness of opportunity may pass and be lost forever. The hour of opportunity, a grand design, and the accomplishment of the design are bound together inseparably.

Exactly.

Once its wad of bombast has been shot, in the best southern-gothic oratorical tradition, *The Fullness of Opportunity* (FOO) actually gets down to some helpful specifics, an array of new facilities for serving 500 undergraduate students, 75 seminary students, and 250 preparatory school students.

The future is difficult to see, obviously, and projections of what is to come often prove wildly inaccurate. In the case of this fiscal planning document, what gets built is dramatically different. But let's see what Sewanee puts on its Christmas Wish-List from 1947 to 1957:

■ Gailor Memorial Hall—already roughed-out.

■ Building the chancel and the sanctuary, at the east end of All Saints' Chapel, building the narthex at its west end, and substantially increasing its overall height.

■ A new chapel bell tower as a memorial to all Sewanee men who served in World War II.

■ A new Science Hall, large enough to house classrooms, laboratories, offices, and special rooms for Biology, Chemistry, Foresty, Geology, and Physics. It will replace Carnegie Hall as the science center; Carnegie will be converted for administrative offices and general classrooms. As it turns out, Forestry and Geology will get their own building, donated by the Snowden family, while the Woods Laboratories will house the rest of the sciences, both hard sciences and soft sciences (anthropology, psychology, etc.).

■ Walsh Hall, says FOO, will remain the principal classroom building of the College of Arts and Sciences.

■ There will be a new two-story wing or addition to the Library (Convocation Hall), with a connecting one-story corridor, creating "a very exquisite small quadrangle." Though the building occupying this spot will turn out to be Guerry Hall—and devoted to art, music, and foreign languages—the quadrangle does materialize into that exquisite space known as Guerry Garth.

■ A new building for the Theological School is sited west of St. Luke's Hall in the middle of what is called Manigault Park. It never materializes. The rendering of this building is interesting: it is signed by Albion W. Knight, the young architect whose photo appears in the Gailor fundraising ad, kinsman of Albion W. Knight, University Vice Chancellor from 1913 to 1922. All the other renderings in FOO seem to be the work of a competent young draftsman signing his name Allan Greasby.

■ FOO says there will also be a Future Building, on the east side of the campus, "the exact purpose of which has not yet been designated." This statement, though showing remarkable truthfulness, is probably not popular in capital fundraising campaigns. It seems to say to prospective donors that we have this big box for you to dump money into. (Why? Because we want it!) Perhaps it is another Parkinson's Law corollary, something like, donations expand with the number of pigeon-holes available for their stuffing.

■ The site for the proposed Fine Arts Building would bring together music, art and dramatics, rather like what Guerry Hall does a decade later. The arts and auditorium site will later be claimed for the large Woods Lab.

■ "If the Phi Delta Theta Fraternity consents, it is the desire of the architects that the proposed Art Gallery and the Museum be constructed around the fraternity house, since this building is directly in line of the buildings on the east side of the campus." FOO's comment is prescient, but almost exactly 50 years premature, since the Purple's first issue for the 2002–2003 academic year divulges the big news that the Phi Delt house has been SOLD! to the University. The fact is, for probably the past 50 years, nobody much liked having a rowdy gang so much in-the-face of the sober-minded campus. Their chapter house needs to be out in the woods, or at least on the campus periphery, so all the various Animal-House funning can go on without grossing out neighbors.

Today's Phi Delta Theta House, waiting for University renovation

■ Finally, on the University's wish-list, FOO says "Five college dormitories to house approximately 250 students will be constructed along Alabama Avenue." With the exception of McCrady Hall, which will be built on the southwest corner of Alabama and St. Augustine, the other new dormitories get built elsewhere, farther east out Georgia Avenue (Trezevant, Malon Courts, and Wiggins), farther east on University (Benedict), and farther south on University (Hunter and Cleveland). Even with only one dormitory, and a clump of apartment units, Alabama never gets improved to handle the amount of vehicular traffic that overloads it now, as one of its residents (moi) cheerfully attests.

The Fullness of Opportunity document does deliver as promised on one of its projected buildings. Gorgas Hall, for Sewanee Military Academy, is designed and built "in the shape of an L." The rest of FOO's projection for the SMA facilities sounds architecturally interesting but does not quite materialize:

> The proposed new Dining Hall is a one-story building east and south of the new dormitory. Thus, in the height of the whole group, there will be a gradual descent from four stories (Quintard) to three stories (Gorgas's west wing), to two stories (Gorgas's east wing), to one story (Dining Hall)

The 1960s will see some unabashed modernism, in the form of Cravens Hall (SMA's dining hall) and Hamilton Hall (SMA's classroom, lecture hall, and faculty offices), designed by Edwin Keeble, one of Tennessee's leading architects. Keeble's contributions to Sewanee merit a chapter by themselves.

Interesting, as well, is the fact that FOO uses Olmsted Brothers' site plans for SMA—thereby superseding an earlier plan bearing the names of the Kessler firm, America's number-two landscape planning firm—and plans for "The Hospital Area"—where a new Nurses' Home is built in the 1950s—and plans for a University Gymnasium which will have a Bowling Alley, Locker Room, Varsity Locker, Swimming Pool, Trophy Room, Gymnasium, Game Room, and an array of Offices.

The gymnasium plan published in FOO appears to be a complete scramble—probably drawn by Warren, Knight & Davis—of an earlier gymnasium plan which bears the name of Olmsted Brothers dated Sept. 4, 1946. The Olmsted Brothers' layout is first published in the *Sewanee Alumni News* issue of Feb. 1947 (p. 8).

FOO's final envoi to the never-failing succession of benefactors is to remind them why Sewanee's campus is out in the middle of nowhere:

> The University Campus is in the center of a forest domain of almost 10,000 acres. The founders selected this domain as the site of the University of the South because it was their conviction that the process of education should not be overshadowed by the life and the activities of a metropolitan area, and because it was their desire that the environment in which young men live should be conducive to the pursuit of learning and to the intellectual and moral development of the individual.

In the middle of the 19th century, when so many states like Illinois deliberately stuck their new state universities out in the sticks, so as to escape the moral contagion of cities, such arguments carried considerable logic with them.

In the middle of the 20th century, where this FOO ineluctably sits, such arguments may seem rather quaint and silly.

TWO GAILOR MEMORIALS

A NEW DINING HALL IS NEEDED RATHER URGENTLY, if anecdotal and photographic evidence is to be believed. The sad fact is that Magnolia Hall, in continuous use since 1873, needs to be gone with the wind.

There is also an obvious obligation, incumbent on the Board of Trustees, to honor Thomas Frank Gailor, Bishop of Tennessee, the only person ever to hold all three of Sewanee's highest offices (Chancellor, Vice-Chancellor, and Chaplain). Gailor served as the University's chancellor from 1908 to 1935. He died in 1935, and is buried in Sewanee's wonderful old cemetery, after a lifetime of service to the University (*The Tennessean*, July 18, 1951).

So these two needs coalesce, happily at first, in a rather formal and dignified Collegiate Gothic building. This rendering, by Allan Greasby, of the Warren Knight & Davis architectural firm, is characterized as "a tentative sketch of the Gailor Memorial" in the two-page ad headed "Why Does Sewanee Need the Gailor Memorial?" (*Sewanee Alumni News*, May 1950, pp. 4–5).

It seems clear from the fenestration—architecturalese for window-arrangement—that the entire front block of the building is to be a large dining hall and nothing else.

The rendering also shows the east wing of what will be intended, according to the ad's program-budget, as lounges, recreation room, student activity offices, and so on.

The one thing impossible to see, according to the final program budget item, is "dormitory rooms for students."

Cross-checking this with the volumes of Proceedings of the Board of Trustees, for 1950–1953, we come across a couple of clues as to what is going on behind the architects' drafting boards:

It was the decision of the Board of Regents at their November Meet-

The original design for Gailor Memorial (U. Archives)

> ing, that the time had come when the construction of the Gailor Memorial Building, a combined dining hall and dormitory for the Military Academy and other new buildings could no longer be delayed. This was further emphasized by the disastrous fire which destroyed the Union Building on March 1.
>
> The Vice-Chancellor, with a special committee, was authorized to begin studies with the architects to complete plans so that actual construction can be begun this fall, even though the money for the buildings is not yet in sight.
>
> The cost of the Gailor Memorial, with the second floor equipped for dormitory space, is placed at $450,000 (Proceedings, 1950, p. 47).

> The concept of Gailor Memorial has been radically changed during the past year. Quite frankly, the University is too poor to have any single-purpose building. According to present plans, the building will have a dining room capacity of serving 550 persons and dormitory facilities for 60 or more students. Much time and effort has been spent in bringing the plans to maturity. Bids have already been received. We are now hard at work with the lowest bidder making revisions that will bring the cost of the building within the range of our possibility (Proceedings, 1951, p. 28).

Okay, putting our guessing caps on, let's try to reconstruct the basic elements of how the building has been "radically changed."

It seems clear from Greasby's tentative sketch, with its high-pitched roof, and smallish dormer elements, that the original idea is to give the hall a high wood-beam ceiling, with beautiful wood trusses, perhaps like St. Luke's Chapel, or at least like Convocation Hall, which has a dormer-lighted attic space above its high wood-beam ceiling.

We also have a floor plan, drawn up by WKD, showing a terrace on either side of the central tower entrance, presumably for dining outdoors on beautiful days.

Above all, in the category marked "expensive," we have a four-story central tower, surmounted by pinnacles, fully crocketed. Inside this, most probably, would be lovely paneled and plastered rooms for faculty dining, plus special spaces for trustees, donors, and other VIP's to eat, to meet, and to greet each other.

All in all, the original first-class version of Gailor Memorial would probably be costed-in at something close to a million dollars—not the $300,000 in the Gailor ad, nor the $450,000 revised figure, nor the $518,750 low bid submitted by Brice Building Company of Birmingham (*Tennessean*, July 18, 1951).

There is no hocus-pocus involved here. The University number-crunchers simply went back to the architects and said, in so many words, strip that baby down to the bare essentials. Forget the big tower. Forget the slate roof. Forget all the fancy heavy-timber expression in the dining hall. It will never happen.

Off goes the high-pitched roof, in favor of a second story of box-top windows identical to the first story, and a flat box-topped roof. Out goes all the expensive cut stone of the original exterior. In comes fieldstone veneer, a first among Sewanee's formal buildings, and cast-cement trim. These two features first appeared in the Gorgas Hall dormitory, setting a precedent that would be followed only once more in an academic building, Snowden Hall.

What results is the remarkably plain, some would say ugly, Gailor Memorial, that gets built and dedicated in November 1953.

Possibly the ugliest feature is the one gigantic entrance arch, outlined in cast stone, whiter than white ought to be, according to the 1953 dedication photos.

There's nothing wrong with stone trim, per se, only here the white frame creates what looks like a gigantic mouth, the maw of a great white whale.

Now those perverse imps of postmodernist architecture, Robert Venturi and Denise Scott-Brown, would clap their hands together delightedly and say: Bravo! This is one of those buildings with a giant sign announcing immediately what its purpose is! Let us come forth and stuff ourselves!

The original floor plan of the dining hall, with WKD's name on it, has survived to show precisely how Gailor's dining hall tables were positioned. Their number, not surprisingly, turns out to be 55, so doing the math, presumably each one seats 10 people.

Gailor Hall today

The problem, when you go into the dining hall now, currently used as a gigantic art studio, is that you see it's a dreary low-ceilinged space, and probably was that way from Day One.

The room is about 200 feet long, about 45 feet wide, flat like a bowling alley, with a ceiling of only about 12 feet above the linoleum floor.

To their credit, perhaps, the architects used huge steel I-beams, encased in plastic, to break up the 200 foot long ceiling into 15 bays. To someone's discredit, a latter-day meddler added faux Tuscan-style fluted columns, which appear to hold up each end of the unornamented slab-like beams.

What seems silliest about the fluted columns is that they are the unique instance of Greco-Roman columns in the University's architecture, instead of the Collegiate Gothic grammar of ornament.

If this were an architectural theme park, a la Walt Disney, the Gailor dining room would be the point where Gothic Land meets Colonial Land.

To complete the disconnect, stylistically, the slate-floored foyer has cloakroom peg racks, made from immense dowel stock, like Shaker pegs on steroids.

As for the 60 students to be housed in Gailor, there are 24 two-man rooms on the second floor, called "Upper Gailor," and 16 two-man rooms in the basement, called "Lower Gailor," as in *Lower Depths* (Nikolai Gogol's proletarian play). Again, however, Warren Knight & Davis make the best of the mandatory cost-cuttting: they take advantage of the downslope on the back side to give full above-ground windows, for the back-basement guys, and turn the "terrace" space on the original Gailor floor plan into a lightwell to give full above-ground windows for the front-basement guys.

My first site visit inside Gailor takes place on September 23, 2002, when Art Department faculty are having an afternoon soiree for a bunch of seniors. Among the fruit, pastries, nuts, and punch there are slices of talk about the future of this building. Several faculty members say they like the space just fine; unfortunately, they will be evicted, under the new master plan, which promises them a new $600,000 metal studio building instead.

The metal building price tag is ironic. It is more than what the 50-year-old Gailor cost.

Gailor Memorial, though getting more amiable with age, serves in this chronological march-of-time to provide a 1950s preview of some other sorry corner-cuttings to come.

EXIT ONE ARCHITECT, ENTER ANOTHER

THE IMPRESSIVE LIFETIME ACHIEVEMENT of the Birmingham firm of Warren, Knight & Davis is ably presented by a Birmingham Museum of Art monograph, *Remembered Past, Discovered Future: The Alabama Architecture of Warren Knight & Davis, 1906–1961* (1999), published in conjunction with BMA's retrospective show of their best work.

So whatever we may say of WKD's work for Sewanee, from roughly 1916 to 1953, John Schnorrenberg's handsomely illustrated book argues that there need be no apologies for their coming to the campus, regardless of the fact that Eugene Knight was a cousin of Vice-Chancellor Albion W. Knight.

But all good things somehow come to an end.

With the completion of Gorgas Hall—a kind of architectural stepsister to the Gailor Memorial, done simultaneously for the Sewanee Military Academy campus and completed for $438,000—and Hunter Hall—a new dormitory completed for $240,000 at the corner of Mitchell and University Avenue—the distinguished firm of Warren, Knight & Davis bids Sewanee farewell.

Actually, they are dismissed, according to Schnorrenberg's research, by a letter from Vice-Chancellor Edward McCrady dated October 26, 1954, one day before the VC dismisses Cram and Ferguson as the architect for All Saints' Chapel. No doubt, posthumously, WKD feel it is in distinguished company.

It is difficult to know, looking at the official record of the annual Proceedings of the Board of Trustees, precisely how Dr. McCrady & Company lead one architecture firm to the red-letter exit sign and usher in another firm.

For one thing, McCrady's style verges towards tight-lipped comment, during his 20-year reign (1951–1971).

Only in the utterly remarkable 1953 Proceedings—completely consumed with the incendiary matter of the School of Theology professors trying to force Sewanee into opening its seminary to Negroes, beginning June 1952, then resigning en-masse when the University fails to validate their courageous act—do we get anything like full disclosure.

But we do know, from all the names on blueprints, and later credit when the buildings are completed, that the Atlanta-based firm of Ayers & Godwin—and its successor firm Godwin & Beckett—designed and supervised Cleveland Hall (1955), Juhan Gymnasium (1955), Harris Stadium (1956), All Saints' Chapel completion (1957–1958), Walsh Hall renovations (1957), Guerry Hall (1961), Benedict Hall (1962), Snowden Forestry Building (1962), Malon Courts (1964), DuPont Library (1965), Trezevant Hall (1968), Woods Laboratories (1968), and Bishops Common (1974).

Nearly all of these 13 building-deals fall squarely within the watch of Vice-Chancellor McCrady. Yet we have as yet no clue as to what the firm's entree is with Sewanee, or McCrady, and why it lasts so long.

The only visibility for Jim Godwin turned up so far comes from a visit to the Atlanta Public Library, where a card-file index turns up an amiable magazine feature, "The Last Architect for the Last Cathedral," written by Margaret Shannon, appearing in *The Atlanta Journal and Constitution Magazine* (June 11, 1972):

> "We expect the cathedral to be here a couple of thousand years."
>
> These are not the words of a visionary or even of a dreamer type, but of James B. Godwin, an Atlanta man who is very businesslike and very direct and is not given to soaring rhetoric or poetic phraseology.
>
> Do not be misled. This modest man—modest in size, modest in demeanor, modest in expression—is the last architect of the last true Gothic cathedral.
>
> Or so it seems now. Godwin and his firm have been selected to complete Washington Cathedral, which has been abuilding in the nation's capital for 65 years. The foundation stone was laid in 1907.
>
> The cathedral is the seat of the presiding bishop of the Episcopal Church in the United States, and will rank, when finished, as one of the world's great cathedrals, larger than Notre Dame or Chartres, almost twice the size of Salisbury, and three-fourths as big as St. John's in New York.
>
> Also, it is faithful to Gothic design and construction, and that is

why there may never be another one like it. The cost of such construction is terribly high these days, and there's the problem of workmen to do the job. Stone masonry, Gothic-style, is an obsolescent trade.

So Jim Godwin must hurry, because the old order is dying and giving way to the new, and for anyone building a 14th century cathedral he is about six centuries late.

It was not easy, even then. It is not easy now, though Washington Cathedral is four-fifths done.

At this point in time, 1972, Godwin's firm has completed 12 of 13 Sewanee buildings, all theme and variations on Collegiate Gothic. Largely on the strength of his work on All Saints Chapel, Godwin is named to oversee completion of the Cathedral of St. Philip in Atlanta, said to be about one-fifth as big as the National Cathedral in Washington.

In the piece, Margaret Shannon sprinkles some intriguing biographical details about the architect, whom she says is 61:

Jim Godwin's interest in Gothic architecture goes back to his youth.

He was born in Columbus, Ga., and his family belonged to Trinity Episcopal Church.

"Back when I was quite a young man, they used to hold summer camp at the University of the South in Sewanee, Tenn." he said. "My two older sisters would go up, and that's how I got hold of a publication showing the proposed completion of the campus there."

Sewanee's campus, with its Gothic-design buildings, is one of the prettiest in the South.

"At that time," said Godwin, "I was working more or less as an office boy. I just made the statement to myself, 'I wish I could do some

> work at Sewanee.' Also, this applied when the original design for St. Philip's was published. I never had any idea that I would be associated with both projects, and of course I never had the remotest notion that I would be called to Washington and asked to work with them."
>
> Godwin says he "studied architecture right over a drafting board." He has been associated with his present firm in Atlanta since 1929, though the firm's name and some of its members have changed.

This is a remarkable detail. Godwin learns architecture on the job, like many of his 19th-century predecessors, not by going to architecture school!

POLYMATH V-C

THERE IS A DELIGHTFUL BIOGRAPHICAL SKETCH of Dr. Edward McCrady penned by Arthur Ben Chitty in the expanded re-issue of *Men Who Made Sewanee* (1981). It shows that the man who served longer as Vice-Chancellor (1951–1971) than anyone else was a true polymath, literally a "many-learned" man.

He majored in Greek and Latin, at the College of Charleston, but after side-tracking in Japanese studies at Columbia University, he pursued a life-long inclination towards biology—the field that brought his grandfather to Sewanee in 1877—by serving as assistant curator of public instruction in the Charleston Museum of Natural History.

From there in 1928 he served as the founding director of the Highlands (N.C.) Museum Association, a mountain biological research station, and then went to the University of Pittsburgh's biology department for a master's degree in genetics (1930). Then he took a Ph.D. at the University of Pennsylvania in embryology and anatomy (1933).

From there, Chitty tells us, McCrady embarked on a lifetime odyssey of self-education:

> McCrady continued the remarkable program of self-education which ultimately qualified him to teach or perform in mathematics, physics, music, painting, sculpture, architecture, theology, philosophy, geology, otolaryngology, botany—all in addition to the major subjects he studied formally.
>
> This was accomplished through prodigious reading backed by a photographic memory. Converting a vast array of knowledge into wisdom and putting that to work for the benefit of man and the glory of God became his life's work (*Men Who Made Sewanee*, 1981, p. 134).

Interesting as this is, it is Dr. McCrady's obsession with architecture that we need to focus our attention on. Rather than merely getting the right architect, plus the ways-and-means necessary for completing the University's new buildings, as any other CEO would have done, McCrady wanted to design the buildings himself!

In any other era, that would have been possible; Thomas Jefferson, for example, had no trouble designing his own mansion and the campus of the University of Virginia. But in our own time—thanks to the century-old credentialist movement requiring professional education, licensing, and board certification for being a lawyer, engineer, accountant, architect, doctor, dentist, or mortician—McCrady perforce ceded the role of "architect" to others.

Here is Sewanee's historiographer again:

> More construction was accomplished in his time than that of all his predecessors combined.
>
> McCrady did the rough sketches for most of these buildings, turning his ideas over to professional architects for blue print detail.
>
> He remained responsible for the general character of the buildings and occasionally even for innovative detail such as the courtyard plan of Benedict and Courts dormitories.
>
> But his personal project of 20 years was the finishing of All Saints' Chapel which had been in use, with wooden floors, temporary east wall and low-beamed roof since 1910. Here he insisted on drawing the tiniest details himself, reworking the blueprints countless times.
>
> Starting in the 1930s he took the original and conflicting designs of Silas McBee and Ralph Adams Cram and reworked them into what was finally built.
>
> The clerestory, fenestration, mullion work, vaulting, choir, and chancel (including the reredos and just-barely-free-standing altar—radical at the time) are entirely McCrady's work.
>
> In addition, he designed a new St. Augustine's Chapel and redesigned the McBee tower to accommodate the 56 bells of the Leonidas Polk Carillon (Chitty, *Men Who…*, p. 141).

As we indicated in the previous chapter, the Birmingham firm of Warren, Knight & Davis was completing its last three Sewanee buildings—Gailor, Gorgas, and Hunter—at the time Dr. McCrady was summoned from his post as senior biologist for the Atomic Energy Commission at its Oak Ridge facility, where he had been since 1948.

Here is the Vice-Chancellor's terse comment on new building progress in 1954:

Hunter Hall today

> The most important building project now underway is the construction of Hunter Hall. The cost will be about $250,000 supplied by the Benwood Foundation of Chattanooga. It probably will not be ready for the opening of school but should be available for use by October 15 (Proceedings, 1954, p. 75).

The date seems significant, on McCrady's personal calendar, for it is close to the date that he dismisses, by letter, the Warren Knight & Davis architectural firm (on October 26, 1954) and the Cram and Ferguson firm (on October 27. 1954). The acrimonious tone is there mostly for the Birmingham firm:

> In accordance with instructions from the Board of Regents this letter is sent as formal notice of termination of the contract between Warren, Knight & Davis and the University of the South made on May 14, 1946.
>
> The plans for all of the buildings have changed considerably in recent years. Some of them are no longer contemplated at all, and others are now conceived in different terms and even in different locations.
>
> And, furthermore, so many criticisms have been made of Gailor, Gorgas, and Hunter Halls that we feel obliged to give some other architects an opportunity to participate in our building program.

WKD's principal, John Eayres Davis, reacts with understandable pique to the termination:

> Having never had this experience since we have been practicing architecture, it naturally comes as a very great shock.

> We think this matter should have been discussed with us before so drastic a move was taken.

At stake is not a whole lot of money, about $5,000, dating back to when architectural renderings were done by WKD for the University's fund-raising brochure, *The Fullness of Opportunity*, printed up for the Five Million Dollar Campaign in 1947. After about $79,000 in architects' fees, work done for more than a million dollars of University buildings, it comes down to a few more hot-letter exchanges, then no more.

By the time of these letters, Dr. McCrady is already plunged into a new relationship with "other architects," specifically Ayers & Godwin, whose letterhead indicates they are physically located in rooms 211–215 of the Bona Allen Building, Atlanta 3, Georgia. (All students of the Rich and Famous need to know that media mogul Ted Turner bought the Bona Allen Building in mid-2002 for one of his penthouses.) Here is the opening chunk of architect James B. Godwin's letter to McCrady dated May 31, 1954:

> In accordance with your request, we have made an estimate of the cost for the completion of All Saints Cathedral for the University of the South.
>
> Of course, it is readily understood that we are unable to make a very accurate estimate since we are having to base the quantities on the present building and do considerable guessing as to the other areas involved. We have based our take off upon the building being completed, more or less as originally designed, using materials which are in keeping with a structure of this magnitude.

General construction:	$602,113.00
Plumbing, Heating, Ventilating:	$80,700.00
Electric Wiring:	$36,400.00
Sub Total:	$731,213.00
10% Contingency	$73,121.00
Total:	$804,334.00
Less Tower:	$128,150.00
Balance of Construction:	$676,184.00

Godwin's wonderful blooper, calling the chapel project "All Saints'

Cathedral," suggests a considerable naivete in the architect. But then this may have been precisely the quality McCrady really liked about the firm.

In a sense, of course, Godwin was very nearly right. All Saints' Chapel was scaled-up to the size of a cathedral, (literally the seat of a bishop, from the Greek kathedra meaning "chair" or "throne"); by implication, the Vice-Chancellor was living vicariously as a bishop-like official occupying a throne of remarkable power and influence.

There seems little doubt that Dr. McCrady put his chair with the upper two "estates"—the aristocracy or the clergy. We have at least one clear declaration on the subject in his 1959 report to the Board of Trustees on the decline of civility on campus:

All Saints' Chapel sacristry wing in a typical Sewanee fog

> Of no less importance than buildings, endowment, quality of the faculty, and academic competence of the students, is the quality of character which is engendered by a university.
>
> If Sewanee cannot, or does not, breed Christian gentlemen, all else will be in vain....
>
> I really believe that with just a little attention we can make the Order of Gownsmen so effective an instrument as to have a marked effect upon the character of our graduates.
>
> Basically what I have in mind is the establishment of what Herbert Ravenel Sass calls an Aristocratic Democracy in contrast to an Equalitarian Democracy.
>
> That is to say, we should make no pretense about all men being equal in either ability or character; we should deliberately establish a privileged class; but the privileges granted should not be hereditary or arbitrary or irrevocable—they should be available to all who qualify and for as long as they show themselves worthy (Proceedings, 1959, pp. 36, 37–38).

The term Aristocratic Democracy is a nice if somewhat oxymoronic phrase. It may actually be more applicable for Sewanee's peculiar architectural style. Sewanee-in-Stone is "high" in its reverence for traditional grammar of ornament and "low" in its use of democratic materials like local sandstone, fieldstone, and concrete. Nowhere else in the history of the University of the South as during McCrady's reign does this architectural duality manifest itself so clearly and unapologetically.

EISENHOWER GOTHIC

THE FIRST EXPRESSION OF ARISTOCRATIC DEMOCRACY in architectural terms may be the coat of arms that is literally the keystone for Cleveland Hall. The new dormitory is cornerstoned on October 11, 1955, by a bishop or two and lots of VIP's, and completed at a cost of $270,000.

Cleveland is the debut for Ayers & Godwin, showing what they can do in the Sewanee stone idiom, but it is also a first test as to how they will get along with Dr. Edward McCrady. Surviving correspondence shows how keen the Vice-Chancellor is on every little detail.

Here, for example, in a letter to Jim Godwin on February 23, 1955, is a checklist of "detailed changes" approved by Mrs. Cleveland. It seems remarkable that the widow of the man memorialized—Alexander Sessums Cleveland, a Houston businessman and civic leader, who dies in January 1954—should be so much in the loop. A cynic might suspect that this third-party may be exercising only virtual approval of what the VC's heart and hand really, really wants. Godwin's reply, to each of the 12 changes, comes as an undated list soon afterwards.

Since this is a church-owned school, with a strong liturgical tradition, let us now compose the 12-item exchange as antiphonal call and

Sessums Cleveland Hall (U. Archives)

response—which readers can either recite or chant as plainsong—with Dr. McCrady as V and Mr. Godwin's vicar (or possibly Godwin himself) as R:

V. Iron work porch running full width of North end of building with access steps and railing.

R. We have designed porch in Gothic style (carrying out theme of local field stone and cut stone trim) which we feel in better keeping with building as a whole. Porch at North end will bring on complications which Mr. Godwin will explain.

V. No porch at front center, but an impressive Gothic door with deep recess possibly providing for storm doors in winter.

R. Provided in revised sketches dated February 11, 1955.

V. Cleveland arms in stone relief over door or under third floor.

R. Can be done directly over doorway.

V. Wide flaring eaves (probably 18 inches) with no gutters—much like those at Johnson Hall.

R. Strenuous objection. Mr. Godwin will discuss.

V. Laundry - Storage Room in basement as previously discussed.

R. Provided in revised sketches dated February 11, 1955.

V. The oblique path probably must be left in front. If necessary, move building back placing front just behind present rear wall. This would save the two best trees, and would not affect relative elevations appreciably—merely reducing them uniformly by about four feet.

R. Mr. Godwin will discuss this item.

V. Picture hanging slot approved.

R. Please direct us in typical suite where picture hanging slot will go, whether in study and bedrooms or no, and on what walls. Suggest side walls of both and not outside and corridor walls. Discuss Matrons suite and attic floor as to picture slot.

V. Linen room, second floor back center, should be Proctor's Study.

R. Provided in revised sketches dated February 11, 1955.

V. Provide cross ventilation in corner bedrooms.

R. Strenuous objection. Mr. Godwin will discuss.

V. Shift Matron's suite across corridor and provide direct access between her living room and main lounge.

R. Can be done with mild objection. Existing location gives Matron better supervision, being adjacent to front entrance, and windows overlooking front in general. Poor planning for Matron to enter or leave apartment through Lounge.

Cleveland Hall today

V. Clear entry and lobby as discussed.
R. Provided in revised sketches dated February 11, 1955.
V. Ventilator fan and duct to take place of mop closet as discussed.
R. Provided in revised sketches dated February 11, 1955.

Despite what may seem like tedious pleading, over some possibly picayune details, Cleveland Hall gets built and looks rather handsome when visited today (October 1, 2002).

Regarding who is the winner and who is the loser, in the as-built Cleveland, let's see:

- The eaves are flared, but only about 12", suggesting a compromise point for each side.
- The porch is on the south; architect prevails.
- The Matron's Suite stays by entrance; architect prevails.
- No cross ventilation in corner bedrooms; architect prevails.
- No impressive Gothic door at entrance; either replaced, in recent years, with nondescript fire-rated doors, or they never made it in the first place. No points for either side.

Cleveland Hall gets six steel sash casement windows, on each side of the front-gabled entrance, on the first and second floors, then five dormer windows on each side of the gable that breaks up the roofline, for the garret-like third floor rooms. Actually these top floor rooms are large single rooms, with good views, while the lower floor rooms are mostly doubles on either side of a "study" room, arranged like suites. What makes the lower-story rooms work, light-wise, is the windows' generous size, about five feet square. Each of these windows is divided vertically into three parts, a crank-out casement window on both sides of fixed panes.

The only odd feature in the exterior of Cleveland Hall is the choice of a cast-iron (grapes and vines) and wrought-iron porch supports for a mansard-like metal roof. The effect is to put a New Orleans style porch on the south end of the Eisenhower Gothic building. Note, however, that the architect's drawing shows a Collegiate Gothic stone arcade on the south end.

Asked about this, Waring McCrady offers the explanation that his father was interested in cast-iron, which he considered to be an important element in 19th-century Southern Architecture: "Determined to incorporate it with stone into a uniquely Southern idiom, he introduced it here, then on the seminary dean's house (now the Spanish House), then in Benedict Hall, and on his own residence (Glen Antrim). In addition to its southernism, he found it lighter and airier than masonry columns and arches, and of course considerably less expensive. But, discouraged, he phased it out of succeeding dormitories, Courts and Trezevant."

Let us end back where we began, with the coat of arms, which McCrady obviously spends a lot of time grappling with, as a great student of heraldry. Here he is, in a letter of May 23, 1955, hammering away at Jim Godwin's skull:

I am returning herewith one signed copy of the Contract for Sessums Cleveland Hall. Under separate cover, I am sending the Coat of Arms which arrived the day you were here, but unfortunately I didn't get it to you then.

Since there will be no color in the sculptured stone, you may be at something of a loss as to how to record the different devices. There is a standardized convention in this connection which we should follow if we mean to be technically accurate, though I don't know how many people would know whether we had been or not. At any rate, I have attached a hasty pencil sketch with notes to explain the system.

My pencil sketch corresponds with the official description of the Arms, not to the painting, which was made by someone who wasn't too informed about such matters.

The top of the cap is supposed to be red and therefore should have vertical parallel lines on the carving.

The coat is supposed to be blue (not green) and therefore should have horizontal parallel lines in the carving.

The three dark bands in the so-called wreath beneath the coat, the upper third roughly of the shield, and the dark chevron are meant to be black not brown and their sculptured key is a set of parallel lines vertical crossed by a set of parallel lines horizontal.

The little devices which represent ermine tails should have approximately the shape shown in my sketch in the sculpture.

The reason these conventions have been standardized is that Arms were very often used as seals and the impression in the wax could convey no identification of the colors except by some such set of rules.

According to the rules of heraldry, the helmet between the wreath and the shield indicates the rank of the owner, and this one should have a closed visor, facing to the left of the observer, which indicates the rank of baron.

Any other details of the shape of the helmet are entirely arbitrary, as are also the ornamental so-called mantel proceeding from it and surrounding the upper part of the shield.

> The motto ribbon is also arbitrary and may be altered in shape at will.
>
> Finally, the shape of the shield has no relative significance and can be altered to suit the artist's fancy.
>
> This little painting should be carefully preserved and returned along with the typed description enclosed.

One can only imagine Godwin's response to each and every one of these niggling details. Nonetheless, the Cleveland coat of arms endures, complete with a latin motto, SEMEL ET SEMPER, or "once and always," something you can't argue with much at all.

JUHAN GYMNASIUM

IT WAS INEVITABLE THAT THE NEW GYMNASIUM should be named for Frank Alexander Juhan.

He was a first-rate athlete, winning varsity letters at Sewanee in boxing, football, baseball, and track. He would also become the fourth Bishop of Florida (1924–1956), eleventh Chancellor of the University (1944–1956), and the University's unpaid Director of Development (1956–1966). His last title, according to Arthur Ben Chitty, was "as consultant to the Athletic Department, undertaken the year before he was named to the National Football Hall of Fame" (*Men Who Made Sewanee*, 1981, p. 112).

Obviously, if you follow the history of the University, it is easy to see how important athletic facilities should be, beginning with the fact that one-half of Convocation Hall (1886) should be used as a gymnasium.

In succeeding decades, the University talks about getting better facilities for its athletic program, but rarely has the financial ways and means to live up to that good intention.

There is a piffling little bracket-shaped building, known as Shaffer Gym (1901), and there is a crackerbox gymnasium, known as Ormond-Simkins Field House (1927), with a bow-truss roof where basketball could be played.

By the time some real money starts to flow into the University's coffers, in the 1950s, two needs jump to the head of the queue. One is a Natatorium, known to non-latinates as a swimming pool, and the other is a Gymnasium, big enough to hold an enthusiastic student body as spectators, and double as an assembly hall.

The Natatorium comes first. A set of blueprints has survived, bearing the date of October 25, 1955, and the signature of Sanford M. Ayers. Also in the University's Physical Plant Services plan room, in the file drawer marked Juhan, are a set of specifications for "Additions and Revisions to

Gymnasium" prepared by Ayers & Godwin and bearing the date of February 6, 1956.

The swimming pool built in the 1950s—not to be confused with the humongous swimming pool built for the Robert Dobbs Fowler Sport and Fitness Center in the early 1990s—gets sandwiched in between Ormond-Simkins (to the west) and Shaffer (to the east). This building measures about 73 feet wide and 116 feet long.

Notable in its high roof are "Naturalite Dome" skylights, about five feet in diameter, fairly high-tech for that day, looking rather like a bunch of jet-plane bubble cockpits sticking out of the roof.

An aerial photograph found in the University Archives shows construction progress, probably in the winter of 1956, when the gymnasium floor is poured, and what looks like a bit of snow has accumulated on the Natatorium roof.

The decidedly anti-gothic structure in the right foreground is a government-surplus Quonset hut—erected shortly after Thompson Union loses its McKellar Little Theatre in the disastrous 1950 fire. This temporary building is known variously as the Barter Theatre, New Sewanee Auditorium, and Swayback Hall, owing to its distinctly sagging ceiling paved with acoustic tiles. Among the University's underground history is the tale that this building burns, set in 1959 by an undergraduate, when he knows that Guerry Hall would soon be providing a new and much improved theatre / concert hall.

Juhan Gymnasium under construction (U. Archives)

Juhan Gymnasium as completed (U. Archives)

Juhan Gymnasium, however, is decidedly Gothic, ruggedly masculine, looking with its two octagonal towers and crenellated battlements rather like a National Guard Armory.

Interestingly enough, keeping up with the Joneses of semi-professional college sports facilities, Juhan Gymnasium gets a number of dormitory rooms for visiting teams added to its upstairs front, overlooking Texas Avenue. At that moment there was still no hotel in Sewanee.

From the narrow focus on Sewanee-in-Stone, that this book often insists on, it is important to note that Juhan Gymnasium returns to coursed ashlar, a stone-setting style not seen on campus since the Carnegie-funded Science Hall (1912), plus two minor appendages, circa-1950, for St. Luke's and for the Torian wing of Emerald Hodgson Hospital.

Here are Ayers & Godwin's specifications for the facing stone on the building:

> 14. Facing Stone. All facing stone on the exterior of the building shall be local sandstone quarried on the University's property at Sewanee, Tennessee. The stone shall be not less than 6" thick with sawed beds and ends, the face to be rocked or pitched as directed and approved by the Architect.
>
> The stone shall be laid up random regular fashion as indicated on the detail drawings.

The face size of the stones shall be approximately as shown but may be varied to fit openings, etc.

The stone shall be tied to the backing with metal anchors every 16" in height and every 16" horizontally.

The stone shall be selected for color. All stone shall meet the Architect's approval before any stone is layed.

18. LAYING STONE VENEER. All stone on all elevations of the building shall be laid up as hereinbefore specified. The veneer shall be tied to the backing every 16" on center vertically and horizontally with 3/16" zinc coated "Z" anchors, in accordance with directions from the Architect.

All stone veneer shall be laid with Combination Mortar and all joints shall be finished with tool of size and shape as directed by Architect.

Stone veneer shall be laid up with mortar joints of color as directed by the Architect.

Stones shall be laid with a shoved joint on full bed of mortar. Running the stone veneer above the backing will not be permitted.

The backing of stone veneer shall be solidly parged to full ½" thickness, then the stone veneer shall be slushed full of mortar forming a solid masonry wall with all joints solid and free of voids of any description.

The parging of back-up shall be of same mortar as used in laying the stone veneer work. The laying of all stone veneer and masonry unit backing shall be executed in a manner to meet the approval of the Architect and in strict accordance with his instructions.

If the Architect's specs sound a bit over-fussy, it is probably a reflection of his nervousness in overseeing a building craft performance that is alien to him and his 1950s contemporaries. The stone masons involved know exactly how to do the work, and get it right, owing to an unbroken tradition of such work passed on for several generations in Sewanee.

The mortar joints on the old part of Juhan Gymnasium are as solid now as they were when set. Regrettably, some of the joints of the 10-year-old Fowler Center stonework are already starting to show signs of distress. But that's a story that can be delayed to another day.

There's one more document, squirreled away in the University Archives, a blue-dittoed job report, circulated among all the contractors on June 17, 1957, some weeks before the gym's scheduled completion.

The first item of nine relating to the Gymnasium (Job No. 2603) is addressed to the stone masons on the job:

> Masons laying stone veneer on Northwest elevation, that is, the side wall of the gymnasium. We are advised that all stone to complete the facing will be delivered to the job during the coming three week period. Based on this, we should complete all stone work in four weeks. Our Superintendent advised Friday that we were out of stone for side stretcher courses; we have stone for pilaster corners. We hope to get additional stretcher stone Monday, June 17, otherwise we can probably use additional stone masons on the Inn.

Other contractors are then addressed: (2), plasterers, Roberts Brothers, Inc.; (3) glaziers, Craig-Morris Glass Company; (4) roofers, Tri-State Roofing Company; (5) tilers, Wallace Tile Company; (6) no one specified; (7) millwork carpenters, O'Neill Manufacturing Company; and (8) painters, Jefferson Painting Company.

The ninth and final item gives a Finishing Schedule, broken down by each sub-contractor, to yield a completion of the building by August 15, 1957.

Some future historian may fact-check this projection to see if the workers do meet the deadline.

What seems more important, however, is the bottom line, reported to the Board of Trustees by Vice-Chancellor in his centennial-year summary that under the current administration there are 21 stone buildings, built or under construction, including "the new Juhan Gymnasium and Swimming Pool which cost $846,000" (Proceedings, 1958, p. 36).

It is an impressive statement, indicative of a building boom, but then by this time the new unpaid Director of Development, Frank Alexander Juhan, is carrying the ball towards a Ten Million Dollar Campaign touchdown.

THIS WAY TO THE VOMITORY

ATTACHED TO THE ARCHITECT'S WEEKLY JOB REPORT for Juhan Gymnasium (Job No. 2603) is a job report for the Stadium (Job No. 2679) and for the Library Stacks, St. Luke's School of Theology (Job No. 2509), showing all are going on concurrently, the week of June 17, 1957.

The coaches wanted new bleachers, and Dr. McCrady jumped at the chance to salute Rome's Coliseum. Considering his love for classical Roman architecture, it is amazing he did not propose rounded arches elsewhere. But this was his chance and he enjoyed it.

Compared with the other jobs Ayers & Godwin will do for Sewanee, the Stadium is simple, like baking cookies, and cheap, costing about $40,000, or roughly 1/20th of the cost of the Gym and Swimming Pool.

But in terms of its symbolic value, what will be called Harris Stadium is immensely important.

To see why, let's go to the flagpole, at the north end of the football field, around which is wrapped a running track.

The flagpole's base is a rock-solid hexagonal prism. On each of its six faces is a bronze plaque. Let us now praise famous football teams. Reading and weeping, with deep nostalgic pleasure, is certainly permissible:

- Team of 1899 / undefeated and untied / won 5 games in 6 days / on a 2,000 mile trip / opponents / Georgia, Georgia Tech / Tennessee, Southwestern / Texas, Texas A&M / Tulane, LSU, Mississippi / Cumberland, Auburn, North Carolina / Champions of the South.
- Team of 1898 / undefeated and untied / Co-Champions of the South.
- This flagpole / erected in 1959 by the / Class of 1901 / in tribute to great Sewanee football teams.
- Team of 1963 / undefeated and untied / and College Athletic Conference champions.
- Team of 1958 / first undefeated / and / untied University team since 1899.

■ Team of 1900 / undefeated in the S.I.A. . . . / Team of 1909 / undefeated and untied / by Southern teams / Champions of the South.

In this era of Superdome Football, where institutions like the University of Arkansas are building stadium additions for $60 million (cheap) with $10 million Jumbo-Tron digital video screens, Sewanee's football field looks as puny as its recent win-loss records, against such mighty opponents as Rose-Hulman.

As a devout non-athlete, the present writer finds this apparent lack of interest in highly paid football players absolutely wonderful. But you can bet there are some a-lums who shake their gray heads sadly at this state of affairs. How are the once-mighty fallen!

Anyway, leaving the flagpole and walking around the edge of the track, counterclockwise, we pass about 100 feet of bleachers, splintery pine slab seats bolted to a steel scaffold which is anchored with big concrete shoes into the Sewanee Conglomerate.

Then, suddenly, there is a splendid little fieldstone structure, about 80 feet of midfield seats, rising as 11 tiers up to the press box.

The best features of this fieldstone stadium are two narrow slots, cut through the rising bank of the grandstand, and rock-faced, looking as if a way has been cut through geologic strata by hard-rock miners.

Harris Stadium vomitorium: the way in is also the way out.

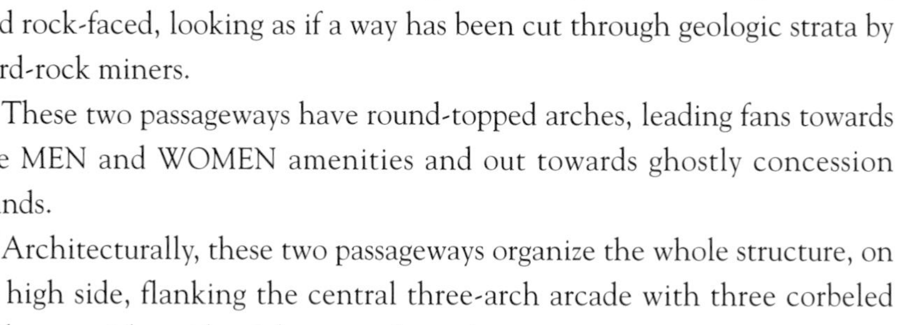

These two passageways have round-topped arches, leading fans towards the MEN and WOMEN amenities and out towards ghostly concession stands.

Architecturally, these two passageways organize the whole structure, on its high side, flanking the central three-arch arcade with three corbeled arches on either side of the central arcade.

This field visit—made at 7 A.M. on October 3, 2002—confirms suspicions made while looking at the stadium blueprints many months ago, namely, that the loveliest part of the structure has the ugliest of names: VOMITORY! The blueprints, signed by Sanford M. Ayers, show a front elevation of the stadium with the notation "line of vomitory above" at a certain point over the two arch-tunnelways.

Not to prolong the jokiness here, it turns out that the word refers not to the spot where drunken fans can vomit over the railing but to the old latin word for "the way out" (vomitorium).

Those who recall the personal interest of Vice-Chancellor Edward McCrady in all such architectural projects, and remember he majored in Greek and Latin as an undergraduate, can easily detect his hand in this little jestful pedantry.

Anyone thinking in deconstructionist terms, today, could take a single linguistic artifact like vomitory and relate it to the whole ignoble Roman tradition of stadium gladiators and their modern helmeted counterparts on today's gridiron. Not being deconstructionists, of course, you and I can forego that intellectual pleasure.

Two other items about the stadium seem worth noting.

One is that the press box, originally designed as an open-air pavilion, heavy timbered with wood-shingle siding, is today tarted up with plate-glass windows and vinyl siding.

YEA SEWANEE'S RIGHT, as the giant sign on the front of the press box screams it, but at this spot it's merely right with the rest of Vinylized America. It would be an easy fix to restore the original skin if anyone cared.

The other item of possible interest is an old-looking bronze plaque bolted to the rock wall beneath the press box window. It has a bas-relief portrait of Shirley Inman Majors (1913–1981), who was head coach for 21 years (1957–1977), coach of the undefeated teams of 1958 and 1963, and

Football Writers National Coach of the Year (1973). "This memorial given in grateful appreciation by his Sewanee players / October 1981."

Anyone who has even a millimeter-deep grasp of football history recognizes immediately that Shirley Majors is the patriarch of the Majors Football Dynasty. Three of his sons (John, Bill, and Bob) played great football for the University of Tennessee and then had distinguished coaching careers. Their sons continue the tradition.

Best, for those of us who like to see home-boys do well, Shirley Majors and his wife (Elizabeth Bobo) grew up, married, and lived close by, in Lynchburg, Tennessee, a town best known as the home of Jack Daniels Whiskey. Majors moved up from high-school coaching—at Huntland, Tennessee, where his teams compiled a 70–7 record—to coaching at the University of the South (www.oskie.com).

The bronze portrait is a mighty-fine likeness, as we say around here, worth the climb up the stadium steps.

TWO EVISCERATIONS

Some time around 1955, with real cash coming into the University's kitty, there begins to be talk of renovating two of the oldest permanent buildings, St. Luke's Hall (1876) and Walsh Memorial Hall (1890).

On October 25, 1955, an Atlanta structural and architectural engineer, William H. Armstrong, writes a letter to Dr. McCrady regarding the "safeness" of Walsh Hall.

Armstrong is guardedly optimistic about the landmark building holding itself up for a while longer, despite "deflections" of various structural members producing uneven floors, and in some cases, "termite damage," causing deflections in original wood beams.

His bottom line, undoubtedly because he knows how the engineering drama should play out, is to say that he recommends "that complete renovation of the building be accomplished as soon as practicable."

Similar surgery is recommended for St. Luke's Hall, in 1955, according to Arthur Ben Chitty's "Sewanee: Then and Now" essay:

> So beloved had St. Luke's Hall become that when age had overtaken it in 1955 the University Regents decided to preserve the outer structure intact and completely rebuild the interior.
>
> Brice Construction Company of Birmingham won the contract, and Mr. Brice himself supervised the complicated task. Partitions and floors were stripped out leaving only the outside walls and roof.
>
> The effect was like a coliseum.
>
> Painstakingly an entirely new interior was constructed and a new wing added on the back so that from the front it was impossible to tell that any changes had been made (Chitty, 1979, p. 9).

Chitty says that in 1979 two of the principals in the St. Luke's and Walsh renovations, contractor Houston Brice Jr. and Gilbert Roberts, the on-site superintendent, gave a taped reminiscence to the University Archive. Here is a condensation of their remarks in Chitty's paraphrase:

> Saint Luke's was in bad shape. We had to remove all inside walls and partitions. The university wanted to save the roof, which was metal covered, and install slate. We took out the stairwells and put in towers to support the roof. We used the old floors to work on while we installed our steel and bar joists. Still using the old floors, we started at

Walsh Hall

> the top and poured the concrete floor slabs, working our way to the bottom level, tearing out each old floor as we finished the new one on top of it.
>
> The roof trusses in Saint Luke's were sound. Later when we did the same sort of job on Walsh Hall, we found the trusses hollow from dry rot. These 12 by 12 timbers looked perfectly good but we had to suspend work while we braced them with steel beams (Chitty, p. 9).

This is a fascinating narrative. Non-engineers might wonder: if the old floors were strong enough to support all the bracing, formwork, equipment and workers, dealing with the floor above, while the steel and concrete was dropped in there, then just possibly the old building was strong enough not to have been eviscerated at all.

Brice and Roberts's reminiscence continues:

Professors' Common Room, Walsh Hall, circa 1920 (U. Archives)

"Back to Saint Luke's. The stone walls had originally been laid up with nothing but lime and sand. The outside stones were uniform but the inside walls were made of the leftover chips. In many places they were so loose that they had to be replaced.

"We had to work carefully for fear the outside walls might topple before we got them tied together.

"When we finally anchored our steel bar joists to them they were stronger than when new.

"We did not have to clean the outside walls at Saint Luke's, but we steam-cleaned Walsh because it had been exposed to the smoke from the old coal heating plant" (Chitty, p. 9).

A decision is made to take the old lecture hall first floor of St. Luke's and split it into two floors, while keeping the two dormitory floors above at the same height, thereby yielding four floors where only three had been before. The only place where a sense of the original floor height remains today is in the old chapel, at the north end of St. Luke's, with a tall barrel-vault ceiling, and five old Corinthian-style wall brackets marking where four gothic arches seem to have been in the original building. The space is now a handsome seminar room.

A similar proposal—getting four stories where only three had been—is put to the Walsh renovation.

It is calculated that adding a fourth floor would cost an additional

$150,000, so this option is scrapped; the three floor original plan is adhered to, at a total project cost of more than $352,000 (Proceedings, 1957, p. 22).

As to the St. Luke's renovation, the Vice-Chancellor reports to the Board of Trustees that it has cost $497,000 (Proceedings, 1958, p. 36).

The pricetag on the 15-foot-high arcade on the south of Walsh (with its reinforced concrete upstairs walkway) comes out to be $53,346, according to a letter from Jim Godwin to Dr. McCrady dated February 13, 1958.

Two other figures may be of interest, square foot costs, as Sewanee's architectural pageant marches inexorably towards the 1990s and beyond. In a letter from Godwin to McCrady, dated May 31, 1957, is the revelation that the renovation of St. Luke's costs approximately $12.15 per square foot, and Walsh Hall, still in process as of that moment, cannot be accomplished "for less than $14.00 per square foot."

Given that McClurg Dining Hall (2000) comes in minimally at about $428 per square foot, and the Chapel of the Apostles (2000) comes in at about $1,000 per square foot, the 1957 costs don't seem extravagant at all.

Walkway along Walsh Hall's Quadrangle side

Regrettably, for historic preservation types, there seems to be nothing left of the original interiors of these two landmark Victorian buildings. The 1950s prove to be a period of historical amnesia, out with the old and in with the new, though to Dr. McCrady's personal credit, the wonderful sandstone shells of the two buildings are preserved, nearly intact. He had to fight the professional architects to achieve that.

A small sense of what is lost, in the twin eviscerations, is this interior photo (p. 190) of the professors' common room, in Walsh Hall. The photo is taken probably before 1920, to judge from the daffodil-shaped telephone receiver in the lower righthand corner, but the furnishings and decor remained unchanged to 1957.

Barely visible is the dark wood-beamed ceiling, with wood strips forming a squared parquet arrangement; the plain but practical chair-rail around the walls (a finish carried throughout the building); the ancient oriental rugs on the floors; the Craftsman or Stickley style chairs, tables, and writing desk; the dark wood-paneled double doors; and a quaint assortment of engravings, paintings, and other wall art, as idiosyncratic as the professors who inhabited this space.

Looking at the stripped-out interiors of St. Luke's and Walsh-Ellett today fills one with sadness, as if seeing a photo of some old family relative who is no longer with us; fortunately, in recent years, some heroic efforts have been made to hang on to some of the historic fabric that once enriched these original buildings.

Less is not always more, to take issue with a truism of modernists, less is sometimes simply less.

ALL SAINTS RESUMED

WE KNOW BY THE LETTER FROM ARCHITECT JIM GODWIN to Sewanee's CEO, Dr. Edward McCrady, that work on All Saints' Chapel is being resumed around May 31, 1954—nearly 50 years after the stop-work order of 1907—when the elaborate budget is prepared as part of what Godwin terms the "planning stages."

Surviving sheets of Ayers & Godwin's blueprints for the Chapel's "alterations and additions" are dated December 9, 1955 (floor plan); March 6, 1956 (lovely elevations south, west, north, and east); August 22, 1956 (elevations of the bell tower); and May 7, 1957 ("room finish schedule," showing what is to be plastered, painted, etc.

Formal approval is requested from the Board of Trustees, and approved at their June 1957 meeting, according to these University minutes:

> The Chairman of the Board of Regents, Mr. Woods, said that the Regents had decided to go ahead with the building of the Chapel, but that they wanted the approval of the Board of Trustees.
>
> The Vice-Chancellor then announced that the estimated time of completion of the Chapel varied from 1 year to 1½ years and that extra money would be needed for the Chapel in about 1 year to 1½ years.
>
> Mr. Kimball then moved that the Board of Trustees give approval of action of the Board of Regents in letting the contract for the Chapel. This motion was seconded by the Rev. Edward B. Guerry and passed unanimously (Proceedings, 1957, p. 23).

The politics of this procedure should not be overlooked.

The Board of Regents is the equivalent of a corporation's board of directors, perhaps a dozen Big Mules (as we say in Alabama), while the Board of Trustees can be seen as more like the corporation's shareholders, numbering more than 100 and representing the University's 22 (then) to 28 (now) dioceses.

Regents deferring to the Trustees is probably a formal and diplomatic way of recognizing that it is the Trustees who will continue to shake their diocesan trees to find the extra money and memorial funds for completing the Chapel, adding stained glass windows, etc.

R. A. Cram's reinforced concrete roof trusses plan circa 1907

It is clear from a variety of sources that All Saint's Chapel is a magnificent obsession for Dr. Edward McCrady. The best authority available is his son, Dr. James Waring McCrady, an emeritus professor of French at Sewanee, and another Renaissance man, as painter, sculptor, musician, historian, linguist, and expert in heraldry.

Here are two brief excerpts from a three-page memorandum (September 25, 1981) that Waring McCrady writes to accompany the gift of his father's drawings and Ayers & Godwin blueprints of All Saints Chapel to the University Archives:

> There are many buildings on campus for which Dr. McCrady did the layout, determined the location and dimensions, and sketched the rough outlines and detail (Hunter, Cleveland, Juhan Gym, Benedict, Courts, the Library, Woods Hall, etc.), but the chapel was the one building over which he imposed his authority and his personal design in every detail, even the placement of the electrical outlets. Everything above the base of the clerestory windows is his own design, as is every detail east of the second bay of the choir. . . .
>
> The mechanics of transferring his hundreds of drawings to working blueprints Dr. McCrady left to Ayers and Godwin. . . . For some technical reason, it is not legally correct to say that Dr. McCrady was an "architect." He had no license. Ayers and Godwin were technically the architects. But every detail of the design, even including the selection of the stone, the placement and weight of the steel beams, the slate of the roof, even the exact composition of the controversial ceiling

bricks, even the flooring and the selection of its marbles were his, all most precisely.

Dr. McCrady's obsession turns out to have started back in the 1930s, when he is a biology professor at Sewanee, and he draws plans and publishes a pen-and-ink drawing of what the Chapel ought to look like. It, and an interior drawing made circa 1950, together bear considerable resemblance to what is completed in 1959.

McCrady's Obsession can get pretty intense, as we hear in his letter (November 30, 1957) to Jim Godwin:

Edward McCrady's design for All Saints' Chapel (U. Archives)

> I have just noticed that in Saint Augustine's vault you have omitted both the ridge and groin ribs which I indicated in my original drawings. The ridge ribs I recognize as dispensable, but the groin ribs are at convex intersections which simply cannot be left without some kind of trim or edging. I don't know what you had in mind, but I am sure that stone ribs would look better than anything else.
>
> Another thing which I have just noticed is that the mullions within what are generally called the petals of the rose in the main West Window are shown with rectangular sections (see section 3, plate A-15) instead of having doubled or coved edges. This is a very crude detail in one of the most elegant parts of the whole structure. I think the specifications ought to be changed and coving indicated along those mullions as we have it on all others.

Dr. McCrady not only argues his points well. He seems to make it impossible for any other viewpoint to prevail. The proof is in checking out such details and seeing that his design wins the day. Here in the same letter is his discussion of the architects' hopelessly big corbel brackets, those ornamental swellings-out at the top of the pier ribs, about two-thirds up the wall from where the great stone arches start to create each roof vault:

> The four foot long corbel brackets on the piers in the nave and in the chancel are nearly twice as big as they ought to be. They ruin the scale of height for the vault, and are one of the factors leading to the decision, which I do not like, of destroying the stone walls already erected between the bases of the clerestory windows.
>
> I have looked through innumerable pictures of Gothic vaults and cannot find any anywhere with such massive terminations of the pier ribs, or any that would be improved by enlarging the corbels to these dimensions.
>
> I know their crowns have to receive the indirect lighting fixtures, but I doubt that they need to be quite as massive as they are and I am sure their vertical height could be reduced considerably with great advantage in their overall effect of the building.
>
> And in the same connection I just don't believe there is any excuse at all for tearing this four feet of stone wall down in order to build that portion of the external buttress as an integral part of the wall.

If the engineers maintain the necessity for this they will have to show me on the basis of their calculations.

Another quick visit to All Saints, always a sensual pleasure, continues to turn up previously unseen charms. This is probably why Waring McCrady likes to give chapel tours, as he does during Sewanee Families Weekend (September 29–30), this past weekend.

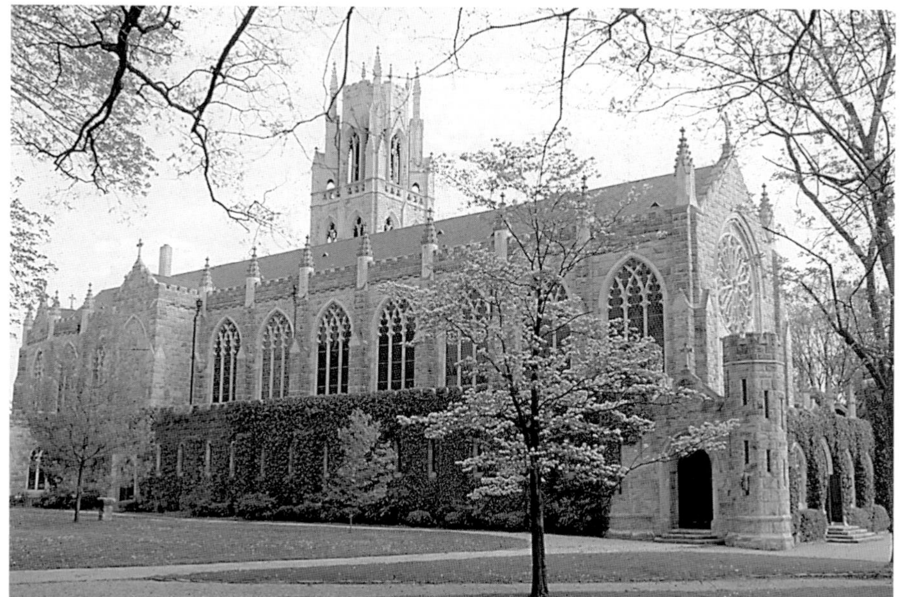

All Saints' Chapel in its finished glory

One example, among many possible, turns up in the ambulatory end of the north-south corridor of the sacristy wing. Here are two sharp-pointed Venetian Gothic stone archways. Their ratio of aperture width to apex height is more pointedly vertical than the standard ratio established for the rest of the Chapel's archways.

What is going on here?

The mystery is solved, quickly, by quoting from the same letter (November 30, 1957):

> The last thing I have on my mind today is the fact that the stone arches which were removed from the hallways at the junction of the old and new portions of St. Luke's have not been used for anything and they ought to be.
>
> There are several places where they could be introduced into All Saints' Chapel. They have an aperture of four feet, but the stones are so thick that the total diameter at the scrolls is six feet ten and above

the scrolls six feet six, so probably the best place for them would be in the two doors of Saint Augustine's Chapel (one entering the priests' sacristy and the other entering the hall).

Or if you feel that the door entering the hall should be of double width, then you could use one of them on each of the two doors for the priests' sacristy. These are the only places where the aperture in the wall could easily be adapted to the dimensions of these stones.

Other places which tempt me are the two ends of the North-South corridor in the sacristy wing, and the two entries into the ambulatory; but in all of these places the thickness of the stone would require it being buried in the walls.

The architect chooses the last option, obviously, perhaps in hopes that the Vice-Chancellor's argument will be buried as well.

Founders' window in All Saints' Chapel

FOUNDERS' DAY

SEWANEE DATES ITS OFFICIAL BEGINNING FROM A MEETING of the founders on Lookout Mountain, July 4, 1857, but it has designated its annual Founders' Day commemoration as falling on the Tuesday nearest October 10, in recognition of the cornerstone dedication on October 10, 1860.

It's a nice way of saying that the University's founding is carved in stone.

What better place to re-live the day than in All Saints' Chapel, a work of art composed of many thousands of stones, consecrated on Founders' Day, October 10, 1975.

Here, for the record, is the official explanation, printed with the consecration's Order of Service:

> The Chapel was brought to its present state in 1959 and stands according to a resolution of the Trustees in 1904 as a "memorial to all benefactors of the University."
>
> It occupies, architecturally, the focal point of campus, establishing visually the nature of this institution as a Christian University.
>
> With the elimination of the debt on the building in August of 1975, its consecration and completion are celebrated today, Founders' Day, 1975.

On another Founders' Day—held October 8, 2002—the main event is an Honors Convocation for the announcement of undergraduate recipients of prizes, honors, and other distinctions, plus the awarding of honorary doctorates to four distinguished individuals:

- Thomas Clark Ely, Bishop of Vermont (Doctor of Divinity);
- Pratima Kale, President of the International Institute of Rural Reconstruction (Doctor of Civil Law);
- Chadwick Dearing Oliver, Distinguished Professor of Forestry at Yale (Doctor of Science);

■ Edward Osborne Wilson, Professor Emeritus of Biology at Harvard (Doctor of Science).

The turnout is not large. Student attendance is visibly optional. The audience is out-numbered by the University Choir, in their white cottas and cardinal red cassocks, and by the University Faculty, in their wizard suits of many colors and textures. Academic processions are always fun to watch, like a Mardi Gras parade, but marching to an organ instead of a brass band, the professors look chock-full of gravid wisdom.

I stand with my back to one of the Chapel's gigantic pillars, which plunge into the marble floor as heptagonal (that magic number seven again) prisms, and in fact continue as rougher stone prisms into the Chapel's undercroft, stopping only when they make a firm-footed contact with the Sewanee Conglomerate bedrock. (It amazes me, one morning in mid-summer, when I follow a workman down into the Chapel basement, to see not the expected block-like piers, but these still geometric masses. All summer the workmen have been excavating around these piers to install a gigantic heating and air-conditioning unit for the Chapel, which explains the disembodied voices issuing from somewhere beneath the Chapel floor, whenever I explore its vacant solitary spaces.) So only when the chisel-edge of the pillar touches my backbone does the dim-bulb in my brain suddenly get brighter, momentarily, to connect the two vertical stacks of stone as one and the same.

After a minimum of liturgical garnish—led by University Chaplain Tom Ward, who happens to be a head taller than everyone else in the procession—there are two riveting anthems performed by the Choir, full of soprano swells that seem to spike up around the high-vaulted ceiling.

Then comes the Founders' Day Address, delivered by Professor Wilson, who among other distinctions, is one of the world's leading authorities on ants, and the man said to have coined the term "biodiversity."

Unfortunately, when he begins speaking, the Chapel's single biggest flaw emerges.

Every single phrase of Wilson's amplified voice reverberates, like acoustical fireworks, hanging in the air to obscure whatever phrase happens to follow it!

For anyone accustomed to the Chapel's acoustical-challenge, it seems probable they soon learn to pace their phrases, pausing for a few milliseconds to let the echoes fade, before plunging on.

But for those of us who admire E. O. Wilson's work, read his books, and hang on every word apt to issue forth from his wise gray head, being able to discriminate only about 40 percent of what he is saying is cruel indeed.

One of the bon-mots that does cut through the acoustical clutter is Wilson saying: "For everyone else to live like an American, at our present levels of consumption, we would need about four Planet Earths." I catch this, in part, because he says precisely the same thing the prior day, in a panel discussion (with Kale and Oliver) in Blackman Auditorium, the big lecture hall in Woods Laboratories with a polychrome Periodic Table of Elements on the wall behind the panelists. After the discussion, when University officials are trying to tug Wilson out of the hall, to speed him on to a black-tie dinner reception, Wilson is asked by me if anyone is preaching asceticism, like first-century Christians, as a way to counter America's over-consumption propensities. He laughs and quips that for Americans to give up present consumer habits is as likely as having the Pope decide to stop being a Catholic.

The point here is that after modern architecture's number-one problem, leaky roofs, the next most intractable problem is bad acoustics. This is something that in All Saints' Chapel cannot be cured, even with great big speakers, that simply pick up the amplified sound and broadcast acoustic confusion.

The same vast stone and glass faces that enhance polyphony in choral and instrumental voices yield something like pure semantic nonsense when we are trying to hear facts, logic, and reasoned discourse.

To recall Beaumarchais's quip about opera, what is too silly to be said must be sung.

Actually, the only silly moment in the Founders' Day ceremony comes when the honorary degrees are conferred, in Latin, a language few of us are fluent in these days.

Honoris Causa!

SHAPARD TOWER

THERE HAS BEEN A BELL TOWER ENVISIONED for the University's chapel since at least 1886. Its shape and size fluctuate, from Woods's plan to McBee and Nixon's plan, to Ralph Adams Cram's insistence that college chapels should not have towers, then to Cram's successor firm which delivers its "proposed plan for the completion of All Saints' Chapel" in the late 1940s, then finally to the version designed by Dr. Edward McCrady—apparently as a riposte to Cram & Ferguson's rejected plan—whose elegant drawings by Ayers & Godwin win the day just in time for Sewanee's centennial celebration. McCrady had decreed Woods's plan too slavishly a copy of St. Mary-the-Virgin at Oxford, McBee's spire too high, Cram's position irrelevant, and his successors' design too much like Breslin. This cleared the drafting table for what won the day.

The important thing is not the tower details, however, but having the tower exist at all. William Morgan, in his book *Collegiate Gothic: The Architecture of Rhodes College* (1989), quotes the donor of the 140-foot-tall Halliburton Tower to Southwestern (as Rhodes was then called) as to the absolute necessity of such a structure:

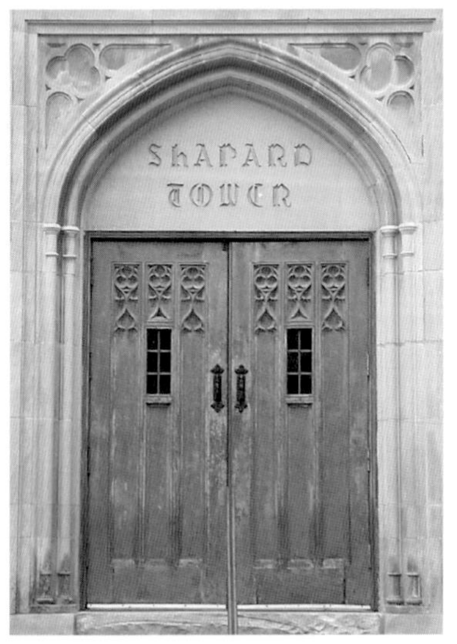

> We must have beauty in our schools and colleges, as well as protecting walls. But as of today, Southwestern is like a charming lady who is becomingly attired, lacking only a hat. Mrs. Halliburton and I decided to buy this lady the hat to complete her sartorial elegance (Wesley Halliburton, quoted at the 1961 dedication of the tower in Morgan, p. 57).

The major donors for the Shapard Tower, a splendid 134-foot-tall tower rising above the south transept of All Saints' Chapel, are the Shapard family of Griffin, Georgia.

But for some reason, known only to the University Relations wind machine, the tower's dedication plays second-fiddle, so to say, to the Leonidas Polk Memorial Carillon stowed away inside it.

Lots of ink gets spilled over the carillon, in the *Sewanee Alumni News* (November 1956, pp. 12–13), and there is an illustrated 12-page brochure printed up for the dedication of the carillon on April 12, 1959, with an abundance of gee-whiz statistical facts:

> The largest bell, the bourdon, weighs nearly four tons and the smallest weighs 22 pounds. An electric motor eliminates bell-pulling by rope, and the motor swings the bourdon. This massive bell will also strike the hour for Breslin Tower's clock.
>
> The 56 bells (total weight: 23 tons) are made of bronze, the larger ones being 78 percent copper and 22 percent tin. To give the high bells more "ring," a greater percentage of tin was used.
>
> The four-story split belfry begins with the bourdon on the bottom, then the seven other bass bells, then the keyboard, officially termed a clavier, and on top the medium and high bells. The keys resemble broom handles and their two rows correspond to the white and black keys of the piano.
>
> At the keyboard the bellmaster is in the midst of his bells, a location of prime importance, according to (carillon designer Arthur) Bigelow. Connections between keys and appropriate bells must be kept within 12 to 15 feet "for the sake of controllability," he explains.

Shapard Tower

Visually, at least, Shapard Tower makes a modest and conventional statement, doing what Gothic does best, expressing its uncompromising verticality.

Its first and second "stories" offer a door and windows that match up with the rest of All Saints' Chapel.

The third story, however, introduces a new kind of fenestration. It is not only tall and slender, remarkably so, but totally open, with only the slenderest stone mullions topped off by light tracery. The openings, of course, allow the bells to give their full voices out over the campus.

The fourth story, the upper belfry, is likewise open for its sounding bells. But its windows also return to a more conventional ratio of height to width, a nice architectural touch, rather like counterpoint for the second story windows.

Shapard's roof also is nicely designed, neatly trimmed out with cut limestone, smooth contrast to the rugged pitched faces of coursed sandstone, plus crocketed pinnacles of sensible size (unlike its neighbor McClurg) and crenellated battlements of quite-peaceable depth.

One of the many tributes to this tower, which has in some ways superseded Breslin Tower as the photographic icon for Sewanee, is that it is the only structure visible for miles around. When you stand on the bluff edge of Lost Cove, perhaps in the vicinity of Rattlesnake Springs Road, the top of Shapard Tower stands tall above the treeline, looking as if it has been there for ever-so-many centuries.

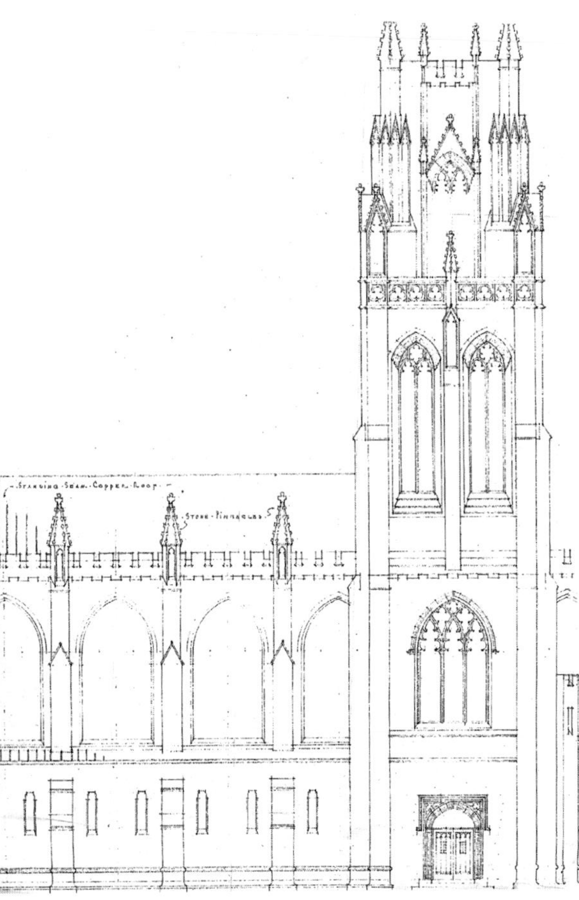

MORE ROOM AT THE INN

WHILE CONSTRUCTION CONTINUES ON ALL SAINTS' Chapel, in the late 1950s, a building very secular in spirit is being constructed at the north end of campus.

It is the new Sewanee Inn.

This one-story structure sprawls like a ranch-house with stables.

It has the familiar cladding of fieldstone, but nearly everything else about it brings a new architectural spirit to town. This may be because its principal outlook is not directed towards the central campus—historically known as University Place—as nearly all of Sewanee's other buildings are.

Instead, the new inn's outlook is towards the golf course, the most secular and hedonistic of places, despite its undoubtedly being blessed by lots of clergy gamboling over its green fairway pastures.

This is not irreverent whimsy; according to a brief historical sketch supplied by Waring McCrady, the new inn's first customers are the House of Bishops convened for the University's 1957 centennial!

Stepping into the Sewanee Inn lobby, on October 14 (Columbus Day), we discover a bronze plaque that says "Sewanee Inn 1957 / Edward McCrady Vice-Chancellor / Frank A. Juhan Developer / Clara Shoemate Manager."

This provides a terse summary of the principals involved. The only puzzler is Bishop Juhan being labeled as the inn's developer. But we remember, from a previous chapter on the Juhan Gymnasium, that after being the University's chancellor, Juhan served as unpaid director of development. Juhan, as Florida's bishop, also may explain how the Sewanee Inn's architects—Kemp Bunch & Jackson—turn out to be from Jacksonville, Florida.

Now the inn is an exceedingly modest-scale project—a lodge with a restaurant and lounge in it and 24 motel-like units broken out as four six-room modules—but it shows the careful attention to detail expected from a good architectural firm.

Noting the firm's name on a sheaf of blueprints in the University's PPS plan room, a few months ago, a quick search from our googly-eyed friend (www.google.com) turns up a wealth of information about who Kemp Bunch & Jackson (now known with the trendy trinitarian initials KBJ Architects) actually are.

First and foremost, in 1954, they design a spectacular high-rise tower, 300 feet tall, for the Prudential Insurance Company's South Central headquarters in Jacksonville. It is the city's first high-rise building, sitting on a choice triangular lot on the St. John's River, and is known today as 841 Prudential Drive, a landmark building refurbished in 2001 by the same firm.

Their website notes that Kemp Bunch & Jackson was established in 1946. With over 50 employees KBJ is now the "largest architecture / interior design firm in Northeast Florida" (www.kbj.com/profile).

Projects in recent years include the Times-Union Center for the Performing Arts, Lamborghini-USA Headquarters, and the United States Courthouse, all in Jacksonville; the Naval Nuclear Power Training Center (Charleston, S.C.), Orlando International Airport Master Plan, Hyatt Hotel and Conference Center (Orlando), and the Savannah International Airport.

So once again, sweet to say, Sewanee snags another young firm at the beginning of its fast rise to the top.

Let's take a quick virtual tour of the inn:

We start in the lobby, which has a warm-feeling floor of very large flagstones, and a big copper-topped fireplace.

This fireplace has two faces, one for the lobby, and one for the dining room behind it.

Sewanee Inn's golf course side

The dining room has great plate-glass windows opening up a nice view to the golf course.

Faux beams cover the functional steel—boxed-up from solid oak planks. They span a good distance over to fieldstone clad piers. The inn no longer operates its restaurant, nor uses its large kitchen, except as a preparation unit for catered oc-

The relaxed 1950s ranch style of the Sewanee Inn

casions, normally by the University food service operator (Aramark).

There is also an amiable "Hearth Room," which has another stone fireplace with a splendid walnut mantel, a peeled and polished log section, with three squared walnut stanchions supporting it. This room serves for groups like the Emeritus Association when they hold their periodic meetings with invited speakers giving an afternoon program.

Outside, detached from the inn's lodge, are four modules containing six rooms each. Each module is canted slightly, to break up any aspect of "motel monotony."

Other nice details, thoughtfully designed by the KBJ firm, are the fact that the fronts of each unit have two small windows high enough on the wall to eliminate unwanted views from passersby. The backs of each unit, in clear contrast, are virtually all-glass. The ten windows, one door, and one air-conditioning unit are arranged in a pleasant Mondrian-like pattern.

Each module has one "deluxe" room equipped with a fireplace and an exposed-beam "half-cathedral" ceiling. These currently go for $82 a night, as opposed to $70 a night for the other units.

Actually, the inn manager says, the fourth module has five rooms (Rooms 20–24) occupied by students, perpetuating the old "dual use" philosophy for its earlier inns, while the sixth room (Room 19) is the innkeepers' linen room. This fourth module is also a later addition: the inn opened in 1957 with only 18 units.

The Sewanee News (April 1957), in its announcement of the new inn, says about $375,000 has been raised for it. Among its amenities will be "a restaurant, two private dining rooms, a lounge, and outside terrace" and the dining capacity will be "200 during the winter and 300 during the summer."

Whatever else may be claimed for the Sewanee Inn (1957), it marks yet another level of increasingly relaxed and casual design, to be followed by similar glass and rock facades such as Van Ness, The Outside Inn (now Ayres Multicultural Center), Lambda Chi Alpha, Beta Theta Pi, many of the newer Woodland apartment units, a host of new professors' residences, and most significantly, the two modernist buildings (Cravens and Hamilton) designed by Edwin A. Keeble.

CONSCIOUSLY ANTIQUARIAN

NEWCOMERS—AND EVEN SOME LONGTIME RESIDENTS of the Sewanee community —are startled to learn that Guerry Hall dates only from 1961.

Guerry Hall looks as if it has been here forever.

This is artful contrivance. Ayers & Godwin, and their behind-the-scenes designer, Dr. Edward McCrady, expressly intend that all buildings on the central campus should look "as if they had always been there"—a deft architectural metaphor for the venerable age of the Church and the Liberal Arts tradition. So they cook up a consciously antiquarian facade for what is a great hulking auditorium / theater / concert hall. Around this 1,000-seat auditorium is wrapped nine new classrooms, nine new offices, and an art gallery, all badly needed by the University for a long time.

Part of the antique-look of Guerry Hall is simply the weathering of the sandstone. Its craggy ashlared faces tend to gather the kind of atmospheric grime your automobile shows when it needs a good washing. There are also the meteorological peculiarities of the Sewanee mountaintop, which enjoys lots of rainfall, and remarkable amounts of fog, which seem to favor the growth of lichens and other colorizers, resulting in a wonderful patina that seems as old as time.

Long before the term post-modern is coined—or at least about 25 years before it, in the case of Guerry Hall, and its 1950s / 1960s siblings—Sewanee is doing post-modernist architecture. Those who pay attention to such labelizing—as the House Un-American Activities Committee did in calling 1930s lefties "premature anti-fascists" in the 1950s blacklisting period—may indict Sewanee for practicing Premature Post-Modernism.

Guerry Hall is dedicated on Founders' Day, October 10, 1961.

The annual ceremonial observance starts in All Saints' Chapel, and then, while everyone is singing Martin Luther's wonderful hymn, "Ein' feste Burg" (A mighty fortress is our God), the congregation processes out the door, across the campus, and into the auditorium of Guerry Hall.

The principal address is given by J. Albert Woods, former chairman of the Board of Regents; his subject, not surprisingly, is a rather eloquently worded encomium on Alexander Guerry, the University's Vice-Chancellor during the transitional period of 1938–1948:

> At the start of the Guerry Administration in 1938, the University was in serious, if not critical, financial condition.
>
> Its invested endowment was a mere $1,552,000, and even that was impaired by a loan of $300,000 from its own endowment funds. In total, the current fund deficit amounted to $474,000, buildings needed repair, the whole domain was run down and dilapidated.
>
> Almost the first act of the new Vice Chancellor was to borrow an additional $125,000, most of which was spent on paint, necessary repairs, and the beautifying of the campus.
>
> He then proceeded to pay off the loans as rapidly as possible, including the $300,000 borrowed from endowment funds, and he told the trustees and regents, and announced far and wide, that henceforth Sewanee could operate within its income.
>
> The hat would no longer be passed to cover constant annual deficits.

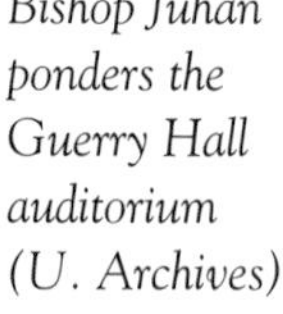

Bishop Juhan ponders the Guerry Hall auditorium (U. Archives)

> His first fiscal year wound up with a surplus of $47,000 and to this very moment, Sewanee has never had another deficit—one of the very few colleges or universities in America which can make that statement (University Archives, vertical file: Guerry Hall, Woods address, p. 4).

Among the other accomplishments of the Guerry Administration, Woods notes two, the commissioning of the Grand Campus Plan, drawn up by the Olmsted Brothers landscape architectural firm, in September 1946, and the launching of the Five Million Dollar Campaign, in February 1947.

So it is inevitable, almost an act of manifest destiny, that Guerry should be so honored by the next major administration.

More interestingly—for this writer so naive in the black magical arts of fundraising—it is a strategic masterstroke to have J. Albert Woods deliver the day's principal address. The strategy is akin to a very big-league baseball game, putting big hitters on deck, in hopes of driving home those teammates who manage to get themselves on base.

Anyway, it can be truly said that J. Albert Woods can jaw with the best.

Woods, of course, becomes the central figure in fundraising efforts, and the honoree for the Woods Laboratories (1968). Similarly, among the Board of Regents on this day in 1961, is Robert G. Snowden, who will be the next big hitter, finding much of the money for the Snowden Forestry Building (1962).

Or to shift metaphorical gears, it is akin to the ecclesiastical principle of apostolic succession, but working backwards, with the big fundraisers laying hands on their predecessors, to canonize them with a building named for them, so they in turn can be so honored after they decide to die.

This remarkably successful principle is formalized in the University Prayer which ends by calling on God to send "a never-failing succession of benefactors."

On a field-trip visit to Guerry Hall, the afternoon of October 16, 2002, the auditorium's backstage doors are open, to accommodate preparations for the evening's concert by Branford Marsalis and his orchestra.

Actually, as Kory Vrieze, coordinator for the Sewanee Summer Music Festival, explains, the original backstage doors can no longer be used, because they are about eight feet above grade. The mystery is quickly cleared up by the fact that in 1961 the original south wall of the auditorium faced onto a parking lot. Trucks could drive up and unload directly into the stag-

Guerry Hall today

ing area with the aid of a hoist. Now, without the drive-up, the only way to haul performance baggage into and out of Guerry is through the main (north) entrance doors.

Other changes to the auditorium include a series of baffles, shaped like large curved plywood shields, installed about three years ago by the Winger Corporation, a Minnesota company that specializes in helping concert halls improve their performance acoustics.

One archival photograph—taken about 1960, with Bishop Juhan cogitating on the steel skeleton and concrete-block walls of Guerry Auditorium (p. 210)—emphasizes the contextual differences between Guerry and its neighbors.

The important difference between it and its two neighbors, Convocation Hall—whose tile roof can be seen in the background—and Walsh-Ellett Hall—just out of camera-view to the left of the photo—is that Guerry Hall is quite honestly a 20th-century ferro-concrete building inside a medieval-looking skin. Convocation starts and stays primarily a 19th-century building of wood, stone, and glass. Walsh starts out the same way, then gets a radical woodectomy, replacing its wonderful wooden viscera with considerably less beautiful reinforced concrete.

Perhaps this is a five-cent synthesis of what Bishop Juhan is thinking. Or perhaps it isn't.

Anyway, in the dozen-plus buildings of Ayers & Godwin, in their Sewanee oeuvre, this building turns out rather nicely indeed.

Wrapped around the auditorium, in an L-shaped fashion, are a first-floor foyer (north) with restrooms; an east corridor composed of a four-room suite of offices on the northeast corner, for the Spanish Department, plus two classrooms; a similar second-floor corridor starting with the four-room suite of offices, for the French Department, plus a long language laboratory, currently filled with computer terminals and other high-tech apparatus to sharpen foreign language skills for Sewanee's students, and three classrooms (one currently occupied by the Sewanee Summer Music Festival operations) on the north corridor; plus a basement that includes other foreign language professors' offices and a classroom or two.

If you like to see languages arrayed in a visible hierarchy, note that the francophones occupy the corner suite with a view; the Spanish-speakers are directly below them, the sole-mia Italian professor (Leslie Richardson) is in the basement office with a window, and the non-western language professors share a suite of windowless offices in the south wall of Guerry's basement, below the defunct loading dock door.

Three of the basement rooms on the south corridor have door-tags identifying their original functions from when Guerry was also a theatrical venue. One says GREEN ROOM, one says WOMEN'S DRESSING ROOM, and one says MEN'S DRESSING ROOM. They are still used to accommodate music performers. The old COSTUME STORAGE ROOM has been moved across campus to the Tennessee Williams Center; in its place are the non-western language professors, occupying a no-frills Third World office ghetto.

Rumors circulating through Guerry that the language professors will all be deported to Gailor Hall provoke sporadic grumbling. At least one of them says that move will come over their dead protesting bodies.

It is, finally, the exterior facade of Guerry Hall that continues to please this particular passerby.

Symbolically, its principal entrance is a three-arch arcade, flanked on either side by two bays; this 2 + 3 +2 central block, coinciding with the auditorium's northernmost bulk, totals up to seven, that old lucky expression of the seven liberal arts. This central block is flanked by six bays on each side, for a 6 + 6 expression of the 12 apostles, leading to a nice theological statement of why it is there at all.

The facade is also trimmed out nicely.

A look at the Guerry blueprints in the University's PPS plan-room reveals that the windows are specified as Hope's "Cotswolds" Casement Sash; there is limestone trim around the windows; sandstone coping along the auditorium parapet; crocketed pinnacles carved out of limestone; and handsome wood batten doors, 2½ inches thick, with leaded glass, and wrought iron hinge plates.

All in all, Guerry Hall seems worth every dollar of the $650,000 spent on its construction.

EXPLORATORIUM

After the formal Collegiate Gothic grammar of ornament of Guerry Hall—with its crenellated battlements, crocketed pinnacles, coursed ashlar cut-stone walls, cannon-like gargoyle downspouts, and voussoir-arched arcades on its north and west sides—it is interesting to encounter the Snowden Forestry Building (1962), constructed just one year after Guerry's completion.

If they were flesh-and-blood people—not constructs of stone, concrete, and steel—Guerry and Snowden might recognize themselves as only distant cousins, despite having a common architectural sire.

A possible clue, as yet not researched, is that Guerry and six predecessors (Cleveland, Juhan, Harris Stadium, St. Luke's renovation, Walsh-Ellett renovation, and All Saints Chapel) are done by the architectural firm of Ayers & Godwin, while Snowden is the first of six works to bear the signature of Godwin & Beckett.

Obviously this successor firm can continue doing Guerry-type buildings—if you hold mental snapshots of duPont Library, Woods Laboratories, and Bishops Common in simultaneous view—but there is a definite note of defiance in Snowden that should not be missed.

For a start, look at the parapet directly above the main entrance, and you can see two perfectly round stones set in the otherwise pure random-shape and random-size chunks of fieldstone. This seems to be the first of a local mason's tradition, rather like a maker's mark, that can be seen elsewhere, as in the stone disks in the two sandstone walkways that angle out from the duPont Library entrance. One longtime Sewanee resident says the stone disks are the work of Columbus Green. They mostly are associated with 1960s buildings like this one.

There's also a nice innovation in the limestone window trim of letting some of the cut stones stick out in random lengths and random positionings.(Such trim is called "tabbed" trim.) That fine act of randomness is

Snowden Forestry Building

also seen in the otherwise orthodox Collegiate Gothic segmental arch entrance to the building.

As to its massing—architecturalese for how a building blocks itself up and out as a three-dimensional solid—Snowden could easily have been laid out as a simple two-story rectangular box—11 monotonous bays for its front and five bays on its side. To its credit, however, the building breaks up this front as a projecting central block and two projecting end-wings, for a nice 2 + 3 + 1 + 3 +2 arrangement of its window and entrance door. It's a simple shtik but it works. That is why, you hope, the client hires an architect to design a building.

Those of us who are architectural numerologists also like the seven-bay central section, as if to say to students that the seven liberal arts can be found in this building too, as well as the 7-come-11 crapshoot of crystallography, that microcosmic dance of molecules, where mysterious architectonic shapes happen by pure chance.

Even better, however, is that Snowden, housing the twinned Department of Forestry and Geology, is wonderful fun to explore. Starting with the heavy rock specimens parked outside the entrance, and proceeding in past a glass cabinet of museum-quality mineral specimens, you suddenly encounter a sawn section of a giant redwood tree about six feet in diameter blocking off half the hallway. Chronological tags trace its dendro-chronology from the year it was felled (1963) back to about 1,200 in its dead-center.

Snowden is a kind of Exploratorium.

Nearly every square foot of wall space gets some visual exhibit, something to engage the student's interest, some further evidence that these rock-and-wood academics are pursuing stuff of more than academic value.

The north stairwell has a geological profile of Sewanee's peculiar strata, measured in millions of years, with explanations of what stuff like Monteagle Limestone and Warren Point Sandstone (the principal material for Sewanee's buildings) are all about.

Wood-lovers roaming the building soon pick up on the fact that different walls and corridors are finished with different hardwoods—oak, pecan, chestnut, yellow poplar, and so on. Little brass plaques say, for example, that this is "Black Cherry donated by Ray M. Johnson, Huntland, Tennessee" (Room 208) or "Wormy Maple donated by Sam Carey Lumber Company, Memphis" (Room 205).

Somewhere in the building—perhaps in Van Ness (built as the Silviculture Laboratory with U.S. Forest Service funds) next door or perhaps in the warehouse portion of the Police Department (originally built for the University Press)—is the department's remarkable collection of about 8,600 species of wood.

There is also the locally famous gavel collection donated by an alumnus; each of these hundreds of lathe-turned gavels represents a different kind of wood.

As you might suspect, by now, a good number of lumber industry executives have given either cash or in-kind donations, not of the wooden nickel variety, but stuff like the $25,000 that Clarence Day (of Columbus, Mississippi, and Memphis, Tennessee) gave to the building fund.

There is also, somewhere, the collection of insect-bearing amber, from the Baltic, 154 pieces in all.

Snowden Forestry Building is itself a kind of artifact-rich museum caught in the virtual forever-amber of scientific curiosity. It invites all who want to know more about the world that shapes our self-endangered species.

WOODLAND

ALSO DATING FROM THE LATE 1950S AND EARLY 1960S—a period for Sewanee utterly studded with building starts—are what is collectively called the Woodland Apartments.

It may seem like a stretch to haul these low-cost buildings into the distinguished company of Sewanee's great sandstone buildings. But there is enough rock-facing, here and there, more than what decorators like to call accent-walls, to be sure they are remembered as well.

We can start with the buildings themselves, clumped together as a mini-village off Roark's Cove Road, or we can start with their paper origins in the basement plan-room of the Physical Plant Services building.

The latter approach shows that most of these buildings started as off-the-shelf plans bought from the Standard Homes Company, Raleigh, N.C.

Each set of plans has a nice model name. They are probably selected by Sewanee officials for their gloriously anglophilic names—Douglas, Durham, Clark, Allen, and Austin.

- The "Douglas" plan is a 57 x 34 foot duplex with a hipped roof and the familiar three-step peek-a-boo pane front door.
- The "Durham" is a 56 x 30 foot duplex with a central gable over a pair of picture windows, flanked by mirror-reversed front porches at each end that are faced with brick. The twin-window bay is clad with "scored plywood," the plans note, another one of those cheap new materials that help date a building forever.
- The "Clark" duplex has two little stoops on each end, triangular vents on the ends of the central block, and lower pitch hipped roofs that probably pour rainwater down over the stoops. It also has two peek-a-boo panes on each entrance door.
- The "Allen" is a 51 x 31 foot duplex with a vented roof similar to the Clark. Its recessed front-porch entries are faced with fieldstone.
- The "Austin" is a 50 x 33⅔ foot duplex, also with recessed porches faced with fieldstone, and a vented peak roof similar to the Clark's plan.

Attached to this plan is a letter, dated August 14, 1964, from James C. Oates, University Business Manager, to Rev. Milton Wood, Canon to the Ordinary, 2744 Peachtree, Atlanta, noting that

> The cost of this three bedroom duplex is $16,810 . . . plus $900–$1,000 for sewer lines, water lines, grading and seeding; $25 for plans; $50 each for water and sewer connections; and $50 for sidewalks.

Another diocesan-financed house, known as the Florida Theolog House, is described as containing 1,000 square feet, @ $9.36 per square

One of the Woodland duplexes

foot, for a total cost of $9,360. This small end-gabled house is faced with "native stone" and has an asymmetric front, with the entrance door (three-step panes) covered with a small gabled porch, on the left half of the front, and two medium-sized windows on the right half.

The Woodland drawer also has plans for a four-building, eight-unit complex. Each building has two-bedroom units, 27 x 33½ feet, costing $14,100 each, or $7,050 per unit. Attached is a memo, dated Nov. 6, 1962, from Arthur Nimitz (University Engineer) to Dr. G. S. Bruton, noting that these were originally designated "Married Faculty Duplex" units. At some point the word Married gets crossed out.

The drawer also has plans, of unnamed but immortal style, that show mirror-reversed units, with a central chimney projecting through the roof. Each unit has a gable on its end, projecting forwards, with a big picture window and an entrance door, cheek to cheek, sort of anti-Palladian in spirit.

When you actually visit Woodland—an aggregation of buildings fronting on Roark's Cove, Kirby-Smith Road, Alston Lane, and Holmes Lane—you discover that many of the above plans are merely paper nightmares, never built, a good omen for this time nigh unto Halloween 2002.

Life is horrifying enough without pretend-goblins.

What is actually built at Woodland are the "Durham" plans, and the "Clark" plans, and fourplex geminations of Durham, mostly on or near Holmes Lane.

Better yet is the fact that all but two of the Woodland buildings are rock-faced. The two exceptions are small redbrick houses at the corner of Roark's Cove and Kirby-Smith roads. Presumably they are there to prove (test) the rock-faced rule ("rule" in the archaic sense, what governs medieval monastic communities, which Sewanee not infrequently resembles).

The point is that good sense prevails, good building sense, avoidance of cheap exterior cladding, and rather remarkable aesthetic sensibilities, something Sewanee seems to possess in abundance.

AN EXPERIMENTAL DORMITORY

THERE'S SOMETHING ABOUT MCCRADY HALL (1964) that immediately strikes one as unusual. Now as modern architecture goes, there's no great virtue in novelty, or looking odd, for its own sake. Good architectural neighbors don't fight with each other, but try to get along visually, co-existing in quiet and congenial ways.

It could be simply that McCrady, as the first Sewanee appearance for Edwin A. Keeble, a Class of 1923 alumnus, is a clear expression of the architect's personality.

But if you look at Keeble's other major works, such as the 400-foot-tall Life & Casualty Tower (1957), a vertical-finned icon in downtown Nashville for about three decades, or his 6,583-seat Memorial Gymnasium (1952) for Vanderbilt University, you might take these markedly different buildings as the expression of an architect with at least three-way split personality.

A better theory of McCrady Hall is that it is an experimental design for a college dormitory. The thick and extensive documentation for this building, preserved in the University Archives, tends to support this theory.

Here, for example, in a letter to Arthur Nimitz, University Engineer, dated December 20, 1962, is Keeble's proposal for actually testing out several approaches to wall construction:

> We notice, as you and I discussed, that the usual wall at Sewanee is built with the block backup to which parging is applied directly and then the stone itself.
>
> There is no waterproofing as such, nor any air space.
>
> We frankly are partial to a cavity wall but realize that this might be difficult, if not impractical, to build with the "pick up" stone.
>
> As a workable compromise, we are thinking that it would be well to introduce a heavy coat of mastic waterproofing on the outer face of the

block into which would be built, on two foot centers, vertically and horizontally, substantial wall ties.

The stone would then be pressed against the waterproofing in absolutely full beds and joints of mortar.

Keeble, as an alumnus with a clear memory of the peculiar mountaintop weather, particularly the fog and heavy rainfall here, knows that dealing with the moisture problem in exterior walls is of paramount importance. Here, he continues, is another wall construction possibility:

> Another thought was to attempt to develop a cavity wall. This might be done by building the block wall approximately three courses at a time. This would be the appropriate interval for placing wall ties.
>
> A two foot wide piece of plywood could be hung over the wall on wires and rest upon the wall ties three courses below. The stone then could be brought up approximately even with the blocks and the plywood removed just before the mortar dried thus leaving an air space.
>
> There would be problems, of course, in arranging to hold the plywood and to remove it readily.
>
> We have done this with bricks satisfactorily in order to keep the mortar out of the air space.
>
> I am not sure how the plywood was handled but believe it was some system of wedges or cams on the ends of rods.
>
> We considered the possibility of using styrofoam or foam glass insulation. We think the styrofoam would absorb some water detrimentally. The foam glass raises the problem of getting around the wall ties and therefore would probably be no safer, moisture-wise, than the layer of waterproofing. Any of these, of course, would provide an important vapor barrier.

Keeble next proposes an actual "testbed" (as the rocket scientists at Redstone Arsenal like to term it) to see how well the wall panels will hold up to an assault by water:

> We would suggest that, if the University would permit it, that you might have some sample panels of wall constructed, perhaps six feet wide and eight feet high; then possibly protected on the sides and top against rain in such a way that the wall might be observed under natu-

McCrady Hall

ral weather conditions—facing into the worst blowing rains, or course.

Then tests could be made with the hose.

If this latter stringent test is passed, we would certainly have a good answer.

In the cavity wall don't forget to have weep holes at the bottom.

We would like to get your reaction to this. If you could go ahead with the experiment, it would be most helpful, as we are hoping to get out for bids very soon after the first of the year.

Nimitz's reply, dated December 28, 1962, indicates that the University would approve the experiment, providing Keeble supplied specifications for the test panels. No correspondence survives, unfortunately, indicating what were the results of the experiment. This practice of a "test panel" wall is being used for the new dormitory under construction in 2003 at Georgia and Mississippi avenues.

McCrady Hall provides a number of other "experiments" for the Keeble / Sewanee collaboration.

One is the use of heat cables in bathroom floors. According to a memo from Nimitz to Vice-Chancellor Edward McCrady, dated January 17, 1964, there are "14 bathrooms with 200 watt cables installed; nine bathrooms have 300 watt cables installed; and five bathrooms have 400 watt cables installed." The memo notes that these installations "have been tested by or in the presence of manufacturer, sales agent, architect, and electrical sub-contractor." Unfortunately, if we read between the lines, the experimental approach to heating is not terribly successful, since "some of these cables have been changed as often as three times."

The memo appears to be in response to a January 16 letter sent to Mr. R. E. Ward, chief electrical inspector, State of Tennessee, by Ben Dozier, of Keeble's firm, summarizing the test results for the heating cables. One of the 14 cables tested—in the presence of a deputy electrical inspector, and

Edwin Keeble sketch of McCrady Hall closet

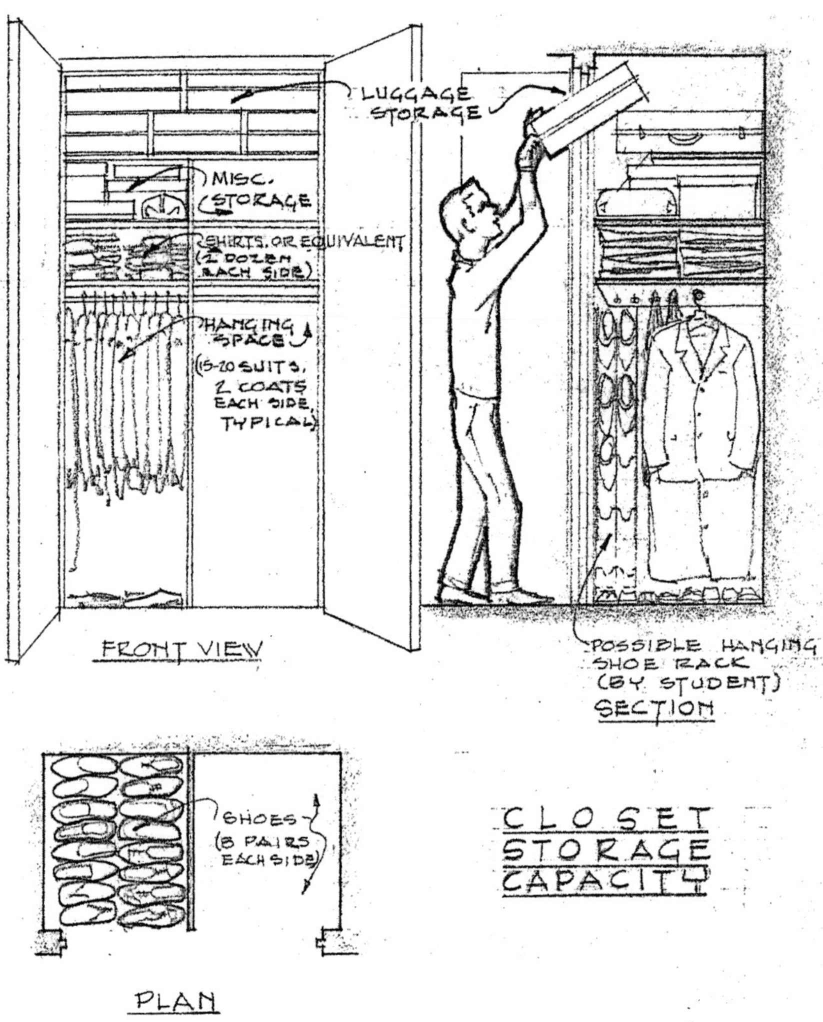

principals of the architect / contractor team—by checking its resistance by saturating the bathroom floor with water—flunked the test:

> One test was positive and it was determined that the insulation on the heat cable was damaged during tile removal. The heat cable was removed back of the damaged portion and a new splice and sleeve installed. This new connection tested negative resistance.

In accordance with standard bureaucratic procedure, copies of the letter to Ward are sent to Dr. McCrady, Arthur Nimitz, and others, resulting in an equally standard response, for Nimitz to clean up.

Another experiment—documented in an exchange between Keeble and the University's business manager, James C. Oates, in September 1963—involves a significant commitment to "built-in" furniture for the rooms.

Keeble sends the University a sheaf of 20 architectural drawings, bound with a plastic spine binder, that show not only the assortment of floor plans for McCrady Hall rooms, but also the design of such things as the "closet storage facility" (p. 224).

Note that Keeble assumes the typical student wardrobe includes 15 to 20 suits, two topcoats, 8 pairs of shoes, and two-dozen dress shirts. Yea, Sewanee's right well dressed!

Keeble's four-page letter of September 18, 1963, to Oates argues that built-in desks "should save a considerable amount of cost" and that their maintenance would be "practically negligible."

He also sends drawings of "modular storage units" including book cases, night stands, chests of drawers, and movable units that can double as coffee tables or ottomans.

Here, again, Keeble shows his empiricist tendencies:

> We have done several types of dormitories and make a point of checking back to see how things have worked out. . . . We have made literally hundreds of studies and are thoroughly convinced that this plan is by far the most functional, desirable and attractive for the money.
>
> The original research included a study of all the outstanding dormitories that we could find in the country. This was accomplished through the use of magazine plates and a considerable number of personal visits.

> We built a typical suite of wallboard and placed the furniture to scale. We had several conferences with the owners, representatives and various people with broad experience in student housing.
>
> This full-scale mock-up was remodeled several times.

The goal, Keeble argues, is to create dormitory spaces for "orderly and dignified living . . . at a small extra cost . . . (to create) a considerable sense of luxury and very valuable privacy." Instead of the "barracks-like effect" and the "regimentation" seen in so many dormitories, Keeble hopes these dormitory rooms and suites will be "homelike, dignified, comfortable, and attractive."

Some of this is brilliant blarney, of course, but then no one will deny that in a pricey product like well-designed buildings one must sometimes sell the sizzle rather than the steak itself. If he had not been an architect, one of Tennessee's better ones, Edwin A. Keeble could have done well as an adman or as a salesman.

But let's go see the building itself, sited on the southwest corner of Alabama and St. Augustine, catercorner to the Snowden Forestry Building. The site provides the inspiration for the name McCrady, since that is where the family has had a lease and a dwelling (simply called "McCrady Hall") since the 1880s. Though the dormitory was never officially dedicated, it is a modest tribute to the Vice-Chancellor, about two-thirds through his 20-year administration, and to those McCradys still living in Sewanee.

What strikes those addicted to architecture-watching is how irregular McCrady is, how asymmetric its layout, how unlike (for example) Snowden across the street

There are two entrance doors. The door to your left, as you stand facing McCrady from the curb on Alabama, is wider and therefore announces itself as the "main" entrance. This is reinforced by the large square tower above it, rising four stories, with a small circular turret sticking up from its roof. Even this turret is asymmetrically placed, on the tower's southwest corner, just visible above the tower's crenellated battlements.

The smaller entrance door provides access to the north wing corridors, and to the Commons Room at the north end of the central (north-south) corridor. This secondary door makes its appearance only by means of a pinched-in entryway. It is as understated as the main entrance is grand.

The two dormitory wings with corridors running east and west terminate on the Alabama Avenue side as massive nearly windowless cliffs with strong vertical rocked ribs and rocked shoulders.

The rooms on the corridor ends of these wings have a pair of aluminum sash windows plus a "light" over each sash to add extra daylighting illumination.

Above these windows, on the corridor ends, are arrays of vent grilles, of patterned tile, in the shape of four-pointed stars. (The pattern is close, but not identical, to the famous and much-copied cement block design that Edward Durell Stone patented for his 1960s buildings all over America. Stone's design was a series of contiguous circles overlaid on a grid of square blocks. The pattern was popular for privacy screens, or sun screens, when applied to the correct side of buildings in Florida, India, and other excessively sunny locales.) Again, it is difficult to know whether Keeble's starbursts are just for fun, as they could well be, or have some utterly functional logic.

Other design elements on the Alabama facade are coved copper standing-seam roofs, providing little hats over the two doorways and over the central block's two bay windows. Like most hats, they are functional without being particularly attractive, and call attention to themselves a bit unnecessarily.

Working from the less-obvious, to the most-obvious, we suddenly focus on McCrady's greatest oddity: it has what looks like zillions of windows!

What the architect has done is to take single sash, each with eight panes, and stick them into narrow slots in the rock wall. Among other things, no doubt, it makes the stone mason a lot more work to fit his stone in between each of these windows, coming as they do every few feet.

On the other hand, these narrow slotted windows are closer to the Gothic Spirit than most windows typically stuck into Collegiate Gothic walls, so again maybe Keeble is taking the less-traveled road to make a real difference.

During my brief visit to McCrady, on October 21, I mention these narrow sash to Sherman King, who is also waiting for the Head Resident there. King has worked on the University's electrical and heating equipment for 30 years, so he has special knowledge of the fact that the windows are too narrow to fit most window-unit air conditioners, for those students who have doctors' statements that they suffer from allergies and need A/C air.

It is also notable that all these crank-openable windows are aluminum, rather than steel, as their window-parents and window-grandparents were from the 1920s onwards.

Again, when archaeologists of some later century come to study the sacred ruins of the Sewanee mountaintop, they will no doubt feel that McCrady Hall is more representative of the Age of Aluminum, as they will no doubt tag this era, mainly because of unearthing billions of perfectly made aluminum drink-cans, sacramental artifacts, hideously deformed and crushed by barbarous brutes of obvious lowland sensibilities.

One more curio, and then we're through, the two stone walkways heading northwest and northeast from McCrady's north entryways also have one stone disk embedded in them.

But we're not through with the work of Edwin Keeble.

Later in the 1960s he will design Cravens and Hamilton, for what was then the Sewanee Military Academy campus; these two buildings are harbingers of the modernist spirit of architecture, which has had to arrive slowly, if at all, creeping on little cat's feet, like the fog, upon the Sewanee mountaintop.

TWO COURTYARD DORMITORIES

SOMETHING OF A DEPARTURE FOR SEWANEE, but common practice at public universities, is taking one basic architectural plan and replicating it for several buildings, typically dormitories.

Charmed by the romance of New Orleans courtyards and his own continuing idea of promoting wrought (or cast) iron in a unique Sewanee idiom, McCrady had Godwin & Beckett, the Atlanta firm doing most of the architectural heavy-lifting for the University during the 1950s and 1960s, do drawings for a new two-story dormitory that wraps about 40 suites around an open courtyard.

The result is, first, Benedict Hall (1963), and then Courts Hall (1966), which has less ironwork.

There are some surface-treatment differences in the two dorms, if you look at the finished buildings. But it's what inside that matters, not so much the two courtyards, but the basic clustering of six cells for a four-person unit, repeated all the way around the two buildings:

- There's a bathroom shared by the four.
- There's a study or living room on both sides of the bath.
- Off of each study is a two-bed bedroom.
- The sixth cell is divided into four closets with a plus-shaped common wall.

The contrast between Godwin & Beckett's symmetric simplicity and Keeble's multiple room-plans in McCrady Hall is remarkable, considering they are designed and constructed at roughly the same time. No inference as to which is the better approach will be made here. That judgment is for facilities managers, head residents (or "matrons" as their title is in the 1960s), and the students themselves to make.

The dramatic difference, to this writer, is one of artistic sensibilities. Godwin & Beckett find a single pattern that seems to work and then apply it with a cookie-cutter industriousness. Keeble, not to be confused with

Keebler's Cookies, multiplies complexity, because that seems to be his way, fitting an unusual number of room configurations into what is also a non-symmetrical floor plan.

Representative dates on the working blueprints for the two courtyard dormitories are May 4, 1962, for Benedict, and June 25, 1964 for Courts. This courtyard rectangular-ring structure will be used again in several subsequent Godwin & Beckett buildings.

The inspiration is of course New Orleans courtyards, especially in the ironwork details on the courtyard balcony railings, on the Benedict plans. But note also the key word "cloister" on the Benedict floor plans. This sounds like Dr. McCrady's often-fervid medievalism is at work and play here. Anyway, Benedict is a kind of marriage-of-convenience of Collegiate Gothic and Bourbon Street.

Eclecticism—that makes America famous in the world of architecture—again rears its cocksure head.

Benedict Hall west wing entrance

Benedict deserves to be remembered for at least two firsts.

In 1969 it becomes the first dormitory to house women, who are admitted for the 1968–1969 academic year. Here is Vice-Chancellor Edward McCrady thinking out loud about how many women to admit:

> As for the number of women to be admitted and the accommodations we shall provide for them, I expressed the opinion that a dozen or so girls would not be considered conscientious compliance with the wishes of the Trustees, and that a hundred girls in the first year would not only be difficult to house, but would require some ten additional faculty members who would also have to be provided with housing, and would increase our rate of growth in total enrollment so greatly

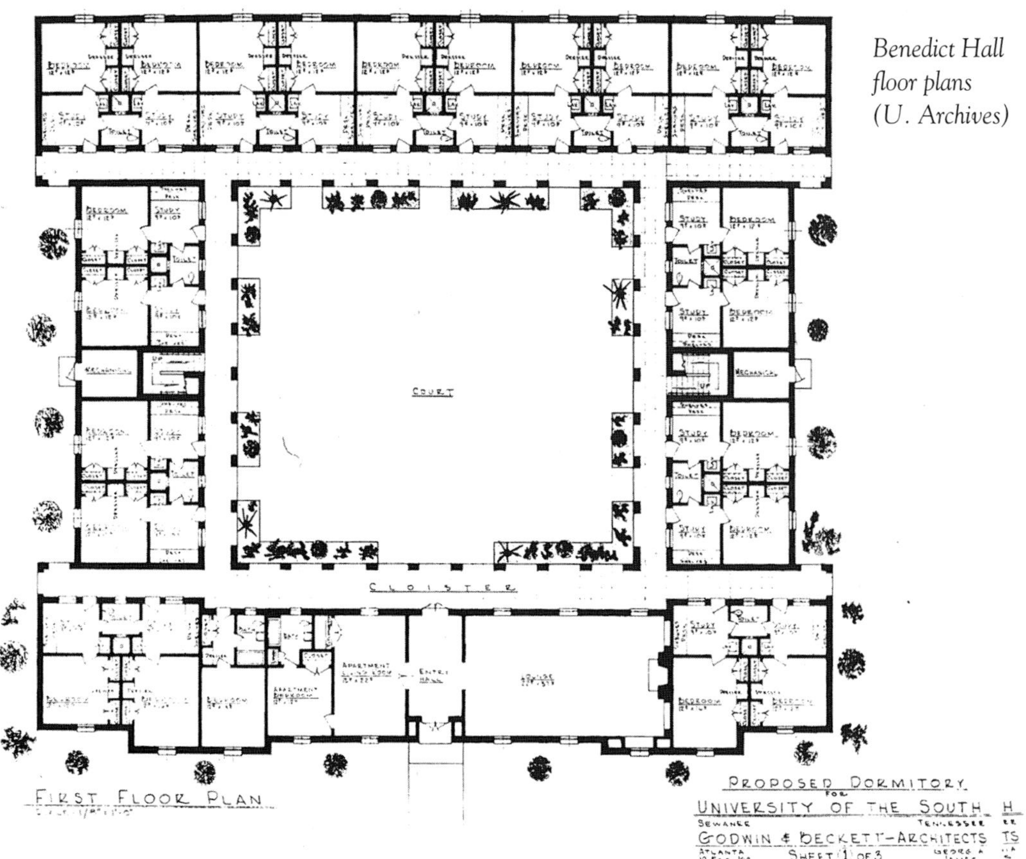

Benedict Hall floor plans (U. Archives)

> as to make it difficult to provide any sort of continuity of tradition. . . .
>
> Accordingly, I recommended at first that we limit the number of women to fifty, because fewer would seem like tokenism, and more would be hard to assimilate. . . . At last I succumbed to the pressure of the faculty and the student body to accept one hundred women and to turn over Benedict Hall to them. The expenses which we shall incur in the way of boudoir facilities and ironing rooms, gates, etc., will be relatively trivial (Proceedings, 1969, p. 39).

In 1982 Benedict Hall becomes the first campus building on the Sewanee campus to participate in a Tennessee Valley Authority demonstration project to use a solar water heating system.

Installed on the south-facing roof are 32 solar panels (3' x 6") to supply preheated water to 13 40-gallon water heaters in the building.

According to the Duck River Electric Cooperative magazine, which features the TVA / Sewanee cost-sharing venture in its August 1982 issue, the collaboration also includes an energy-use survey that recommends "adding insulation, weatherstripping, caulking, storm windows, and in some cases the changing of heating and cooling systems to electric heat pumps" (p. 14).

A veteran of that era (no names please) recalls on October 23, 2002, that the TVA solar water heater program proved to be a failure here. Why? "Not enough sun in Sewanee," she opines, with a small smile, "and maybe those women took too many showers."

Courts Hall is dedicated on November 6, 1966. It is named in honor of Malon Courts, an Atlanta investment counselor, according to a brief article in *The Chattanooga Times*, and costs about $300,000.

Cost, as usual, is a big issue for the University bean-counters.

In a project memorandum from the contractor firm (H. A. Brice of Birmingham) written by Harold J. Roberts, on August 5, 1964, he notes:

> Dr. Bruton was disturbed because our cost is above $14.00 (per square foot) and explained that they were able to do residential work for $10.00 / sf. Of course, their residential construction consisted of one-story units, wood frame, composition shingle roofs and stone veneer.
>
> Mr. Godwin stated that we could design and build one story units with a slab on grade, using wood studs and framing, composition shingle roof, stone veneer and other residential type construction for about $10.00 / sf,

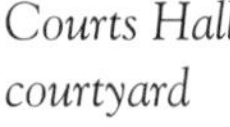

Courts Hall courtyard

Courts Hall east entrance

but Mr. Godwin did not think the University was interested in this type of construction for these new campus buildings.

The memorandum includes a couple of other interesting details, including the fact that Courts has a gross interior building area of 19,132 sf and a gross area of interior walk of 4,332 sf, and that Courts's $301,183 cost is about $19,000 above Benedict's cost for roughly the same area.

The significant place for Courts, in the University's institutional history, is that it is intended to be the first key piece of Dr. McCrady's plan for a New College, based on his firm belief that the ideal size for residential colleges at Oxford and Cambridge is about 500 students.

With the plan brewing to admit women, and gradually increase the enrollment as the University's new facilities would allow, two sites for the New College present themselves. One is the hallowed ground inside Louisiana Circle. The other is out at the end of Georgia Avenue, about 300 yards east of its intersection with Alabama, and that, it turns out, is where Courts and other new buildings will go. At least one "plan" survives, from 1909, showing a bird's eye view of perhaps two dozen buildings arranged as a "women's college in affiliation with the University of the South," presumably on the Harvard/Radcliffe and Columbia/Barnard plan.

A central amenity for this new college campus will be a small lake. Here is a bit of insider history provided by Jan Drake-Lowther, head resident of

Courts from 1992 to 2002 (when she takes over as head resident at Tuckaway Inn):

> Courts Hall faces on a small lake which attracts water birds and has a resident muskrat. It was originally known as Finney Lake. Recent custom finds the lake named annually for the winner in canoe competition between Courts and Trezevant at Courts's famous Thursday afternoon "Shrimp and Beer" party, which has been kicking off Sewanee's Spring Party Weekend for well over a decade (Drake-Lowther, "Malon Courts Hall," 1997, a four-page typescript in the University Archives).

It is not clear precisely why the New College plan doesn't flesh out beyond the addition of Trezevant Hall (1968), the last dormitory the University will build for 33 years, and Wiggins Hall; this is a small building across Georgia Avenue which originally housed a regional location for the College Entrance Examination Board testing service. The building gets sold in 1967 to the University for $82,310.31 (Proceedings, 1967, p. 40) and is renamed in honor of Benjamin Lawton Wiggins (Vice-Chancellor from 1893 to 1909).

Perhaps the University's successors to Dr. McCrady do not share his hopes for a multi-college university.

Perhaps the students think the new college campus is too far away from the center of old-campus life. Walking 300 yards, three football fields, in this motor-driven age, does seem like a hardship.

Or perhaps, as usual, the explanation is Something Else.

But it is significant that the new Unnamed Dormitory, under construction in 2002-2003, is physically clumped with the New College, which is now nearly 40 years old. Maybe there's life in the old idea yet.

MODERN IN DESIGN

POSSIBLY THE FIRST OUTCROPPING OF "MODERNISM" pops up at Sewanee's airfield in 1959.

Let's be clear, however, this is not the modernism of Frank Lloyd Wright, or of LeCorbusier, or Mies van der Rohe, or any of those boys, pushing the design envelope in all directions. It is Mid-Century Modernism, young in spirit, less linked to Grandfather Eisenhower than to Young Father Kennedy, not particularly daring, but 100 percent American.

The *Sewanee News* (April 1959) describes the new general aviation facility as "a pilots' ready room, a classroom for flight instruction, and for meetings of local units of Civil Defense, Civil Air Patrol, and the Tennessee National Guard, Aviation Section."

The drawing by architect Edwin A. Keeble shows a bird's eye view of a low-pitched roof, looking rather like an airfoil flying wing waiting for take-off. The cutline accompanying the illustration explains that Keeble and his Nashville architectural associates are interested in long-range planning for small airports, and in "using Sewanee sandstone in modern-type construction," and therefore they are donating their design and plans for the project.

Well, as it turns out, the only sandstone used in the building is the free-standing fireplace, that anchors the pilots' lounge. The rest is plate glass, and wallboard, and structural materials used in all the small offices that can be found in their parking-lot puddles of asphalt all over Mid-Century America.

After his adventures with McCrady Hall, experimental inside and a quirky Collegiate Gothic outside, Ed Keeble launches a serious assault on the mountain's architectural mossbackery with Cravens Hall (1967).

This building may be less familiar to visitors to the Sewanee campus today because it is less-well utilized than when it was completed, as the dining hall and auditorium for the Sewanee Military Academy campus.

Cravens Hall's "bluff shelter" cantilever

Cravens Hall is dedicated on Parents' Weekend in the 100th year of the secondary school's existence, 1968.

A bronze plaque explains that it is named in honor of Col. DuVal Garland Cravens (1875–1946), who was SMA's superintendent from 1912 to 1932 and its assistant superintendent from 1932 to 1946.

If you stand today where the crowd stood for its dedication, in the middle of Kentucky Avenue by Cravens's west entrance, the dramatic cantilevering of the upper story suggests we are solidly in the Structural Steel Age.

This side, today, marks the entrance point to what is known as Lower Cravens (p. 238). The recessed foyer space beneath the cantilevered mass is rather like a bluff shelter or perhaps like a big squared-off sandstone quarry, with a couple of massive side pillars to keep the ceiling from collapsing on the quarrymen.

Inside the entrance doors is an auditorium, about 65 feet by 80 feet, with a small stage, doubling as a bandstand for dances, or a focal point for a movie screen, with a projector booth at the north end.

The interest here is in the four immense reinforced concrete trusses, shaped like giant staples, holding the big dining hall floor up overhead. The ballroom chairs lined up around the wall seem to offer time-warp clues to all those magical weekends when the uniformed cadets got to ask their gowned-up dates to dance.

If you walk out the front doors, around the building's outside, clockwise, you will go up a 10 to 12 foot grade and find yourselves staring in through large windows into a small gathering space, a reception room that still serves as entrance hall to major banquets. This is the first glimpse into what is called Upper Cravens.

The view from inside the glass is now mainly towards the wonderful old main building, Quintard Hall, with a bit of the Parade Ground as well.

If you continue in a clockwise fashion, the building opens up further, with bigger windows, in what is obviously the Main Dining Hall. It is as light and cheery as the lower entrance is dark and dreary.

Inside the dining hall is more unabashed modernism, gigantic wood-beams, glue-laminated and pressure-bent to create crucks that not even the biggest old oak trees in medieval times could yield to a builder.

Even the finish of the coved ceiling is modern, large panels of wood fiber bonded with cement, a hot new building material that was widely used in the 1960s, and then mysteriously disappears a decade or so later. Just so you know what's on the ceiling, Keeble stipulates that it not be painted, expressing the material with brutalist honesty, and unpainted the ceiling stays to this day.

One clue as to what seems to have happened, an architectural false-start for Cravens, is found on an undated blueprint in the University Archives. The sheet shows a plan to add a dining hall to the front (that is, south, facing the parade ground) of Quintard Hall.

It's one of those bad ideas gone wrong.

Keeble probably works up this bellying-out scheme just to show how horrible it would be, turning that grand old landmark, Quintard, into the stone and glass equivalent of a pregnant fat man.

Fortunately, for our story, good sense prevails, and a new multipurpose facility anchors the west edge of the Parade Ground.

Along the Parade Ground's eastern edge is another Keeble design, Hamilton Hall (1969), a 32-classroom academic building.

An eight-page and well-illustrated commemorative booklet, distributed for the dedication on October 4, 1969, shows Hamilton in its pristine condition. (In the fall of 1999, when I was teaching the "Writing About Architecture" course at the University of Arkansas's School of Architecture, a Fayetteville architect named Ernie Jacks, a longtime associate of Edward Durell Stone, said that architects should NEVER go back to the buildings they have designed; his implication was that building deterioration, and thoughtless changes made to the original plan, invariably distress the architect deeply.) Not that Hamilton has been mangled by its current occupants, the School of Theology, but it is immensely valuable to see documentation as to the original configurations and furnishings of the interior spaces. If only Sewanee's other buildings were as richly documented, by text and photo/illustration, as Hamilton Hall is, then this architectural historian's work would be of much better quality.

Off the soapbox, sorry, let's prowl through what is now a pleasant monastery-like space, as serenely quiet as Hamilton must have been noisy when hundreds of uniformed SMA cadets were changing classes.

Up a broad set of seven stone steps, we enter Hamilton under another big cantilevered cave, like Lower Cravens, but this time it folds up, archway-like, as a vault-like ceiling. This vaulting continues in through the entire length of the administrative block of the building.

At the end of the first corridor to the right (reaching west) is the Headmaster's Office. The delights here are the window walls inset with ecclesiastical and military seals of stained glass. Not coincidentally, perhaps, the new SMA headmaster when the building is dedicated in 1969 is the Rev. James R. McDowell, the first "man of the cloth" to head the school in half a century. McDowell's address in the back of the booklet is headed FOR

Exterior view of Hargrove Auditorium, Hamilton Hall

GOD AND GOOD EDUCATION, a good rallying cry for a year that seems wracked by protests, rabid anti-militarism, and other symptoms that challenge the institutional commitment to its historic mission.

Hamilton's northeast corner is dominated by a cylindrical lecture hall, Hargrove Auditorium, undoubtedly the best feature of the building, at least to the few uncompromising modernists among us.

It's not the novelty of the cylinder, inside which can be seated 96, or its multi-purpose features (for lectures, movies, concerts, and so on), but the elegant simplicity of its geometric shapes, and the wonderful rock-facing of its mostly windowless exterior extending about four-fifths of its circumference.

Hargrove may remind you of the MIT Chapel, another cylindrical structure, designed by Eero Saarinen in 1955, but that's okay. Hargrove improves on its windowless Cambridge stepsister by having four tall slotted windows—two on the SE compass point and two on the NW compass point—whose ratio (width to height) is reminiscent of those narrow single-sash windows we see all over McCrady Hall.

Elsewhere, in the 1969 building, the academic wing is painted "in daring modern colors (that) add to the feeling of space." Other modernisms are what the booklet calls "forced ventilation" and "large windows and fluorescent lighting" and a number of classrooms arranged "seminar style" with tables and chairs instead of the traditional chair-desk seating.

Today, if we look again, Hamilton Hall seems to have weathered the years rather well. Keeble's adroit use of the hilly site puts the headmaster's office up on the head of the hill, and wraps the two-story wing of classrooms around a tree-shaded garden, on lower ground, offering a modest lower-profile for the wing.

Two of many interesting features of the School of Theology, SOT for short, are the on-site day care center, at the south end of the first-floor classroom wing, and the still-used kitchen and dining room, where hungry theologs are gathered, shortly before noon on October 24, 2002, waiting to chow down on a hot lunch.

As in the early days of the monastic church, mutatis mutandis, it may be that the best way to a churchman's head is still through his or her stomach.

THE duPONT LIBRARY

It is a distinct pleasure to arrive at the duPont Library (1965). Trumpet fanfare, maestro, please.

This is one of my very favorite buildings on campus, not so much for its handsome exterior, but for all the wonderful stuff inside the building. Also, you should know that librarians are my very favorite category of professionals (writers are among my least favorite), and duPont Library is the very best place to encounter lots of them daily.

It is also the place, at a computer terminal in the Main Reading Room, where this magnum-opus has been written, from page 1 onwards.

The duPont Library's arcaded entrance

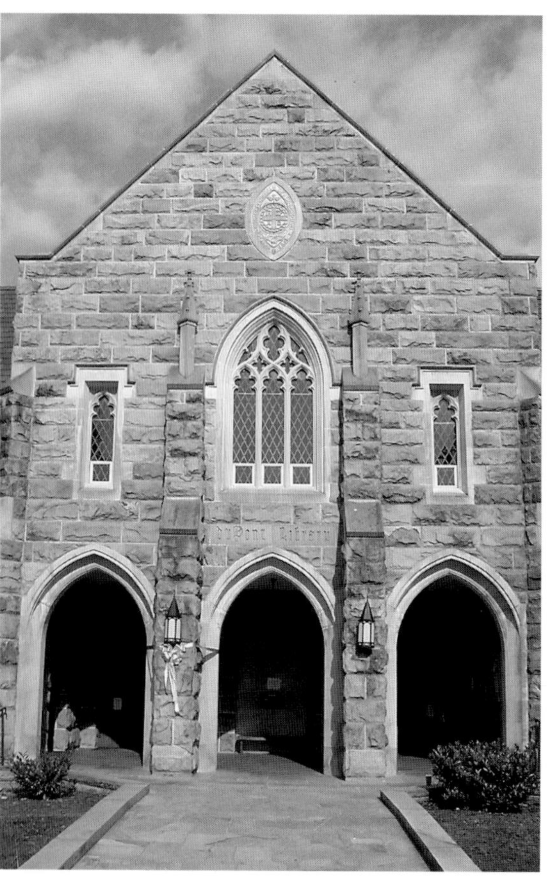

Vice-Chancellor Edward McCrady also seemed to hold this library in highest regard. Here is his rational exuberance for the start of duPont, in his report to the Trustees:

> The great new Library is under construction at last. When it is finished in September 1964, we shall have proper space for 400,000 books, plus another 200,000 on the top floor, which will not be needed for a number of years and for which furnishings will not be purchased at present.
>
> It will also have an abundant supply of carrels for student use, research rooms for the faculty, seminar rooms for small classes, a lecture room for a hundred people, an archives room plus adjoining stacks, microfilm facilities, as well as the usual reading rooms, night study room, smoking room, and so forth.

Torian Room of the library (Coulson Studios)

> The Library has been named for our greatest benefactor, Mrs. Jessie Ball duPont, but we are still greatly in need of major gifts for named memorials in it, and also for the purchase of the great research collections and basic library which will make possible our future expansion at both the undergraduate and graduate levels (Proceedings, 1963, p. 35).

How do I love thee, duPont; let me count the ways:

■ On any given day, there are hundreds of thousands of books, magazines, newspapers, government documents, videotapes, books on tape, waiting just for me. The sole exception to this sweeping generalization is that a book or other item can be checked out to a faculty member for up to three years!

■ The place is inhabited by quiet, courteous, civilized souls. If you park your belongings at a terminal, or in a carrel, you know they will be there when you return, an hour or days later.

■ The library is clean and well-lighted. It is cool on hot days, and more importantly for me, warm on cold damp days, unlike most places I have lived in much of my life. Nationwide, of course, libraries are the favorite place of homeless men, who sometimes can not be distinguished from venerable scholars, though the latter do not doze off as much. Sewanee, with virtually no homeless people, as yet, sees virtually no grubbiness, except my old trenchcoat. Under new University rules, as well, dogs are barred from entering the library, as are smokers.

■ The library's computerized system, known as Gabriel, is a fast and efficient way of finding the resources you need, while its Internet connection to the world-wide-web of information resources is fast and reliable.

■ Its librarians and other support staff, particularly the computer-savvy souls in the basement, are invariably helpful and do not give simple types like me a hard time at asking stupid how-do-I questions.

■ Best of all, for this work, is the University Archives operation run by Annie Armour and her student staff.

Okay, but let's try to imagine, for a moment, a duPont Library utterly empty. No books, no shelving, no chairs and tables, no librarians or patrons.

Doing this will enable us to focus our minds on what is architecturally a really fine array of interior spaces.

One of Sewanee's sleeping dogs outside the library (U. Archives)

It looks, quite frankly, as if the architectural firm of Godwin & Beckett is moving rapidly up the learning curve. It is probable that they are doing their homework well, studying other libraries that "work," something a few architects (like Edwin Keeble) say is a key to good design. Anyway, when the first sheets of working drawings are being created, in January 1963, the architects are really doing a wonderful job.

Entering the library through its main triple-arch arcaded entrance, there is an amiable little cloistered space now used for smokers, banished from the building; or parking wet umbrellas, so they don't drip into the building itself; or dogs who are likewise banished, but told to wait patiently for their owners; or just a spot for small-talk, posting bulletins on the board, and other vestibular matters.

Off this porch to the north is a little room with two telephone booths for free on-campus and off-campus local calls.

In through the handsome and solid oak

doors, a pair of which flank the book-depository chute, the next space is a heated / cooled foyer room with a lovely Tudor-style plaster ceiling, raised in a tesellated pattern, the first hint that the interior will be richly ornamented. Another elaborate ceiling pattern can be seen in the Torian seminar room (p. 241) immediately above this space on the mezzanine floor.

Note also the rope-pattern corners on all the plastered Tudor arches, tall and splendid formal elements that shape the interior three sides of the Main Reading Room. This, like the oak-paneling and wainscot—plus its

The crew fabricating oak paneling in the east end of the library's main reading room (U. Archives)

formal series of dentil-like brackets, along the mezzanine floor edges, suggesting exposed "bullnose" ends of timber floor joists—indicate a wealth of finish-treatment that will probably not be seen again until McClurg Dining Hall (2000) gets completed.

Interesting to note, the library's main lobby is essentially like a ceilinged "courtyard," with oak-paneled balcony all around its mezzanine floor. This feature makes a neat architectural link to the Vice-Chancellor's two courtyard-centered dormitories, Benedict and Courts, on the drawing board at roughly the same time as DuPont. We will see another courtyard in the north half of Woods Laboratories (1968) as well.

This duality of possibilities—having a vertical space either full-height, for the grand effect, or divided into first and second (mezzanine) floors, for efficiency and functionality—gets carried northwards into the Main Reading Room on the north side of the library lobby.

Here is a truly wonderful space, with five tall stone-mullioned windows pouring northern light into the room, then equally tall bay windows at both the Periodicals Room end and the Reference Room end.

Again, for us numerologists, with 1 + 5 + 1, this is duPont's best face. Here is the magic seven-bay expression of the Liberal Arts. If a library—as literally containing the sum totality of the liberal arts and sciences—cannot make this symbolic statement, then no building on the University of the South campus should be able to make the statement.

The duPont Library is a steel reinforced structure, with hidden cement block inside walls and coursed ashlar sandstone outside walls. But it is also, if we study the 1960s photos made during its construction (above), a real craftsman's labor of love, top-quality work by masons, carpenter/joiners, plasterers, and so on.

The key question beyond that, of course, is whether it functions well as an undergraduate library.

My answer, as a "heavy user" during the year 2002, is that it functions remarkably well.

A few more clues emerge from delving into the ton of blueprints made for duPont Library. The 28 "A" series of sheets are dated January 15, 1963. At this point, without a donor / honoree, the blueprints are simply designated as "A Library Building" for the University.

Dr. McCrady's enigmatic comments (above) about a night study room, a smoking room, and so on, are explained in the basement floor plan (Sheet A-1). The room immediately beneath the Periodicals Room is designated as a smoking room; east of it is the "night study room." (The first floor plan shows a separate stair leading to the basement as the "night stair" presumably with a separate entrance from the rest of the library.) There is also in the southwest corner of the basement a "music room" with eight listening booths.

The main floor and the second floor are used today much like the original configuration, except that next to the Torian Memorial Room to the south is designated in 1963 as space for "special collections."

The third floor is designated as "unassigned attic space"; this third floor is not converted, for the School of Theology Library, until 1981, with the University Archives moving into the top floor's south end.

Specifications indicated in the blueprints argue the architect and client are going first-class all the way. The stair handrails, for example, are Julius Blum No. 4530 bronze handrails, while the balusters beneath them are ⅝" x ⅝" twisted Swedish iron, put 5¼" o.c. The front doors are specified as red oak batten doors, v-jointed, with leaded glass panes. Godwin & Beckett designed them from scratch rather than off-the-shelfing them. The only element missing from these entrance doors is a drawing of the dog (p. 242) that invariably lounges outside them.

North-facing windows light up the Current Periodicals room.

The most ornate element of duPont Library is the central block containing the entrance, with a lovely stone-mullioned window (p. 241), plus doors leading to the front parapet battlements on either side of this projecting block. Also in this front parapeted gable is the University seal and a big stone nameplate block specified by the architects as requiring an "inscription not to exceed 30 Gothic letters."

Since the name is not known, at this point in 1963, 30 letters seem like a safe number. If, for example, the winning entry would be the "Waldemar Higginbotham Memorial Library," the University would have to reject the offer, or at least go back to the drawing board.

The name that does get carved there, duPont Library, is but one of many variants of arguably the most distinguished name in Plutocratic America. There is the DuPont Company founder, of course, Eleuthere Irenee du Pont (1771–1834). There is also the Dupont name, favored by a lot of folks (according to a www.google. com search). But since the DuPont Company turns 200, in this year of living dangerously, 2002, it seems almost right to use to honor the makers of Kevlar and Teflon by using the company's very own orthography.

On the other hand, that would be a slight to Jessie Ball duPont (1884–1970), who married Alfred I. duPont (1864–1935) in 1921 and outlived him by 35 years. According to a website at Washington & Lee University, Mrs. duPont gave over $100 million to charitable causes during her lifetime.

Anyway, duPont Library is dedicated on April 3, 1965, and it is a fine building, regardless how you capitalize it, about $1.5 million to be exact.

J. ALBERT WOODS LABORATORIES

The building known formally as the J. Albert Woods Laboratories (1969), and known familiarly as Woods Lab, is not a great architectural work.

Woods Lab does have the virtue of being much more handsome than its original design. Whether out of budget fattening, expanded programming, or just plain Occam's Razor reasoning to keep-it-simple, this new science classroom and laboratory building scrapped an awful plan—two wings that reach around, like stone lobster claws, and attempt to capture a bit of quadrangular turf—in favor of a plain rectangular building, 151 feet by 252 feet, wrapped around an auditorium and an interior courtyard.

Unfortunately, we do not have any recollections by the principals involved—neither the architects (Godwin & Beckett) nor the prime movers (Dr. Edward McCrady and the Board of Regents)—as to why this change happened. The original design and floor plans for the "Science Hall" date from 1963 during the fund-raising effort for what is essentially a $2 million building. We can only rejoice and be glad that all those concerned, in the mid-1960s, come to their esthetic senses.

Woods Lab's entrance tower

Still, Woods shows a little hamhandedness when compared with its slightly older sibling, duPont Library, which it was intended to reflect. All of us favored with good looks

Original design for Woods Laboratories (U. Archives)

by Mother Nature always try to feel charitable towards our plainer siblings, as it is meet and right to do, and our bounden duty. The problem, architecturally, is that these two siblings sit across the street from each other, from here to eternity, inviting comparisons that don't take place when the twain are 600 miles removed from each other, as my brother and I happen to be.

To get the worst feature out of the way, first, Woods Lab's corridors are a dreary march of cement block walls, the lower half of which are painted a mud-pie brown, while low drop ceilings glare down with high-intensity fluorescent lighting. Off of these corridors one expects prison cells instead of doors to classrooms and laboratories.

Even the central feature of Woods Lab's main entrance, a large square tower with crenellated battlements, beneath which is a salient squared-off oriel window, turns out to be disappointing, when you see what happens to the space inside that promised prominence. You cannot see out of the oriel window, since it is set too high in the wall, and the tower room has been captured by the Chemistry Department for equipment and chemical storage; the tower room enjoys no ceremonial rank or respect at all.

The very best feature, the stone-arcaded Benedict Courtyard surrounded by two stories of windows, has as its central feature a lily pond, the size of a kiddie pool. Around it are two circular walks arrayed like a bull's eye. At the first-floor level there are Tudor-arch reveals, six to give visual interest to the courtyard's east and west walls and four such arches doing likewise for the north and south walls. Unfortunately, only in the south and east rows do the arches fully define and fill the windows; on the other two sides, north and west, the arches are mostly stone set in around rectangular double windows.

The main problem with this courtyard is it doesn't seem to be appreciated. The only time I have ever seen anyone in this lovely courtyard space is during the summer of 2002, when a student attending the Sewanee Summer Music Festival, is practicing her violin works. If her esthetic sensibilities count for anything, and they should, she will grow up to be a virtuoso.

On the south side of Woods's central corridor, which does have oak paneling of a kind comparable to that seen everywhere inside duPont Library, is a large lecture hall known as Blackman Auditorium. One enters at the hall's high end; the hall's low end is burrowed into the building's basement, a neat use of the natural lay of the land. Above the roof of Blackman Auditorium, at the second story level, the "courtyard" shape reappears, though it is not a roof that can be utilized. As everyone knows, in the building game, the quickest way to ruin a flat roof is to walk on it a lot.

If you stand in or near the middle of Alabama Avenue, and try not to get run over by an SUV drive-by, you can see immediately the grammar of ornament shared by the duPont and Woods facades.

There is, of course, the handsome coursed ashlar sandstone, with window surrounds of oolitic limestone. There are also the dentiled cornices, underneath eaves that project just enough to throw water off the roofs without the need for guttering, but not so much as to look un-gothic.

The dormer windows on the roofs of duPont and Woods are slightly different in design, and less attractive in their finishes than the rest of the exteriors. But it's doubtful these dormers even get noticed. As a matter of fact, this "third floor" of Woods (really a garret-like space under what is technically a two and a half story building) doesn't even get converted to usable office and classroom space until about 1990, a good number of years after the May 10, 1969 dedication.

Woods Lab's courtyard

Look again at the original 1963 rendering for the

"Science Hall" building (p. 248). You notice that there are projecting parapeted gables nearly identical to the projecting gables on duPont Library, and on their even younger sibling, Bishops Common (1974), just north of the library on Georgia Avenue. For some reason, cost perhaps, all but two of these lovely parapeted gables are stripped off the flanks of Woods Laboratories. The result, not having those triangular gable-tops rising up to punctuate the roofline, around the other three sides, makes for a less-interesting building.

On the other hand, the mysterious maker of stone disks strikes again, installing one in the walkway from Woods straight towards the street.

Let's take a quick virtual tour of Woods Lab just to see what's inside its 62,000 square feet.

In the oak-paneled foyer, just inside the main entrance, the building directory announces that this is home to the departments of biology, chemistry, physics, mathematics, anthropology, and psychology, six strangely interesting academic bedfellows.

Just outside the twin entrance doors to Blackman Auditorium, you get to meet J. Albert Woods (1897–1964), in a rather informal oil portrait and two bronze plaques, reciting the bare essentials of his and his brother Cecil's lives. You should also know—according to a press release circulated the week that construction began on the building—that

> The late J. Albert Woods, for whom the building is named, served until his death in 1964 as co-chairman with his brother, G. Cecil Woods of Chattanooga, of the University's recent ten million dollar campaign.
>
> Mr. Woods's career included terms as president of the Chilean Nitrate Company, the Wilson-Toomer Fertilizer Company, and Commercial Solvents' Corporation. For nine years, he was the North American representative of Courtlands, the British equivalent of duPont.

Biology occupies the entire first-floor ring of offices and classrooms. It also offers the most visual interest, including a wonderful collection of birds and small mammals (west and south corridors) stuffed with considerable taxidermy skill by biology professor emeritus Dr. Harry Yeatman, and a great collection of skulls donated by Dr. Edward McCrady's son John (northwest corner) a family full of amateur naturalists.

The second floor ring houses chemistry on the south and west corridor, mathematics on the east corridor, and physics in the northwest and north corridor.

The third-floor ring, with a bite taken out of it where the square tower is, has the softer-scientist anthropology and psychology professors.

The basement is excavated only on its south end, much lower in grade than the building's north end; this south L-shaped corridor houses the mysterious workings of the Landscape Analysis Lab and provides access to the Waring Webb Greenhouse.

Detail over Woods Lab door

Actually, the best course for real visitors is to pop in, through any opened door, announcing you are the Inspector General (as Nikolai Gogol's farce and comedian Danny Kaye depicts him), and maybe you will get a quick explanation of what is actually going on there. With a good faculty, such as Sewanee has, whatever is conveyed is likely to be quite interesting.

A DORM TOO FAR

THE LAST DORMITORY BUILT ON THE SEWANEE CAMPUS, Trezevant Hall, is dedicated on April 6, 1972.

It is part of Dr. Edward McCrady's largely unrealized New College, or "second campus," begun at a moment when he is ending his 20-year administration, the longest of any Vice-Chancellor in the University's history.

In the superlatives department, Trezevant is also billed as the University's "largest dormitory," according to a press release issued forth on April 7, 1972.

Trezevant will also be the first Sewanee building to be given a "permanent endowment for its upkeep."

That act of generosity comes on top of the original donation, from Edward Herman Little, retired president of Colgate-Palmolive. Little gives a half-million dollars for the dormitory to be named in memory of his wife, Suzanne Trezevant Little, and her brother, Stanley Trezevant, a Sewanee alumnus.

Trezevant Hall is also—though not so designated by the University's official wind-machine—the dormitory farthest from anything else on campus.

On a cold and rainy day (November 6, 2002) this weary pilgrim trudges to the shrine. It is located out near the shank end of Georgia Avenue, and is reached either by a great loop counter-clockwise around the lake, or by an even longer loop, on the road past Courts Hall, clockwise around the lake down an empty street called Parsons Lane.

The only building Trezevant is close to, ironically, is Emerald-Hodgson Hospital, whose fieldstone backside can be seen through the pine trees to the north of Parsons.

In layout, at least, Trezevant resembles nothing so much as a fieldstone-clad motel. It has a matched pair of long two-story wings (p. 254)—with doors opening onto double-decker balconies instead of closed-in

Trezevant Hall today

corridors—reaching out from the commons room (east) end, rather like a turkey's wishbone. This odd shape may be an admission that the enclosed courtyards of Benedict and Courts had proven far too noisy. In the interests of peace, and New Age tranquility, their square shape has been pried open.

The architects (Godwin & Beckett) do at least one remarkable thing with this rather unremarkable structure: they site the U- or V-shaped building on three sides of a knoll. It is picturesque most of the time, except when there has been a lot of rain, which tends to dump itself into a moat-du-jour in front of the hall's U- or V-shaped floor slab.

Though the 90 male students who live in Trezevant tend to like it there, as freshmen and sophomores, they tend to want to move in closer to the central campus, according to its matron (head resident) Pam Lytle.

She also shoots down my short-list of superlatives by noting that when the University takes over the Sewanee Military Academy campus, circa 1981, its two dormitories (Quintard and Gorgas) are both larger (in population) and farther away from the center of campus than Trezevant is.

Though there are about 65 vehicles owned by Trezevant's residents, only a handful are visible in the parking lot, immediately east of the dormitory, during this field visit at 10 A.M. The vaguely scientific conclusion

Trezevant's motel-like or barracks-like gallery

from this data tends to indicate that the students drive themselves over to the campus, not more than 10 minutes' walk away from their residence hall, assuming of course they do attend classes with regularity.

Anyway, that's essentially all there is to say, about what will prove to be the last dormitory the University of the South builds for 30 years. The new dormitory, christened Humphreys Hall, rising slowly at the corner of Georgia and Mississippi during this academic year 2002–2003, will be too late for inclusion in this work.

McCRADY'S LAST, GODWIN'S LAST

FOR A NUMBER OF REASONS NOT TERRIBLY CLEAR, Bishop's Common goes slower than its predecessors.

It could be that the never failing succession of benefactors, prayed for perennially, are putting their money elsewhere.

Or it could be simply that the two warhorses, Dr. Edward McCrady and Mr. Jim Godwin, are slowing down themselves.

Bishop's Common, dedicated on May 3, 1975, will be both gents' last building collaboration.

In what proves to be his last report to the Board of Trustees, as Vice-Chancellor, Dr. McCrady delivers his detailed explanation of what is going on with the Bishop's Common project. Since this may be the last time we hear from him, let's quote him *in extenso,* as he himself might say it:

> Last April, when I was in Detroit for the meeting of the Association of Episcopal Colleges, Mr. Welteck and I called on the Kresge Foundation on April 13 to explore the possibility of getting a grant to cover part of the cost of construction of the Bishop's Common.
>
> We were told that there was no use presenting any application before January, 1971, but they encouraged us to believe that they would take a serious look at such an application at that time. We did present a proposal in which we asked for $140,000.
>
> On May 24, I received a letter from Mr. William H. Baldwin, the President, advising us that the trustees of the Kresge Foundation had approved a grant of $50,000 toward that building.
>
> Payment of the grant is conditioned upon our certification on or before September 15, 1972, that the balance of the required funds has been raised, and that the project contract price is within the available resources.
>
> Since that date is a year and a quarter away, I think we should be able to have the funds.

Bishop's Common

As to what the contract price will be, I have no way of knowing, though I am sure we should make the scale of the project fit the available funds by that time. This additional $50,000 raises our total of funds in cash and pledges to approximately $730,000.

Our original expectation was that the building itself would cost $750,000, not counting furnishings and landscaping and architects' fees.

Mr. Godwin, on May 31, brought some revised drawings in which the total square footage was reduced and it began to look as if we might be able to proceed with the working drawings and get bids this summer so as to be able to start construction in the fall, provided agreement could be reached between the Delegate Assembly, the Faculty Building Committee, and the Regents Building Committee, on a floor plan and a site.

After two years of confused negotiations, the Regents finally appointed a committee which they asked to make final decisions on all the moot points so that there would not be any further delay.

I do not know at the time of dictating this report what decision the Regents will make, but if there is any delay which will necessitate the drawing of a new set of plans I am afraid we shall lose not only the Kresge Foundation $50,000 grant but we will also lose the prospect of a matching grant of $30,000 which has been offered by General Williams if we proceed within the next few months to signing a contract for this memorial to Bishop Juhan (Proceedings, 1971, pp. 40–41).

When the new Vice-Chancellor, J. Jefferson Bennett, gives his first Report to the Board of Trustees, in June 1972, he issues what sounds like an imperial decree that the development-frontier is about to be closed:

> In my opinion the physical plant of the University will be basically complete when the new Bishop's Common is built and occupied.
>
> That facility will be a most welcome addition. The quality of experience outside the classroom is a very important part of the academic experience of every student. Extracurricular programs and constructive leisure activities will be vastly strengthened when this facility is available to us....
>
> We have every hope to have bids in hand by next August 15, with construction to begin very soon thereafter (Proceedings, 1972, p. 41).

Bennett's next report, in June 1973, reveals that a major benefactor has arrived, in the form of Niles Trammell, the legendary president of NBC:

> I am delighted to report, at long last, the Bishop's Common is now under construction.
>
> It is anticipated that the building will have been completed by the time we meet in 1974.
>
> Sufficient money is in hand or assured so that the building, its furnishings and equipment, and necessary site improvement are funded.
>
> This is in spite of the fact that the construction contract ran far higher than estimated.
>
> The execution of the construction contract was made possible, after the construction bid was received, by notification to us by the trustee, that the University of the South was named sole beneficiary of an *inter vivos* trust created by the late, beloved Niles Trammell, and which vested in the University following his death last month.
>
> Proceeds from the trust ($370,000–$400,000) will be applied to the cost of the building for which Mr. Trammell had worked so hard as a gift solicitor.
>
> In the meantime, other gifts are being solicited for the purpose of diverting as much as possible of Mr. Trammell's gift to our permanent en-

dowment, thereby assuring perpetual support to the University's operating budget (Proceedings, 1973, pp. 34–35).

But let us ask the obvious question, implicit in the V-C's two remarks, as to what "extra-curricular programs and constructive leisure activities" are programmed in to the original Bishop's Common, and what the building has evolved into today.

Answering the question on November 7, 2002, is Barbara Banks. She has been manager of the student center for 12 years, and knows the place, past and present, as well as anyone.

The building's basic arrangement is a square, with corridors running along its south (entrance), west, and east sides. There is a small kitchen on the back side, now unused, and closed off to student center traffic.

Bishop's Common entrance

Like any good multipurpose building, BC has an information desk just inside the main entrance, to field all sorts of Q&A issues about every student organization's location and other kinds of issues (like toilets).

If you head west, from there, you come to two rooms on the southwest corner, that are originally used as the St. Luke's Bookstore, relocated from St. Luke's Hall. A charming feature here is that the bookish atmosphere of one of the two rooms was intentionally enhanced by a fireplace, oak-paneled like much of the BC's interior, an amenity not generally found in bookstores anywhere today.

The fact that this space later became a dining room suggests the highly movable "program" of the building, which probably changes lots of times from the moment the architect gets the first go-ahead to start drawing plans.

As a matter of fact, there are four fireplaces in the BC, one on each corner, two facing west and two facing east. Actually, it turns out that the southeast corner has only a pretend-fireplace, which exists as a handsome stone chimney on the outside, but no hearth or inside chimney breast. Either the chimney is there for the sake of symmetry (which BC has a lot of) or gets X-ed out during a last round of redrawing the plans. The actual number is four, however, since the northeast stack serves a first-floor fireplace, in the lovely oak-paneled lounge, and a basement stone-breasted fireplace immediately below in the Tiger Pub.

There is also an oak-paneled fireplace in the northwest corner, serving a space that early on becomes a secondary dining hall, when Gailor gets overcrowded with the additional enrollment from 1969 onward.

Sadly, the three doors that seem to open onto a stone patio outside this dining hall can no longer be used, thanks to a change in state health laws, which say they don't want flies to wander in, much less dogs, who are no longer welcome in all university buildings as they were by sanctified tradition.

Banks's wonderful ten-dollar tour leaves me with the impression that the main contrast between past (circa 1975) and present (circa 2002) is that the serious side of Sewanee seems to be overwhelming the frivolous side. The small dining hall is now "heavily utilized" in the afternoons for speakers and student group meetings, as is its counterpart, the oak-paneled lounge, on the far side of the unused kitchen.

The manager's office, west of the information desk, used to be a recorded sound listening room. On the other side of the info-desk is a lay chaplain's office. The two rooms on the southeast corner used to have billiard tables and ping-pong tables. Now they serve Student Activities and the Sewanee Outing Program.

Bishop's Common right front bay

On the inside of this east corridor is the Community Service office, which has always been there. What is originally a chair-storage closet is now home to the director of Community Outreach.

Responding to my comment about the handsome interior of the BC—as a possible statement by the architects knowing it will be their final Sewanee building—Barbara Banks recalls that the corridor walls are originally covered with grass-cloth, a burlap-like material that proves to be a bad-maintenance surface. One of her first tasks, as facilities manager there, is to swap out the grass-cloth (everywhere the paneling isn't) with a high-gloss paint surface. Some guy sold the University miles of grass-cloth during the 1960s / 1970s.

We go upstairs, past a bronze plaque announcing that is where the Trammell Communications Center will be; sure enough, the first door unlocked is originally the Recording Studio, with a glass-windowed control booth at its north end. Sadly, nobody seems interested in sound recording anymore.

Near the southeast corner is a photographic dark room, still used, mainly by staff of *The Sewanee Purple*, whose offices are just across the hall.

Along the front garret-space are rooms that used to be for student organizations, but are now given over to faculty offices, an indication perhaps that there are fewer Organization Men and Organization Women today.

The inside suite of rooms at the southwest turning of this upstairs corridor is occupied by the campus radio station (WUTS). This basically concludes the Trammell-Com facilities; sorry to say, there is no campus television broadcasting studio up here.

Down in the basement, as previously mentioned, is the Tiger Pub, occupying the only windowed section of this lowest floor. It is open from 5 P.M. to 2 A.M. and includes a variety of beverages, plus two pool tables, and a jukebox. It has a great big Sewanee Tiger as well possibly related to the great big Sewanee Tiger in the lobby of the Juhan Gymnasium. Maybe the Bishop liked great big tigers.

The dreariest part of the basement is the Student Post Office, which used to be in Thompson Union, but got moved here and is overcrowded with boxes and service rooms. Rumor is it will expand, or maybe move upstairs, in the indefinite future.

There is also a two-bay truck loading dock in the back of Bishop's Commons with a quarry-tile corridor now serving only the two basement tenants.

Stepping back outside, to ramble around its public faces, it seems safe to say that as a final statement ($750,000 plus furnishings) of the dynamic McCrady-Godwin duo, Bishop's Commons makes an elegant valedictory indeed.

There are, first and foremost, the three projecting parapeted gables on the front (facing Georgia Avenue), and two projecting gables on the east

Bishop's Common east face

and the west sides, making this not only a House of Seven Gables, but also, for us architectural numerologists, an expression of the Seven Liberal Arts, seeing no dichotomy between academic duty and student conviviality.

Saying this may be a stretch—like hundreds of other iffy statements in this book—but in the absence of any more compelling theory this one about Sewanee's "architectural septenaries" will have to do.

The sandstone—all Crab Orchard stone from the Crossville, Tennessee area, according to master mason Carl Reid—is again laid in coursed ashlar, but the building gets a generous helping of oolitic limestone as dressings around its windows, as stone mullions for its two front-gable bay windows, as capstone for its buttresses (twinned at each corner for all gables except the main entrance), and as coping for its seven parapeted gables, for its front terrace wall and its east-side retaining wall, and even as handsomely expressed drip mouldings over its east and west side entrances.

It seems right to ask Jim Godwin and Edward McCrady to come out for a final bow, to applaud them, and give a loud BRAVO! to them and their large supporting cast of stone masons, carpenter/joiners, and all their crew.

PLANS, PLANS, PLANS

SUDDENLY, IT SEEMS, THERE IS NO CONSTRUCTION going on at all.

It is Vice-Chancellor J. Jefferson Bennett's belief, at the beginning of his reign, that "the physical plant of the University will be basically complete when the new Bishop's Common is built and occupied" (Proceedings, 1972, p. 41). At the end of Bennett's reign, University Treasurer H. E. Dodd confirm's the V-C's decree:

> Building Program? No construction is in progress. The most recent buildings are the new hospital (1976—$1.6 million) and the Bishop's Common (1974—$1.3 million). Building efforts in recent years have been devoted to dormitory renovations (Proceedings, 1979, p. 48).

What happens when no construction is in progress?

Why, we make plans, of course. And more plans. And yet more plans.

That way, if the ways and means, not to mention the programmatic push, appear to justify a new building or two, then we already have the paper documentation to satisfy those squinty-eyed bean counters in the front office.

In the beginning, the veriest beginning, the founders of the University of the South send out what we would today call an RFP, that is, a request for proposals:

> To Architects / University Place / Franklin Co. Tenn. AUG. 1, 1860:
>
> Designs for the building of the University of the South are invited from the Architects of the United States.
>
> The building, for which designs are more immediately required, is the main building of the group.
>
> The designs for this building must contemplate a central structure, flanked by two wings, the whole to be two stories high.

T. K. Wharton's design for Sewanee's first building in 1860 (U. Archives)

The upper story of the central structure is to be used as an Exhibition Hall. It must be constructed with galleries, upon the plan of the Academy of Music, with sittings for 2,500 persons.

The lower story to be divided into offices for the business departments of the University.

One of the wings must be arranged for a Library, with rooms underneath for unpacking, storing, etc.

The other wing to be constructed as a Gallery of Art, the lower story of which is to be used as an Academy of Design.

The plans must contemplate a building of stone, which shall be fireproof throughout. The wings to be constructed as to admit of extension.

For further particulars, in reference to this and the other buildings to be erected, applications must be made to the Executive Committee.

The design which may be adopted will be paid for; all others will be held subject to the order of the Architects.

All designs must be forwarded so as to erect University Place by the 1st of October and must be addressed to the Executive Committee, University Place, Franklin County, Tennessee.

By order of the Executive Committee / Leonidas Polk / Stephen Elliott / Geo. R. Fairbanks (subcommittee).

It is fortunate for the University, and for this narrative, that the building thus described does not get built; owing to the war (pronounced woe-wah) and the total wipe-out of the donors' pledges, the University's founders get the opportunity to re-think their basic Idea of a University.

A distinguished response is submitted by a respected New Orleans architect, T. K. Wharton, though his 1860 design looks more than a little like the U.S. Capitol Building, minus the great cast-iron dome that was added to it circa 1868.

The antebellum dream of the RFP obviously elevates three main elements—an academy of design, an immense auditorium for 2,500 persons, and a perhaps equally large library.

Considering that the University of the South starts in 1868 with nine students, set out in a wilderness community, it is a jolly good thing that this Main Building does not get constructed.

Instead, Sewanee's planning proceeds in an ad-hoc fashion, small in scale and frugal in budget.

As we have seen, in this book's earliest chapters, the "permanent buildings" appear slowly. The burden for nearly all of the classrooms, lodging, and other daily functioning of the University falls on much humbler structures, built of logs (like Rebels' Rest) and frame (like St. Augustine's Chapel), modest and serviceable, though always at risk of burning down.

It is not until the late 1880s, when a measure of optimism about the future of the University's survival seems assured, that the first of many real "plans" start appearing. It is, as you recall, the planning war waged by Telfair Hodgson and Silas McBee. Hodgson wants the new Convocation Hall (1886) yoked to the new stone Chapel. Silas McBee's 1890 quadrangular plan puts Walsh Memorial Hall in in place of the Chapel, and pushes the Chapel a bit farther south, to anchor a second and larger quadrangle. The so-called "McBee-Nixon" plan wins the support of the University's governing bodies and remains the main organizing principle for University site planning until the Olmsted Brothers landscape plan of 1946.

The campus plan for the Sewanee Military Academy, prepared by Eugene Knight and William Kessler before the First World War, is still in place after the Second World War, but has little influence beyond suggesting the placement of the buildings around the Parade Ground.

There is nothing terribly new or strikingly original in the Olmsted plan. Its ancestry can be traced back to the first two campus plans in the United States—Joseph Jacques Ramee's 1813 plan for Union College in Schenectady, New York, and Thomas Jefferson's 1818 plan for the University of Virginia in Charlottesville—and to the hundreds of campus plans that appeared perennially ever afterwards.

The fact that George R. Fairbanks was a graduate of Union College may have fitted him quite early for becoming "Architect of the Domain" for Sewanee. After the great George Fairbanks dies in 1906—leaving behind not only a vision for the campus but a lively and readable history of the University—there is no one person attuned to the virtues of campus planning, until Dr. Edward McCrady comes along, first as a professor (when he does his pre-war pen and ink drawings of the Chapel and its quadrangle) and then as Vice-Chancellor, from 1951 to 1971.

As soon as McCrady retires, however, there seems to be a great stirring of interest in campus planning. Here is an introductory sketch to the 219-page *Report on the University of the South Land Use Study*, dated April 1979 and done with substantial assistance from the Tennessee Valley Authority:

> The planning process for this study was initiated in 1972 by former Vice-Chancellor Bennett. In late 1977, Vice-Chancellor Ayres, with encouragement from the Regents, determined to seek an early completion of the study. A steering committee was appointed consisting of the Provost (as chairman), the Deans of the College and the School of Theology, and the Headmaster of the Sewanee Academy. Mr. (Charles) Baird of the Department of Forestry and Geology was asked to coordinate the study.
>
> In a real sense, this report is a product of the people of Sewanee. More than 90 Sewanee residents are responsible for its findings and recommendations (Baird Report, p. i).

Work on this 1970s study is divvied up into 20 "technical advisory group" (TAG) committees—Agriculture / Arboriculture, Airport, Athletics / Outdoor Recreation, Biological / Other Scientific, Business / Commercial, Campus Planning, Cemeteries, Faculty / Staff New Housing Areas, Forest Management, Geology / Soils / Building Stone, Historic / Scenic / Natural Trails / Caves / Trails, Lakes / Watersheds, Leases / Nonresidential / Noncommercial / Easements, Population Growth Forecasts, Public Utilities, Real Estate Development, Special Housing Concerns, Special Projects, Wildlife Management and Wood Energy Study.

Rather than being a long-haul proposition, however, the study introduction says that the work of the TAG teams "was conducted between April and December of 1978."

This 1979 study really deserves careful re-reading, a quarter-century later, because it provides a valuable baseline for saying where Sewanee was, in contrast to where it is now, in the 2002–2003 academic year.

It's also a fine model for citizen-based planning, remarkably inclusive, done out of love for this remarkable mountaintop community.

Two counter-examples of campus planning, done out of love for whatever money might be cadged here, include the Dober & Associates plan (1987) and "The Domain 2020 Land Use Study," done by The Architects Collaborative (TAC) and dated January 1, 1992.

Now, make no mistake, the lead-guy of the Dober firm, Richard P. Dober, is one of the best-known names in the campus planning field. He is known principally as the author of *Campus Planning* (1963), *Campus Design* (1992), *Campus Architecture* (1996), and *Campus Landscape* (2000). All four books are in the Sewanee library, proving if nothing else, that he and his firm still have their following here on campus.

This last-mentioned fact is good circumstantial evidence that Dober does a plan for Sewanee. Yet nowhere can we find a copy of this plan, and nowhere is Sewanee mentioned in Dober, Lidsky, Craig & Associates' website (www.dlca.com) as one of its clients.

Still, there is a long report on three special sessions on campus and strategic planning held for the Board of Trustees, held April 29 and April 30, 1987, which involves Dober's representative, Arthur Lidsky (misspelled in the Proceedings, 1987, pp. 21–30, as Litzsky).

Insofar as the Dober plan document seems not to have survived—despite the usual trashy rumors that the University paid big bucks for it—we must rely on what is said in the 1987 Proceedings. Three speakers are introduced—Director of Campus Planning, Tom Kepple, Theater Department professor Peter Smith, and Sewanee alumnus and consulting architect, Dan Randle:

> Mr. Randle spoke to explain why a campus plan was needed. He said that Sewanee was about to undertake major new construction and that there were complex problems relating to this construction that had to be solved.
>
> "It represented good stewardship to do a plan," he said, and for this reason the University had retained the firm of Dober and Associates of Boston to assist in devising a formal campus plan. Dober had been

The historic "core campus" silhouetted at sunset

> chosen because of their extensive knowledge of institutions similar to Sewanee (Proceedings, 1987, p. 21).

Presumably, Randle is referring to the major pumping-up of Sewanee's athletic muscles, with the Fowler Center, plus a new theater complex, and a new dining hall. As is customary with such hired-gun-expert moments, a great deal of hoopla is offered for the visual delectation of the client audience:

> For the occasion of this Special Session, the north and south walls of Convocation Hall had been used to display some 50 large and brightly colored maps, drawings, and charts of University topography, traffic and pedestrian patterns, residential and academic buildings, social and athletic facilities, and administrative and support structures.
>
> The focus of these displays was a "core campus" area extending from Gailor Hall to St. Luke's Hall and from University Avenue to duPont Library; a few of the displays focused on special areas such as the gymnasium and the Hamilton Hall-Gorgas Hall area (p. 21–22).

The session's high point or low point, depending on your view of Sewanee's historic campus, is Lidsky proposing the "construction of a theatre facility immediately north of Convocation Hall and Guerry Auditorium."

That is, if you know the site in question, the majestic stand of old oaks, tulip poplars, and white pines we know as Manigault Park would be obliterated for what one observer later describes as a "six-story-tall building"!

Anyway, Lidsky tells the assembly that it will take "approximately 12 months to complete a detailed campus plan and another 12 to 24 months to complete several renovation projects provided that money for these projects could be raised" while a "separate timetable was projected for major new construction" (p. 23).

Diligent search and inquiry in the University Archives turns up a skimpy six-page "Campus Plan Report" that is noted to be a Summary for Trustee Discussion May 1988. Presumably this is the promised detailed campus plan just mentioned by Lidsky. It says remarkably little. Its project budget page lists 11 capital projects with a total project cost range of from $38.2 to $55.3 million. Curiously, it lowballs significantly what is proposed for "Athletics / Recreation" ($6.0 to $8.5 million) and the Dining Hall ($1.7 to $2.3 million). The wide spread between Dober's low and high estimates for each project sound as if they have been pulled out of the top of the head.

A candid reaction to the Dober work appears in the *Sewanee News* (June 1988, p. 3):

> When the celebrated Campus Plan was unveiled last year, a few dyspeptic voices were soon joined by a chorus of opposition.
>
> The planners (Dober and Associates) learned that Sewanee's myths and legends have a subtle existence even in the curve of streets and the face of buildings.
>
> The attempt to open a new quadrangle, on the model of a Duke or a Virginia, seemed reasonable and even laudatory at first.
>
> But to close Georgia Avenue, build a performing arts center in Manigault Park, and give permanent official blessing to a pedestrian channel from Gailor Hall to the Bishop's Common offended too many sensibilities.

When in doubt, institutional wisdom says, commission another study. *The Domain 2020 Land Use Study* (1992) prepared by The Architects Collaborative (TAC)—a Cambridge design firm, in association with GA/Partners (Washington), a subsidiary of the Arthur Andersen Real Estate Services Group, and Ellers, Oakley, Chester and Rike (Memphis), an engineering firm—appears to be another one of those quick-sketch works done with

Magic Marker colored pens and large sheets of paper, suitable for tacking up on the wall and mystifying the non-planner client.

Domain 2020 is a 65-page document printed on 11 x 17 inch paper. Half of each sheet is blankest white, as if it is a work of minimalist art, but there are some interesting comments to be dug out by the curious. For example, TAC recommends a 60-acre parcel next to the golf course reserved for a future Office Research and Development business campus:

> This acreage will allow for five office buildings, each on 12-acre parcels, with sufficient area for on-grade parking. Located near the airport, Route 64, and four miles from Interstate 24, this is a prime location (Domain 2020, p. 46).

Less happy is TAC's recommendation to devote 755 acres for 604 single family residences (p. 44). That idea of one-acre lots seems to have perpetuated itself, in the Wiggins Creek development, Phase II of which seems destined to get built out (in 2003–2004) in a hellish determination to perpetuate suburban sprawl on the Domain.

There is a show of community involvement, forming up myriad committees, to capture a sense of legitimacy for the plan's recommendations, but a great deal of it (like the 60-acre R&D campus, as TAC concedes) simply borrows from the 1979 Baird Report study.

It is entirely possible that the University of the South gets even less for whatever it pays TAC than for what it pays Dober & Associates. But then nobody seems to know. Those who do know won't say. Maybe in a half-century, when all the principals involved in this deal are shuffled off the mortal coil, someone will unlock the University's vault of financial secrets and future-we will learn what the going price is for these Games Planners Play.

THE MAN AND THE HALL

AFTER A 15-YEAR HIATUS, 1975–1990, IN WHICH no new buildings are constructed, there is a remarkable new Sewanee residence dedicated, Clement Chen Hall.

Considerably more remarkable, however, is the biography of the honoree. He tells his own tale well, on October 25, 1985, when he receives the year's "Outstanding Alumnus" award:

> On the morning of May 19, 1949, I received a telegram telling me that Sewanee not only had given me an admission, but also a scholarship of $500, without which I would never be able to come, because my father had a large family to support, and he had lost much of his savings during the Second World War.
>
> By that time, the City of Shanghai was totally surrounded by the Red Army. Three out of four airfields had fallen to the Liberation Army. My mother gathered all the money we had at the house, totaling about $450, and she sewed them into my undershirt. I was lucky enough to get a ticket on the very last airplane that left Shanghai on the 21st of May. As I flew out, I could hear the loud thuds of bombardment all around the city. Two days later, the city fell.
>
> From that point on, I was totally cut off from my family. I was on my own. By way of Hong Kong, I finally arrived in Sewanee in late August, 1949 (Typescript, Clement Chen speech, Chen Hall vertical file, University Archives, p. 4).

So what is Clement Chen's connection to Sewanee?

Chen's long and wonderfully moving speech explains that he is in his last year at an Episcopal school in Shanghai, and he wants to go study in the United States, so his English teacher, Miss Grace Brady, puts him in touch with Mr. Ellis Tucker, whose brother is the Bishop of Virginia, who is a good friend of Dr. Alex Guerry.

Among his favorite Sewanee teachers—Professors Frierson (French), Petry (Physics), and Woods (English)—it is Professor Charles Cheston who teaches Clement Chen engineering drawing.

> Then the Korean War broke out, and I found myself, like so many Chinese students in this country, having to take up a technical or engineering profession so that we could make a living, as we were not allowed to return to China.
>
> Since Sewanee did not have an engineering school, I transferred to Rensselaer Polytechnic Institute in Troy, New York, and studied architecture (Chen speech, p. 6).

Chen finishes his degree, moves to California, marries his childhood sweetheart June, and starts an architectural practice in California. He starts to win several architectural design competitions and gets the chance to work on large projects, including hotels. His first big breakthrough is the Holiday Inn Financial District (1971), a 30-story hotel with 565 guest rooms and suites. From this work, Chen gets to design "many Holiday Inn hotels both in this country and in Asia" and become "an owner of several Holiday Inns and a Hilton Hotel as well."

Following the historic trip of President Nixon to China (February 1972), and the opening of trade relations between the two nations, comes the invitation from the Chinese Government to joint-venture a major hotel in Beijing:

> In 1978, the Chinese government invited me to China and to explore the possibility of building hotels there. That was the beginning of a new policy of opening the country to foreign investment as well as to the foreign travellers. It was a very exciting time, and I found myself right there at the frontier of that new policy. I proposed to build a hotel with them, in a 10-year joint venture.
>
> My proposed hotel was more or less an experiment of this open-door policy, and I knew that there was a great deal of responsibility on my part, as my project was the very first hotel joint venture they ever attempted. If my project succeeded, it would be an affirmation of the correctness of that policy, and I wanted to do everything possible to make it a success.

> After many trans-Pacific journeys, and much hard work, my Jianguo Hotel opened in Beijing in April 1982 (Chen speech, p. 8).

For those of us who like instant gratification, a virtual visit to the Jianguo Hotel is possible immediately through its website (www.hoteljianguo.com). The hotel is currently celebrating its 20th anniversary and describes itself as having "469 well appointed rooms and elegantly furnished suites" and being "an upscale four-star business hotel located right in the Beijing Central Business District within 10 minutes walking distance to the major diplomatic and government areas and prime shopping centers."

In his 1985 speech, Chen notes that among those present for the award are Kemmons Wilson, founder of Holiday Inns, and Xie Shi Gang, representing China's ambassador to the United States, Han Xu.

As for the hotel, after three years of operation, Chen notes that the Jianguo Hotel is a success beyond his wildest expectations:

> Occupancy has been over 97 percent for three and a half years now. Among our long-term tenants are the U.S. State Department, U.S. Department of Commerce, 18 international banks, and eight of the largest oil companies in the world.
>
> It is regarded as the best hotel in China, both in terms of facilities and services. Two years ago, the Chinese government has declared it the model hotel for all of their other hotels to emulate (Chen speech, p. 11).

The official dedication of Clement Chen Hall, as the new Vice-Chancellor's residence, is held on November 17, 1990, with the family of Mr. Chen in attendance. Clement Chen III—a graduate of Stanford with an MBA from Harvard and now president of a large hotel management firm—gives a brief but powerful statement which re-tells how his father happened to come to Sewanee, and includes a sketch of his last moments:

> I wish that my father could be here to see the house and to share this joyous occasion with us; nevertheless, I know that it meant the world to him to talk with Bob Ayres, only two hours before my father died, and to know that Sewanee had received his gift.
>
> Sewanee meant a lot to my father, and, it has meant a lot to all of us. This occasion is an opportunity for all of us to reflect upon how

> good luck—and divine help—change all of our lives (Clement Chen III, letter, Dec. 3, 1990, enclosing dedicatory remarks, in Chen Hall vertical file, University Archives).

As to Clement Chen, the hall not the man, it is clearly a departure for Sewanee's architectural tradition, showing if nothing else that the only constant in architectural fashion is one of continual change.

Despite the University's early embrace of what we have previously called Premature Post-Modernism, by the time Vice-Chancellor Robert Ayres raises the money, for an 8,500-square foot residence, to be enjoyed by his successor, Sam Williamson and his family, Fully Ripe Post-Modernism is all the national rage.

Clement Chen Hall east gable end (above) and the Harvard Lampoon Castle (below left)

Looking at the elevations done by architect Randolph C. Marks, we see some design features that proclaim to Dorothy and Toto, at least, that we are no longer in Kansas.

There is the curious resemblance, in the east (front) elevation, to that of a large stylized face. There are two oculi for eyes, a Jacobethan chimney as a nose, a stepped gable as a frizzy haircut, and even a set of choppers fashioned out of French doors. The resemblance to the famous anthropomorphic Harvard Lampoon Castle (1909) seems rather remarkable.

Behind this projecting front bay is a Living Room, about 44 feet by 20 feet, used for receptions by the reigning Vice-Chancellor. Larger crowds tend to spill into the Grand Hall, an octagonal "crossing" (in the ecclesiastical sense) with a nice coffered ceiling formed by the intersection of the Dining Room, Foyer, and Living Room.

When the ceremonial scale of the Dining

North side of Chen Hall (U. Archives)

Room (18 x 21 feet) seems wrong, the VC can dine en-famille in the Family Dining Room, a much smaller alcove-like space with a 5'6" radius bay window.

The kitchen seems enormous—19 feet square—but then the Vice-Chancellor's Residence (VCR) is at its jolliest when a lot of food and drink is being served.

Balancing the kitchen on the north side of the Gallery (central east west corridor) is a Family Room, also 19 feet and also quite square.

Flanking the Rear Entry, which leads out to the parking lot behind the house, is a pantry (south) and a laundry (north), both roughly 8 by 11 feet.

One can get to the second floor of the VCR either by a stairway or by an elevator.

Remembering the layout of the first floor, architect Randy Marks has cunningly placed the Master Bedroom above the Dining Hall, the Master Bath above the Family Dining, Bedrooms 2 and 3 above the Kitchen and Family Room, a Sitting Room above the Grand Hall, and a Study above the Foyer. Bedroom No. 1 is smaller (14'10" x 11'10") and immediately above the Screened Porch.

There are also Baths 1, 2, and, 3 playing supporting roles for the three bedrooms.

The south elevation of the VCR, rather Chateauesque in look, has several nice features, including a Terrace, outside the Living Room, for dining alfresco, cocktail mixing, or schmoozing. Below the Terrace is a three-bay Tudor arched Covered Parking Garage. The rest of this lower level space is reserved for mechanical stuff and crawl space. This handsome face presents itself in close-up to North Carolina Avenue.

Marks notes on this south elevation sheet some interesting specifications:

> Eggshell cream is the Dryvit color. Sandblast texture to belt course, pilasters, as well as window and door trims. All other Dryvit surface areas are Quartzputz.
>
> Sloped roofing surfaces are to have 290 to 310 fiberglass shingles with felt underlayment.
>
> Elastomeric membrane single-ply roofing material is to be used on flat roof areas.

On the north elevation (p. 274), with its two stepped gables speaking Dutch or Flemish, Marks specifies a "crimson terra cotta Flemish Bond chimney stack" and "crimson terra cotta brick arches with limestone accents (keys and voussoirs)" and "coursed sandstone stepped gables."

So far, at least, no reliable cost figure has turned itself in to this observer, besides the $500,000 given by the Chen family. Let us be patient: the final figure may turn up later.

Randolph C. Marks's south elevation for Chen Hall (U. Archives)

THE $11 MILLION SPORT & FITNESS CENTER

THE SANDSTONE SLAB SIGN SAYS FOWLER CENTER / 1994. But the $11.3 million monument to Sewanee's longterm commitment to Muscular Christianity begins at least as far back as July 14, 1989, a century after a gym is put in the east half of Convocation Hall. This 1989 date is on the detailed site plan of the ground around the Juhan Gymnasium, surveying work done by Betts Land Engineering for Hastings + Chivetta, a highly successful St. Louis architectural firm specializing in sports complexes.

The *Sewanee News* announces on the front page of its November 1989 issue that the University of the South "has received a $5 million gift from an anonymous donor to build a multipurpose sports and fitness complex."

In the SN article, mostly quoting VC Sam Williamson and Athletic Director Bill Huyck, it is stressed that the new complex is badly needed so Sewanee can remain competitive with its liberal arts peers.

Curiously, however, there is reference to a "multi-purpose forum" for volleyball, basketball, and badminton, surrounded by an indoor track.

Could we be talking, like, you know, Roman Forum? Mens sana, in corpore sano, and all that?

Now my unabridged dictionary says that the Forum was a place for carrying on business, judicial, and civic affairs in Rome. Could it be that the principal business of Sewanee is competitive sports, narcissistic agonies of personal fitness, and athletic performance as public spectacle?

This is an interesting leap into the future, where cities' central business districts are being designated as "urban entertainment centers," and we seem bent on "amusing ourselves to death," as Neil Postman's troubling book titles the trend of media-driven life in Post-Industrial America.

Possibly in defense of the expense, the SN piece says:

> "Students today are taking a far greater interest in intramural programs," Williamson said.
>
> "These programs are very important here; it gets dark early and it gets

cold; the campus is isolated, and the students need something to do."

Fowler Center

Presumably this quote is not for export, but to belay alumni doubts about the unprecedented project cost, since the bum weather and isolation on campus could conceivably drive applicants elsewhere.

We next hear from Sewanee's Vice President for Business and Community Relations, Tom Kepple, saying on March 30, 1992 that the Sports & Fitness Center architect is hard at work completing the plans for the facility:

> At their February 1992 meeting the Regents approved the issue of $5,000,000 in bonds to cover the interim financing for pledges to the Sports & Fitness Center and to complete approximately $3,000,000 in deferred maintenance projects. Our plan is to issue tax-exempt, 10 year, fixed interest rate bonds in April. We expect the interest rate to be under six percent. Morgan Keegan of Memphis, which handled our 1990 Bond Issue, will again be underwriter.

In his April 1992 report to the Trustees, Provost Fred Croom reports a full project cost figure, apparently for the first time: "This $11 million facility will be vitally important in providing athletic and recreational programs and opportunities consistent with the high quality of our offerings in the academic programs and other areas of University life."

This leads, from what seems like a solid cash-nexus, to lots more sheets from Hastings + Chivetta, during the summer of 1992.

One (dated June 30, 1992) shows the "Multi-Sport Center" where a six-lane indoor track wraps around three basketball courts. To the architects' credit, the building is not just a box big enough to contain the regulation size running track, but uses the lovely curve of the 160-meter track's east flank to bow out the SFC's front and clad it in coursed ashlar sandstone. This addition to the north side of the Juhan Gymnasium is about 30 feet below the older gym and excavated out of the Sewanee Conglomerate bedrock.

Another (dated July 29, 1992) shows the north elevation, where the buff sandstone wraps around from its front, then transitions to a complementary buff-color brick for the north wall. The windows are an amiable blend of tradition (vaguely Palladian) and modernity (glass-block inside the lower three mullions) with cast-stone arched heads. There are also belt courses and copings of sandstone to ornament this otherwise business-like north wall.

As possibly mentioned earlier, in the chapter on Juhan Gymnasium, the coursed sandstone ashlar on this 1990s building comes from the exterior walls of the older gyms that the Fowler Center wraps around. They are removed, according to Fowler Center director Bill Barry, shipped to Nashville to be cleaned up, for $2 a stone, and then re-set on the new facade.

The olympiad-scale swimming pool, with nine racing lanes, added onto the south flank of Juhan, has similar exterior features, plus crenellated battlements on its parapet that are spaced out just a bit longer than the original Juhan crenellations.

Hastings + Chivetta's northeast elevation for the Fowler Center (U. Archives)

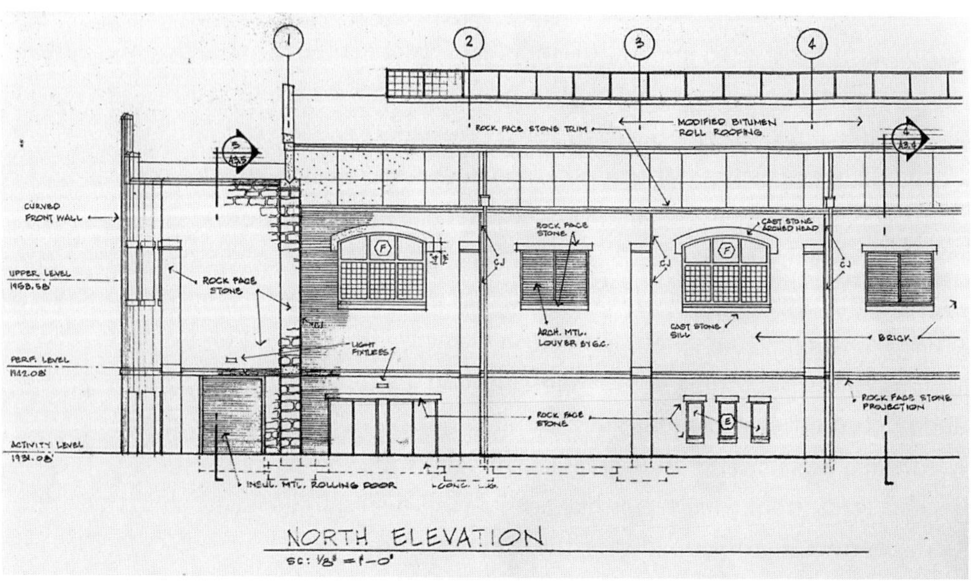

For the least visible elements of the exterior, Dryvit is used, but with Panzermesh (for extra strength), and brick is used "where it doesn't show," as Barry tells it.

There are lots of other elements in Fowler Center—the old 1,000 seat basketball and volleyball "performance gym," three racquetball courts, one squash court, a dance studio, a fitness gym, classroom space, locker rooms, and three indoor tennis courts. But we really need to plunge down into the lowest and westernmost rooms of the complex, those spaces equipped with torture devices of motorized treadmills, weight-lifting gear, and other highly evolved aids to giving us flatter abs, thinner thighs, cuter buns, and sexier pecs.

One wonders what the original perpetrators of Muscular Christianity—Charles Kingsley, Thomas Hughes *(Tom Brown's School Days)*, the Young Men's Christian Association, the Boy Scouts, Teddy Roosevelt, and many other enthusiasts flourishing from 1880 to 1920—would think of this $11.3 million complex.

TENNESSEE WILLIAMS CENTER

IT IS A RAINY FRIDAY AFTERNOON, NOVEMBER 15, 2002, and the campus is bailing out for the weekend, but somehow the Tennessee Williams Center (1998) seems at its elegiac best.

The architects, a Nashville firm styling itself Street Dixon Rick, have done a cunning wall treatment for what otherwise would be a giant windowless box.

The reason there are no windows is that this projecting block is a 150-seat "black box theater," which means literally that the interior walls and ceiling of the performing space are painted black. This presumably gives total control to those who do the stage lighting, set decoration, and so on. If you happen to like black-box theaters, then the Proctor Hill Theatre may be one of the best.

So outside this big box the architects have the problem of how to make the three windowless walls visually interesting. Their solution is to provide horizontal bands in two complementary materials, a buff glazed brick, and a pink and yellow stone, laid in coursed ashlar blocks.

The result is to offer an illusionistic wall that seems to be slices of geologic strata:

At the base are six courses of stone.

Above them are two courses of brick.

Then come six thinner courses of stone.

Then three courses of brick.

Then three courses of stone.

Then six courses of brick.

Then two courses of stone.

Then, the rest of the wall, up to the top coping, is all brick.

Only when you look at the architects' elevations, dating from May 1998, do you realize that this is "synthetic stone," that is, cast stone, artfully made by a Nashville company, and even more artfully given pitched faces in the best Sewanee building tradition.

The elevation also indicates that the glass curtain wall of the Tennessee Williams Center foyer has "aluminum storefront" muntins.

Behind these two new dramatically contrasting blocks—one unglazed masonry and one all-glazed—is what used to be an old gymnasium used by Sewanee Military Academy. It has been given adaptive re-use for classroom space, a dance studio, studio theater space, large dressing rooms, and lots of storage space for props, sets, costumes, and other materials. There is even a CADD (computer assisted drafting and design) lab for helping students and professors work out set designs.

Groundbreaking for the TWC takes place on May 2, 1997. It is significant that the initial site plans, dated April 16, 1997, designate the project as the Tennessee Williams Center. This is unusual; it means that the money and the honoree are already known, on the front end, unlike most of Sewanee's buildings, which start off with a generic name (e.g. New Dormitory or Sport & Fitness Center), then find their funding, before getting a formal christening.

Tennessee's link to Sewanee was his beloved grandfather Walter Dakin, pictured back on page 145.

The reason for the project being named for the great playwright is that he wills the University of the South the remainder of his $7 million estate—upon the death of his sister Rose—and rather more astonishingly, the copyrights to all of his plays.

These latter assets earn Sewanee about $500,000 a year in royalties, ac-

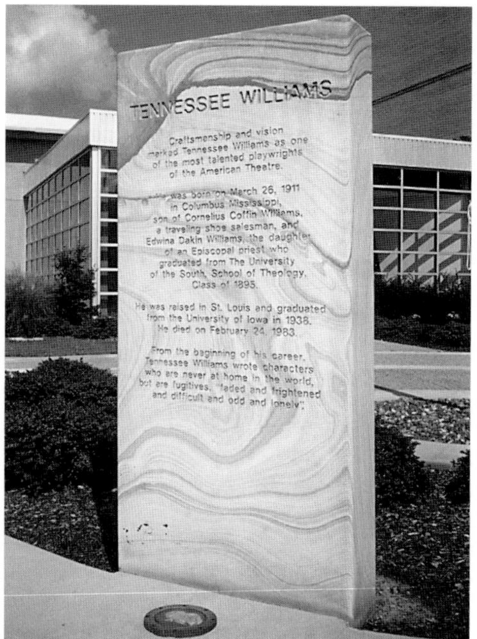

Sandstone monolith summarizing Tennessee Williams's life

cording to University communications director Joe Romano (*The Sewanee Purple*, October 28, 2002, p. 3).

For the past seven years, says the story reprinted from *The Chattanooga Times Free Press*, Sewanee "has used the money to fund the Sewanee Writers' Conference, Tennessee Williams Fellows, and Tennessee Williams Scholarship Fund."

Outside the entrance to the TWC complex are three exquisite banded sandstone slabs telling a bit of the life and works of Tennessee Williams. They stand tall, in a semicircle, near the periphery of a circular Memorial Garden. The iron swirls are particularly lovely on this wet autumn afternoon.

Inside the Proctor Hill Theatre, this weekend, Sewanee's immensely talented Theater Department, under the direction of David Landon, are performing *Lysistrata*, a classic play always revived in time of war, as this historical moment seems to be. Aristophanes' timeless comedy revolves around a woman who urges her friends to go on strike, sexually speaking, to get their husbands and lovers to stop the war before it kills or mutilates them all.

If only the spouses of our current national leadership had such similar determination!

CATHEDRAL TO GLUTTONY

THE LAST FEW YEARS OF THE MILLENNIUM see a firestorm of controversy over what is provisionally called the University Commons.

Sewanee lifers consider it bad form to lose their equanimity. Nothing is worth getting too upset about, except possibly getting an inferior bottle of wine from the sommelier, and certainly nothing is so important as to provoke yelling and throwing mud at each other.

Yet following the annual meeting of the Alumni Council of the Associated Alumni, on August 16, 1997, all heck breaks loose. The date is highly significant, being the last day of Thermidor, on the French revolutionary calendar, that month in which Robespierre is overthrown (July 27 or Thermidor 9) by the moderates, after which the reactionaries take over.

In this case, of course, it is the inner circle of University administrators pushing a dining hall design that promises to overthrow the 120-year-old tradition of Collegiate Gothic in the name of Post-Modernism Über Alles.

Not a spade of dirt is turned, until May 2, 1998. By then an acrimonious nine months have passed, with a lot of mud flung, not only at the dining hall and its architect, but at longtime colleagues, many of whom have never taken a political stand in their lives, beyond going to the polls when told to do so.

Leader of the opposition is Dr. James Waring McCrady, who has spent a lifetime on the Sewanee mountaintop, and two decades watching his father, Dr. Edward McCrady, bring the best of the Collegiate Gothic tradition in line with mid-20th-century construction techniques.

On October 29, 1997, Waring McCrady composes a critique of the design, titled "Some Comments on the Aesthetics of the Proposed Dining Hall," and distributes its 110 copies to 91 faculty members and others who express interest in this critical viewpoint.

The critique's target is mostly Hardy Holzman Pfeiffer & Associates (HHPA), the blue-chip New York architectural firm that has been chosen

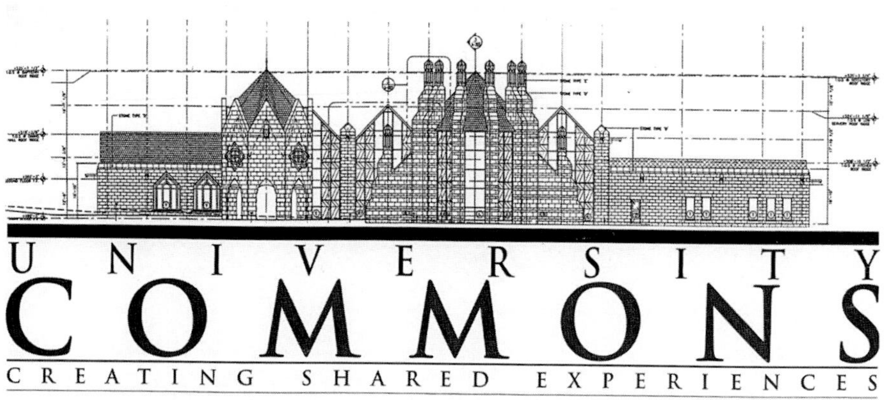

A 1997 information sheet on the "University Commons" dining hall plan (U. Archives)

to do the University Commons job, but is also indirectly aimed at the administrative insiders surrounding Vice-Chancellor Sam Williamson, clearly the Mr. Big in this high-stakes deal. Ironically, or not, Williamson will be rescued from this pressure-cooker of duty in the summer of 2000, before what is nearing completion as McClurg Hall gets dedicated (on May 3, 2001, exactly three years after groundbreaking). Williamson's successor, Dr. Joel Cunningham, is blessed by not having a dog in the fight, as we hillbillies like to put it up here.

McCrady does a remarkably elegant job of taking the HHPA drawings, all done in the Post-Modernist idiom, and "translates" them back into the Collegiate Gothic idiom, with identical measurements, window placements, etc., just to show what the University is losing in adopting HHPA's approach.

In many cases, he places "The Architect's Proposal" side by side with "A Collegiate Gothic Treatment," drawn skillfully and to scale, not with the CADD system his opposition uses, but by his own talented hand.

McCrady is also capable of first-rate architectural criticism:

Post-modern idioms (such as blank walls or cut-out effects) can be rectified by a more interesting articulation of the surfaces (such as drip-courses over the windows, etc. — see my drawings) at no greater expense at all.

Every stone in the building has to be cut on all six sides in any case, and having a row stick out a few extra inches has nothing to do with cost. Buttresses such as those on Guerry are simply a matter of shifting stones outwards, not at significantly greater exense.

The reference to Ego: A really tasteful building will blend graciously and sympathetically with its neighbors. It should look so right that one would think it had always been there.

In this particular setting, a building should defer politely to the chapel.

This is not to say it should be a Plain-Jane. It could be quite charming and thoughtful.

The dining hall currently proposed has the egotism of much contemporary work in that it comes across as intrusive and defiant of earlier work.

It has a distinct flavor of "Hey, look at me!"

That's from the quasi-gothic eastern perspective. As to the other two-thirds of the exterior, they ignore (defy) entirely the rest of the campus (McCrady, e-mail, October 31, 1997, 5:35 P.M.).

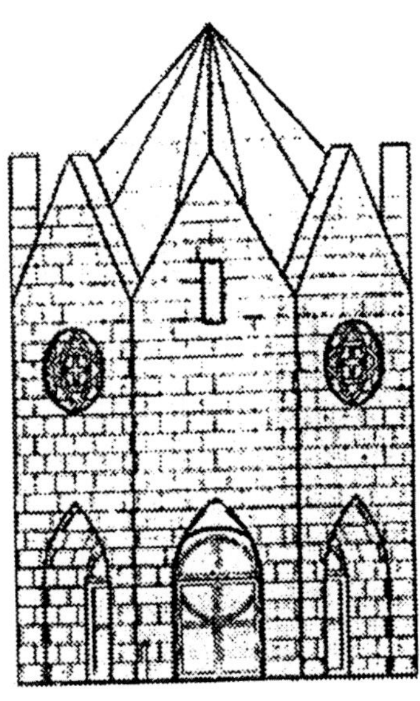

Waring McCrady's "Collegiate Gothic" alternative to HHPA's design (U. Archives)

Let's also tune in to McCrady's stirring conclusion in his "Some Comments" pamphlet:

> The University, wary of local talent and politics, understandably decided that the way to assure our having a fine and appropriate building was to obtain an architect of national experience, versed in collegiate needs, and having experience with stonework.
>
> We discover a bit late that the architect thus hired is profoundly unsympathetic with the ethos of this community and rather anxious to impose a "signature" building entirely inappropriate to our heritage.
>
> In spite of our having spent serious money on the many frustrating revisions so far circulated, we must swallow our pride, admit our error, and go after what we want.
>
> Let us not commit a 13 or 14 million dollar mistake which will irretrievably distort our central campus, offend our constituency, and embarrass us in the eyes of the future.
>
> We do not want future generations to say, "Lo!—a 1990s building!"
>
> We want them to appreciate a building that looked right when it was built and will continue to look right as long as it stands ("Some comments…", University Archives, McClurg vertical file).

Among the "many frustrating revisions" in the design—from its early iterations to what passes through the community gauntlet and gets built—are some jazzy purple glass zigzags that show up on early information sheets circulated to raise funds and build support for the University Commons.

A three-inch-thick stack of e-mail printouts, in the University Archives's McClurg vertical files, refers to this information sheet as an "apology sheet" and a "propaganda handout," by faculty and townspeople, according to McCrady's compilation of work disseminated on October 29, 1997 at 3:57 P.M. (p. 3).

It is interesting, possibly significant, that the earlier of two versions of the sheet—with the purple lightning bolts on the windows—contains the architect's thoughts on "Gothic Design and the New Dining Hall," while the later version—minus the purple lightning—removes Malcolm Holzman's bylined text, summarizes a few of his main talking points and adds them to "observations" by Dean of Students Rob Pearigen (C'76), ex-VC Bob Ayres (C'49), Board of Regents chair David Beecken (C'68), and three Regents board members, Blucher B. Lines (C'71), Maibeth J. Porter (C'77), and Jerry B. Adams (C'65).

The insistence on quoting only bona-fide Sewanee alumns seems to say, see, all these Good Ole Boys and Good Ole Gals like the building, so shouldn't you feel the same way?

It is probably a tough sell, one of the toughest selling jobs the University Relations Office has had in a while, maybe since the admission of women back in 1969. This may or may not explain why Stephen Becker, vice president for university relations, and Thomas R. Kepple, vice president for business and community relations, both announce the same day they are leaving Sewanee, according to a January 26, 1998 press release. Kepple seems to be getting a nice promotion, becoming president of Juniata College (in Pennsylvania) in July, while Becker goes to be a vice president for development and college relations at Whitman College (Walla Walla, Washington) in March, hardly a promotional move.

Faculty and students are polled, early in December 1997, about their feelings on the dining hall. The poll results are circulated by Waring McCrady on December 12 at 5:41 P.M.:

■ Of the 81 faculty who express their opinions, 70 percent are against, 16 percent for, and the rest indifferent.

■ Of 277 student responses, on a 1 to 5 scale, 1 percent (3) say a great design; 4 percent (11) say a good-enough design; 6 percent (17) have no opinion; 5 percent (13) say it's a poor design but not worth fighting about; and 84 percent (233) say it's a bad design for Sewanee, something it will ultimately be embarrassed by.

Sooner or later, it becomes necessary to make a field-visit to each building, and *de gustibus*, there is no disputing that McClurg is the most delicious building on campus.

McClurg Hall turns out to be a cathedral to gluttony.

For the paltry sum of $6.50, a total alien being like myself can land on this spot, fill up the tray, and then eat enough to die, theoretically speaking.

Even those who possess admirable self-restraint, never taking more than can be consumed, so as to stay a member of the Clean Plate Club, may find it hard to deal with the 100 *(mas o menos)* food items that get set out by the Aramark food services employees on a typical lunch-day.

A good meal, such as is had on November 19, 2002, is bound to soften the judgment towards the place.

The first observation, post-prandial, is that McClurg Hall is surely interesting to look at, even if no food is on the serving counters and none of those photogenic young men and women are in the building.

McClurg is interesting, first, because, the architects have indeed created a cathedral-like structure.

The innovation of Gothic wall construction over Roman wall construction is the buttressing at right angles to the way the wall is running. McClurg expresses this Gothic wall treatment in elegant minimalist form.

McClurg's main axiality is east, where the food-laden altars are, and west, where the buttressed congregation sits in what is known as the refectory.

At the west end, where the narthex should be, is an apse-like termination, shaped by six tall buttresses in a radial array, with clear glass windows in between them.

At right angles to the main dining hall's length are much deeper alcoves, formed up by massive sandstone pier-walls. Each alcove terminates with a window seat; these small "side-chapel" dining-room spaces are popular with the students, and with all kind of groups, and tend to fill up before the "nave" tables do.

There are openings pierced in each of these pier-walls, rather like the passages of a cathedral's side-aisles, except that there is a foot-high stone sill creating a stumbling block to anyone trying to walk through them.

Artificial lighting in this large space comes primarily from two enormous lens-shaped chandeliers shaped like the University's seal. The design adopted by HHPA comes over the protest from University traditionalists, who find the whole idea of a cross (the central figure) made up of lightbulbs pure blasphemy. At one stage in the design, McCrady counts more than 40 "parodies" of the University seal in the building.

When totally abstracted from its Sewanee iconography, the chandeliers look remarkably like those spaceships that hover above Earth's surface and suck up terrestrials into their underbelly.

Another lens-shaped structure—constructed of unpainted wood strips and suspended from the ceiling between the dining hall "nave" and the servery "altar"—may simply be a way of announcing (as Frank Lloyd

McClurg's south flank: Patriot missiles ready to launch?

Wright used to do with his choked-down hallway corridors) that we are moving from Room Experience #1 to Room Experience #2, or vice versa.

The servery is a wild-looking architectural experience, nearly impossible to describe, without either wads of snapshots or great rolls of blueprints.

One suspects immediately, upon looking at the compound curves of the gothic-arch-shaped steel beams, that they are designed by a computer CADD system, hideously difficult to fabricate in the steelyard, and obscenely expensive for the client.

Not to keep anyone in suspense, what is described as "$13.8 million" for "approximately 42,000 square feet," according to the official University Commons info-sheet in 1997 soon escalates to a publicly admitted $18 million. (By the time of its completion the actual cost is generally seen as much higher.) Doing the basic bonehead math leads one to believe this building costs a breathtaking $428 per square foot!

If you take a magnifying glass to this same University Commons info-sheet (p. 284), and look in the top lefthand corner of the reproduced west elevation of the building, you can make out the words "Baptistry Roof Ridge."

Baptistry?

So that's what this wild and crazy looking octagonal entrance (p. 290) to the dining hall is! Again, it offers a monster's visage, with two eyes (oculi in architect-speak), and a mouth you enter to get yourself gluttonized.

Those who are amateur deconstructionists may wonder out loud what is the "baptismal" experience being simulated once one decides to enter the gustatory kingdom of McClurg/Aramark.

Certainly, we know, a good meal can restore someone's soul, for a good five or six hours, at least.

McClurg's entrance seems to want to swallow those entering its great stone head

It is less likely a feeling of being born again, offered or even implied, since mankind shall not live by bread alone, even if it is buttered and jammed.

Perhaps the baptistry joke is on the University of the South. Possibly: 1) You are now entering into the kingdom of the Soaked Client, or 2) sprinkled with the jokes of the Goober who doesn't know much about art, or 3) something entirely else, known only to the Architect and his closest cocktail-party friends.

As to #1, the usual unconfirmable rumors say that the REAL price of McClurg actually is somewhere in the realm of $26 million, with a lot of project-cost stuff squirreled away in other drawers.

As to #2, here is a semi-anonymous comment delivered by e-mail on November 11, 1997:

> Why should we care about the taste of those who built Frog Manor (the new VC's residence), or who have hired a New York-Los Angeles architectural firm to share their willing interpretation of Collegiate-Gothic-Meets-Philip-Johnson dining hall?
>
> The architect isn't the goober, by the way, the goobers are the ones who see the emperor nattily attired. Art—in Los Angeles and New York—is what you can get away with (University Archives, McClurg file).

We might be able to discount #3 when we pick up Malcolm Holzman's handsome and lavishly illustrated coffee table book, *Stone Work* (Images Publishing, 2001, 210 pages). It tends to argue, with cleverness and gorgeous color photographs, how deeply and devoutly he believes in the sacramental acts of stone.

McClurg Hall is one of 17 buildings showcased by Holzman, and his large supporting cast at HHPA, and he cannot say enough good things about those buildings, or what stone brings to them.

Here is what he recalls about how sandstone got revived at Sewanee after a 20-year slumber:

> Following a design review meeting with faculty, students, and other individuals interested in the project, university stonemason Houston King asked me about the possibility of using stone from the campus for the new dining hall.
>
> This was an unexpected proposition, as I knew stone in any quantity had not been available for at least 20 years, except for modest repairs to existing structures.
>
> From his inquiry came a new building that is clad in 750 tons of sandstone from the reopened campus quarries and a sizable amount from other nearby sources.
>
> All but 300 tons of the material, excluding the decorative limestone finials, was fabricated on campus.
>
> Getting from a dozen pieces of sandstone mocked up for review by the university regents to a completed structure in four years' time was an intricate process. . . .
>
> The most compelling aspect of this remarkable enterprise was the university's unflagging interest in reviving the use of sandstone from their campus to a major project.
>
> The dining hall, in making visual and physical reference to Sewanee's most revered buildings, could not have paid such stunning homage to this educational institution's heritage with any other material (Holzman, p. 109).

Amen to all that.

The only point at which Holzman lets down his rhetorical guard, perhaps unconsciously, is when he argues that a revival of stonework for today's architecture is made possible when "the stone industry fully embraced Henry Ford's two basic production principles: make standard, interchangeable parts, and assemble them with a minimum of handcraft labor." Further, he says, the "latest improvements in stone-processing equipment whittle away at production costs and reduce material waste with little impact on the quality of the final product." Finally, we can now ship stone anywhere, like plums or cheese, thanks to the global marketplace, where "it is often the case that stone blocks are quarried on one continent, cut and fabricated on another, and installed on a third" (Holzman, p. 72).

Holzman may not realize, or may not care, that he is flatly insulting Sewanee's venerable tradition of quarrying its mountaintop sandstone and setting it on that same mountaintop in a 120-year series of memorable stone buildings. It is precisely that pride of place, honored by stoneworkers since the beginnings of time, that seems to be violated by the Holzman ship-anywhere dictum.

This kind of arrogance leads Holzman into what may be his greatest blunder, so far as McClurg Hall is concerned, his use of limestone from the Gillis Quarries Ltd. (Winnepeg, Manitoba, Canada) for the silly ithyphallic pinnacles erected along McClurg's main dining hall rooftline.

These nine-foot-tall finials look to most cynical observers like rows of gigantic stone penises. That simple fact has led campus wags to some semi-unmentionable nicknames for McClurg like the "Phallus Palace," and "Viagra Valhalla."

It may be better, in these times of National Security Paranoia, to re-direct the visual symbolism of the stone finials by making McClurg into an expression of our nation's Anti-Ballistic Missile defense readiness.

When the light is right, or with insignia painted on their sides, they could look like a classic Cold War battery of surface-to-air missiles, Patriots perhaps. Dr. Helen Caldicott deconstructed that symbolism in her delightful book *Missile Envy* (1984).

Collectively, the finials could be stone poster-boys for our next United We Hate campaign against some far-off terrorist nation, emblematic of our first line of defense.

Anything is better, for this University owned and controlled by the bishops of 28 dioceses, than seeing them as Comedy Central jokes representing 28 bishoprics.

An alternative nomenclature may be in order. We could, with impeccable logic, call it "All Sins Chapel." Such a name, for the closest stone-kin to All Saints Chapel, would recognize the old Manichean notion of good and evil having equal sway in this world.

After all, the dining hall exemplifies all of the Seven Deadly Sins: 1) Gluttony (in excelsis); 2) Pride (architectural ego); 3) Anger (betraying a 120-year-old Collegiate Gothic tradition); 4) Greed (spending $428 or more per square foot); 5) Envy (my finial is bigger than yours); 6) Lust (ditto); and 7) Sloth (what slugs we feel like after the too-big-a-meal buffet experience).

A coda should be added, lest anyone think editorial-we don't like McClurg Hall, or are faulting the generosity of its many donors, notably Lakeland banker C. V. McClurg and distinguished others.

There are a lot of fun and interesting design elements in the building. It is like a mini-theme park for contemporary architectural ideas. Its wall treatments are never dull. Its creative shapes and wrinkles—like the big sculptural-steel gate that closes off the refectory half of the building when that area isn't needed—are really quite wonderful.

Less successful are some of the following:

■ The clerestory windows are too small and sit beneath too much roof overhang to give enough daylighting into the refectory.

■ The blind-window arcades—that is, the "cut-out" window-shapes without windows—of the kitchen wing sandstone walls are uglier than necessary. McCrady's critique about "articulation" could have made these walls more appealing.

■ The triangular-prism bay windows, with the anodized bronze curls, are a 1990s mannerism that will seem silly, like the 1950s airfoil shapes of the Air Force Academy Chapel, in the future.

But the building is deuced clever, as the hundreds of architects' drawings show, indicating a depth of imaginative talent inside HHPA that will succeed elsewhere.

Time will tell how the building succeeds, whether it wins acceptance with its stone neighbors, and if it can last long enough (say a century or more) to offer a lower "life-cycle" cost that justifies the humongous capital investment put into it.

At the very least, no doubt, McClurg Hall will outlast this book and all the cheap-shots made about it!

CHAPEL OF THE APOSTLES

THE NAME CHAPEL OF THE APOSTLES, BUILT TO SERVE Sewanee's School of Theology, may be a double-play of words, since it is designed by the two leading apostles of E. Fay Jones. It is not by the great Arkansas architect himself, the man who gets credit in the Sewanee "Catalog & Announcements, 2001–2002":

> The Chapel of the Apostles (2000) was designed by renowned Arkansas architect E. Fay Jones, and serves as a center of worship for the university's School of Theology, providing an important space for the training of priests.
>
> The building seats approximately 250 people and is flexible to meet the varied needs of the liturgies of the Episcopal Church.
>
> Funding for the chapel was aided by an anonymous $1 million donation, as well as a major gift from Paul and Evelyn Howell of Houston, Texas, whose contribution honors Bishop Allin, presiding bishop of the Episcopal Church, 1973–1985 (Catalog, pp. 74–75).

The Chapel of the Apostles is actually the work of Maurice Jennings and David McKee, two talented architects working in Fay Jones's old office in Fayetteville, Arkansas. Their work so far, however, has remained loyal to the design parameters of the firm's ex-senior partner, Fay Jones, who has come very near to canonization, for work including the Thorncrown Chapel (1980), and the private residence (1960 and 1972) of Sam Walton, the founder of Wal-Mart and the scion of the wealthiest family in this shopping-mad world.

One might argue that we are niggling here, since Fay Jones is himself the best-remembered apostle of Frank Lloyd Wright, and sometimes it is difficult to distinguish the Master from the Pupil.

Such, we understand, is the principle of apostolic succession, something Sewanee's theologs know well.

Chapel of the Apostles

One approach to Fay Jones is through Robert Ivy. His book *Fay Jones*, is first issued in 1992 after the American Institute of Architects gives Fay Jones its coveted Gold Medal for 1990 as the most significant building of the previous decade. Ivy's handsome 224-page coffee-table book is re-issued in 2001, shortly after Fay Jones retires from his partnership with Maurice Jennings, as a $40 paperback.

If you look at the six "sacred spaces" that Ivy showcases—Thorncrown Chapel (Eureka Springs, Arkansas, 1980), Thorncrown Worship Center (Eureka Springs, 1989), Mildred B. Cooper Memorial Chapel, Bella Vista, Arkansas, 1988), Marty Leonard Community Chapel, Fort Worth, Texas, 1990), Pinecote Pavilion (Picayune, Mississippi, 1987), and Pine Eagle (Wiggins, Mississippi, 1991)—you see a strong personal style and a mature grammar of ornament that is never deviated from in the Jennings + McKee chapel for Sewanee. Fay Jones's work, by any other hands, would still be the work of Jones himself.

Regardless of the paternity of the Chapel of the Apostles—we should never forget the still-lively theological controversy over the paternity of Jesus himself—we have a beautiful expression of spirituality that does homage to any hand, eye, head, and heart.

Unlike the Thorncrown Chapel, which sits on the natural limestone knoll of a wooded mountaintop in the Ozarks, the Chapel of the Apostles sits on a stereobate, a classical temple podium that levels the architectural playing field, sitting on sharply down-sloping ground.

This steel and masonry basement platform (3,500 square feet), which contributes virtually nothing to the 4,000 square-foot chapel's sacramental use, undoubtedly helps elevate the $4.2 million project cost to something near $1,000 per square foot.

Chapel of the Apostles interior

The platform is necessitated by the simple hydrological fact that the site chosen has a virtual river that runs through it.

The chapel's cantilevered floor—both inside the glass and redwood walls and on the two balconies (north and south) outside it—is flagstone. That qualifies it for this Sewanee in Stone architectural theme park.

There are also L-shaped retaining walls, flanking the front entrance, of Crossville sandstone.

The rest is wood (redwood outside and oak inside), big sheets of glass, small slate roof tiles, and metal fittings (gussets, brackets, diamond-shaped hollow metal joints, etc.) that hold the various wood members together to form the lattice-like trusses of the Chapel's amazing-grace of a roof.

Under this roof, and standing very still on the Chapel floor, you can begin to sort out what looks at first like unending complexity, like explosions in a lumber-mill factory frozen in mid-air forever.

When you concentrate, you start seeing patterns, recurring motifs, order and harmony, deeper meaning.

There are 12 bays, for the 12 apostles, formed as the spaces between the roof trusses.

Within each bay there are three cross-braces, their X-arms spanning between the inner members of the parallel-spar trusses, whose members are at 60 degrees to the horizontal. There are also three more cross-braces, positioned vertically, connecting the structural members above and below them.

Each bay gets three pairs of skylight panes at the ridgeline.

There are also cross-shaped mullions in the tall glass curtain walls, again intersecting at 60 degrees, to form repeating suggestions of equilateral triangles, a nice statement of trinitarian equity, theologically speaking.

The Chapel of the Apostles is a lovely structure, but there are some flaws, introduced not by original sin but by something like pilot-error, probably remediable by some actions in the indefinite future.

One is the fact that the all-glass altar-end of the chapel gives not a million-dollar view of the Cumberland mountains, or the valley below, as one gets at every edge of the Sewanee mountaintop, but a remarkably pedestrian view of three electrical transformer pots mounted on a pole, and a string of three unremarkable outbuildings spaced out southwards behind a residence on Tennessee Avenue. The obvious remedy for this would be to plant a lovely sacred grove of fast-growing tulip poplar trees, or hemlock trees, to hide the unsightly middle-distance with mountain greenery. Regrettably, because of the 20-foot tall platform on which the Chapel sits, it will be 30 years before trees of suitable height can stand tall enough to fill that optical trajectory.

Another problem—to this low-church semi-lapsed Anglican at least—is the rather conventionally depicted and painted-up Crucified Christ, as the central focal point at the altar end. Its semi-realistic, semi-stylized cartoon-like depiction seems to be at war, aesthetically at least, with the universalist details of the rest of the Chapel.

The best effect, let it be said upon entering the building at 4 P.M. on November 22, 2002, is that the setting sun, entering the Chapel through its all-glass west end, beams a blinding reflection of itself on the east-end glass behind the carved / sculpted figure on the cross! This blaze of solar glory transfigures the crucifix!

Throughout the Chapel, and in the forecourt in front of it, are handsome geometric constructions with opal glass insets that serve as lighting sconces and pavement lighting. Their latticework casing, whether of oak, or square bronzed rods, or other material, shows the clear lineage of Wright -begat-Jones-begat-Apostles, as does the fact that the wall-planes of glass intersect each other at right angles, on the Chapel's four corners.

There is lots more to say about the Chapel of the Apostles, but many professors or students at the School of Theology may have already said it, so it seems best to urge you, Gentle Reader, to come and see for yourself.

You may disregard the wording of the parking space in front of the Chapel, which says "CHAPEL/ VISITOR / 20 / MIN / LIMIT" You should feel the religious impulse to stay as long as you like here.

One of many afterthoughts about the Chapel of the Apostles pops up after reading in *Outside the Pale*, a 1999 catalog done by the Department of Arkansas Heritage, for a retrospective on Fay Jones's architecture held at the Old State House in Little Rock.

The biographical note following Robert Adams Ivy, Jr.'s foreword to this catalog says that the "native Mississippian is a graduate of the University of the South, where he majored in English, and Tulane University in New Orleans, where he received a degree in architecture."

It's a great pity that Ivy got both these nice works into print before getting a chance to write up his thoughts on the Chapel of the Apostles.

Robert Ivy would also be a good advocate for Sewanee establishing a "pre-architecture" course of study for undergraduates—perhaps akin to its 3 + 2 pre-engineering program—who would move on to some place where they could complete a degree in architecture. The University should invite Ivy back to help inaugurate such an initiative and perhaps give him an honorary degree.

A CALL FOR LITHOPHILES

THE MAIN PURPOSE OF THIS WRAP-UP CHAPTER is to call for more lithophiles.

Maybe it's obvious, or maybe it's not, but such a book as Sewanee in Stone can never claim to be definitive. There's always more to be learned, more insights to be gained from digging into the archives, and above all, more understanding to be won from careful and repeated observations of these wonderful stone creations.

Sewanee in Stone will have to serve, *ex tempore,* until someone else comes along and does it better.

Let me offer a few exhortations for further research by stone-lovers:

■ In the course of my fieldwork, 2002–2003, I continued to notice that there were no two buildings on Sewanee's campus that had identical arched openings for their entryways. The only ways to capture that remarkable diversity would be through 1) a series of measured drawings, registering the centerpoints of the radii of each curved element, as a way to plot their varying geometries and shapes, or 2) a series of photographs arranged as an exhibit of the joyfulness of the work by their masons and designers.

■ There's a similar playfulness in individual design elements, which may lurk unnoticed by the same observer for a long time, then pop out suddenly as quite remarkable.

One example, quickly verifiable, concerns the stone window lintels on the south face of Walsh Hall. The lintels on the first and third floor windows of Walsh are all gigantic sandstone slabs about five feet long. The lintels above the second floor windows are composed of five interlocking jigsaw-puzzle pieces. These five look rather as if they had all been hammered by identical thunderbolts. We see these zig-zag stone joints nowhere else on campus.

If we focus on the plinths, or bases, of the stone jambs on each side of

University entranceways, we start seeing some charming touches as well. Snowden's plinth tops, for example, have a triangular projection that curves like an S-shaped ski slope. All Saints' east-door plinth tops, by contrast, are elegantly simple downward curving arcs.

■ There are also innumerable stone artifacts, less important than whole buildings, but quite remarkable in themselves as contributing features of Sewanee's cultural landscape.

The University's stone bridges, for example, are quite lovely, as they cross the little creek in Abbo's Alley. A good part of this ravine garden's beauty is contributed by the bridges periodically punctuating the walkways. A lesser known stone arch bridge spans the little creek behind (that is,

Elliott Hall's twin-peaks gable end

west of) McCrady Hall. Historically, of course, the bridge and path has seen a lot of foot traffic to and from Gailor Memorial.

Other obvious artifacts are the stone walkways, some laid in herringbone patterns, as with the walk from All Saints' Chapel to University Avenue, or as random geometric slabs. The colors and bands of these slabs show up brightly during rainfall, which on Sewanee's mountaintop, means they show their best faces often.

And of course there are all the benches, ranging from those made from immense lichen-covered monoliths, to the latter-day benches slabbed and then inscribed as memorials.

This last word leads us to the University Cemetery, whose stone monuments are as distinctive in their own way as the personalities they aim to memorialize.

My favorite cemetery stone, one among many, is a lichen-covered monolith, rising out of the ground, with a bronze plaque saying simply KIRBY-SMITH on its front. On its backside is a remarkable latticework, raised ridges of ironstone intersecting each other at more or less regular intervals, like a rune of crystallography writ very large.

■ Someone might devise an "architectural scavenger hunt" with a list of items to locate on or around the Sewanee campus. It might include, for example, the twin peaks (twinned gables) curios on several Warren & Knight buildings—Sewanee Inn, New Hoffman, and two mirror-twin houses on Florida Avenue. Such an exercise might be used during freshman orientation, or for alumni reunions, for "bonding" new friendships.

Such examples should encourage us to exercise our powers of observation, that is, open our eyes and see, always as if for the first time.

One encouraging sign, in the past year, has been the emergence of the Sewanee Trust for Historic Preservation. This new group can have a great deal of influence in preserving, protecting, and educating us all as to what is best about this remarkable cultural landscape we call Sewanee. Clearly a top priority will be renovation of the Phi Delta Theta House (1928).

At this point, it's best for the lithophile to stop burbling; put the book down, and go see it all for yourselves!

ACKNOWLEDGMENTS

LIKE MY FAVORITE DRAMATIC CHARACTER, Blanche DuBois, I have always depended on the kindness of strangers.

Since late February, 2002, I have been a fixture in the Main Reading Room of the duPont Library, writing this book on the University's computers, in a 120-day period (August 1 to December 1), working like a maniac. So it seems right to begin by thanking the librarians who have cheerfully put up with me and the book project for nearly a year—Sue Armentrout, John Janeway, Heidi Lowry, Wayne Maxson, Andrew Moser, Mary O'Neill, and Kevin Reynolds. Thanks also to Barbara Dykes, who keeps the circulation staff at their best, when a book cannot be found and needs to be.

Upstairs, in the third floor garret that calls itself the University Archives, is Annie Armour, one of at least three people without whom this book literally could not have been done. Her mental map of the collection, which continues to reconfigure itself as new materials are added, is quite remarkable. Her memory of Sewanee, of matters large and small, is considerably more amazing.

My mentor and guide to Sewanee stonework is Carl Reid. He has been everything from laborer to university stone mason to Superintendent of Buildings and Lands. His wry comments on the good, the bad, and the ugly have also been delightful. Best of all, he has taught me to read the grammar, syntax, and orthography of sandstone masonry.

As a man of overarching interests, but most importantly a lifelong Sewanee resident and ultimate insider, James Waring McCrady has always provided me with precise and focussed insights as to the buildings and their makers, including his remarkable father, Vice-Chancellor Edward McCrady, whose administration (1951–1971) changed the shape of the campus more than all his predecessors or successors combined. His critical reading of this final draft was invaluable.

Beyond these three there are another five immensely helpful souls—Katrina (Trink) Beasley, John Bratton, Lucas Myers, Jill Carpenter, and David Clough—who probably represent about two centuries of coming to understand Sewanee as well as the rest of the world beyond the mountaintop.

As with everyone else mentioned in this section, however, none of these folks are in any way responsible for any outrageous judgments or wildly inaccurate opinions expressed in this book. Errors of fact, as well, are mine alone.

Thanks also to my distinguished professor friends from Memphis—Dale Richardson (English) and Leslie Richardson (Italian)—and to their wonderfully helpful University colleagues—Henrietta Croom (Biology), Bran Potter and Martin Knoll (Geology), Gerald Smith (Religion), Celeste Ray (Anthopology), Laurence Alvarez (Mathematics), Mishoe Brennecke and Elizabeth Mansfield (Art History), Major McCollough and David Michaels (Archaeology), and others who helped one way or the other.

Also in the utterly indispensable category are the good folks who run Physical Plant Services—especially Marvin Pate, Dan Henon, Karen Singer, and Kathy Backlund—and their stone mason colleague Houston King, who keeps the University's stone-setting tradition alive from its start at least four generations ago.

Thanks, finally, to all of the University officials, particularly Vice-Chancellor Joel Cunningham and his staff, his executive assistant, Sarah Stapleton, and the University's communications director, Joe Romano.

Latham Davis designed this book, after a long stint of service to the Sewanee community, and persevered with the author's sometimes-quirky choice of text and illustrations.

Not to be forgotten are all those editors and publishers who humored my 30-year obsession with writing about architecture, historic preservation, urban environment, and livable places, including Gerald Murley *(Center City)*, Ken DeCell, Bob Towery, and Kenneth Neill *(Memphis)*, Barney DuBois *(Memphis Business Journal)*, Bob McNulty *(Place)*, Bob Hall *(Southern Exposure)*, Lee Woodward, Budd McLaughlin, Bill Green, and Bob Ludwig *(Huntsville News)*, Bob Qualls and Betty Barker Smith *(The Baxter Bulletin)*, Jim Morriss and Rusty Turner *(Morning News of Northwest Arkansas)*, and Scott Stewart and Steve Lake *(Giles Free-Press)*. Thanks also to David Buege, and his colleagues in the University of Arkansas School of Architecture, for allowing me to teach "Writing About Architecture" in the Fall 1999 term.

One truly awkward acknowledgment cannot be avoided. That is to give credit where it is due, to those goo-goo-googly eyes (www.google.com), the search engine that never sleeps, gets tired or cranky, and nearly always links me up to information of great value. Thanks also to everyone who built the websites or provided content that I have made use of in this study.

Thanks to you all, friends and family, for grinning and bearing with me.

David Bowman
April Fool's Day 2003

North side window of ATO House

BIBLIOGRAPHY

A. Architectural Background

Blodgett, Geoffrey. "Oberlin College Architecture" (www.oberlin.edu), a condensation of his 1985 book .

Bond, Francis. *Gothic Architecture in England*. Batsford 1912. 782 pp.

Brand, Stewart. *How Buildings Learn*. Viking 1994. 243 pp.

Conservation of Stone Buildings. National Academy Press 1982. 365 pp.

Fletcher, Banister. *A History of Architecture*. 17th edition, Scribner 1961. 1366 pp. A classic first published in 1896.

Hamlin, Talbot. *Greek Revivial Architecture in America*. Oxford 1944, Dover 1964. 439 pp.

Haneman, John Theodore. *Pictorial Encyclopedia of Historic Architectural Plans, Details and Elements*. Wenzel & Krakow 1923. Dover 1984. 70 plates, usually with two dozen illustrations each, and detailed descriptions.

Hitchcock, Henry-Russell. *Architecture: Nineteenth and Twentieth Centuries*. Penguin Books 1958, 1978. 687 pp.

Howard, Maurice. *The Early Tudor Country House: Architecture and Politics, 1450–1550*. G. Philip 1987. 232 pp.

McAlester, Virginia and Lee. *A Field Guide to American Houses*. Knopf 1984. 526 pp.

McCoy, Esther and Barbara Goldstein. *Guide to U.S. Architecture: 1940–1980*. Arts + Architecture Press 1982. 166 pp.

McRaven, Charles. *Building with Stone*. Storey Books 1989. 192 pp.

Morgan, William. *Collegiate Gothic: The Architecture of Rhodes College*. University of Tennessee Press 1989. 105 pp.

Pevsner, Nikolaus. *An Outline of European Architecture*. Pelican 1943. Seventh edition 1963. 496 pp.

Scully, Vincent. *The Shingle Style and the Stick Style*. Yale 1955, 1971. 184 pp.

The Secretary of the Interior's Standards for the Treatment of Historic Properties with Guidelines for the Treatment of Cultural Landscapes. National Park Service, Historic Landscape Initiative 1996. 146 pp. Charles A. Birnbaum and others.

Stern, Robert A. M., Thomas Mellins and David Fishman. *New York 1880: Architecture and Urbanism in the Gilded Age*. Monacelli Press 1997. 652 pp.

B. Sewanee

"All Saints Chapel" tour brochure (undated).

American Places, ed. William Leuchtenberg. Oxford 2000. Chapter on Sewanee, pp. 365–389.

Bradford, Robert. "Romancing the Stone," *Sewanee*, April 1997, pp. 14-19. Appreciation of Sewanee's long stone-building tradition. With introductory notes on p. 2.

Bulletin of the University of the South. 1875 to date. Also known as the Catalog.

Cap and Gown. Yearbook from 1891 to date.

Chitty, Arthur Ben. *Reconstruction at Sewanee, 1857–1872*. Proctor's Hall Press 1993. 206 pp.

Chitty, Arthur Ben. "Sewanee: Then and Now." *Tennessee Historical Quarterly*, Winter 1979 (No. 4), pp. 3-20.

Choi, Susan. *The Foreign Student*. HarperPerennial 1998. 325 pp.

Domain 2020 Land Use Study. The Architects Collaborative 1992. 65 pp.

Fairbanks, George R. *The History of the University of the South*. Drew 1905. 403 pp. See especially his "Plans of the Founders of the University," pp. 248–263, a major policy statement given to the Trustees in 1886.

"The Fullness of Opportunity." Ilustrated fundraising brochure for the University's $5,000,000 campaign (1947). 22 pp.

Green, Ely. *Ely*. Seabury Press 1966. 236 pp.

Hill, James Otto. *Sewanee, a unique community*. M.A. thesis, Middle Tennessee State, 1952. 106 pp.

Hoffman, Charles Frederick. *Christ, the patron of all true education*. Young 1893. 209 pp. Hoffman donated funds for Hoffman Hall (1898).

Guerry, Moultrie. *Men Who Made Sewanee*. University of the South Press 1932, 1981. Additional chapters by Arthur Ben Chitty and Elizabeth N. Chitty. 163 pp.

Spencer Judd's photo album of Sewanee, undated, circa World War One. University Archives.

Knoll, Martin A. and Donald B. Potter. "Introduction to the Geology of the Sewanee, Tennessee Area." In the 1998 *National Speleological Society Convention Guidebook*, pp. 144–152.

"Lease Policies and Procedures." May 2000. 20 pp.

Lynch, Arthur Joseph. *George Rainsford Fairbanks*. The Shambles Press 1999. 192 pp.

Makris, Patricia. *The Other Side of Sewanee*. Dogwood 1997. 197 pp.

Makris, Patricia. *Sewanee, Echoes of Its Past*. Makris 1999. 223 pp.

McCrady, James Waring. *Under the Sun at Sewanee*. University Press 1967. 117 pp.

Percy, William Alexander. *Lanterns on the Levee*. Knopf 1941. Chapter on "Sewanee," p. 92 et seq.

Potter, Donald Brandreth. "Franklin County Geology." *Franklin County Historical Review*, XVI, 2 (1985)122–130.

Proceedings of the Board of Trustees. Published annually from 1868 onwards. Invaluable.

Purple Sewanee. Charlotte Gailor and others. APTA 1932, 1961. 169 pp.

Randle, Daniel Wilson. *A Question of Style: The Architectural Competition for the Central Building of the University of the South* (1860). M.A. thesis, University of Texas (Austin) 1978, 294 pp.

Rossi, Mary K. *Spatial perception, memory, and meaning: utilizing cognitive maps to understand the gothic elements of All Saints' Chapel in Sewanee TN*. M.A. thesis, Western Washington University, 1998. 142 pp.

Sewanee Alumni News. 1946 to date. Variously titled through the years. Articles by Arthur Ben Chitty, often unsigned, and many others.

Sewanee Messenger. 1984 to date. Tabloid weekly newspaper.

Sewanee Purple. 1904 to date. Student newspaper.

Sewanee: Seasons on the Domain. Photographed by Tommy L. Thompson. Harmony House 1993. 112 pp. With an introductory essay by Gerald L. Smith.

Sewanee Siren. 1967 to 1984. An eight-page mimeographed community newsletter.

Sewanee: University of the South. Harmony House, 1984. Unpaged. A beautiful coffee-table book of color photographs by William Strode, with an introduction by Andrew Lytle, undeservedly out of print.

Siddons, Anne Rivers. *Hill Towns*. HarperCollins 1993. Fictional portrait of Sewanee, as Trinity College, pp. 6–8. 356 pp.

Warriner, Alfred Louis. *The Way It Was*. Privately printed 1975. Chapter on 1915 building of "The Cliffs" with excellent photographs of the progress of the stone building, p. 102–118.

C. Architects and Planners

Dober, Richard P. *Campus Architecture*. McGraw-Hill 1996. 258 pp.

Dober, Richard P. *Campus Landscape*. John Wiley 2000. 259 pp.

Dober, Richard P. *Campus Planning*. Reinhold 1963. 314 pp.

Eastlake, Charles Locke. *Hints on Household Taste in Furniture*. . . Longmans Green 1868. Dover 1969. 304 pp.

Githens, Alfred Morton. "American Campus," *Brickbuilder*, July 1906-December 1907.

Githens, Alfred Morton. *Forms and Functions of Twentieth Century Architecture*, Vol. 3. Columbia University Press 1952.

Hall, Lee. *Olmsted's America*. Rizzoli 1995. 270 pp.

Holly, Henry Hudson. *Holly's Picturesque Country Seats*. Appleton 1863. Dover 1993. 171 pp.

Holly, Henry Hudson. *Modern Dwellings in Town and Country*. Harper & Brothers 1878. 219 pp.

Holzman, Malcolm. *Stone Work*. Images Publishing Group 2001. 210 pp.

Ivy, Robert Adams Ivy. *Fay Jones*. AIA Press 1992. McGraw-Hill 2001. 224 pp.

Schnorrenberg, John M. *Remembered Past, Discovered Future: The Alabama Architecture of Warren Knight and Davis*, 1906–1961. Birmingham Museum of Art 1998. Unpaged.

D. Cultural Matrix

Brooks, David. *Bobos in Paradise: The New Upper Class and How They Got There*. Simon & Schuster 2000. 285 pp.

Carnegie, Andrew. "Wealth," *North American Review*, June 1889, 653–664.

Florida, Richard. *The Rise of the Creative Class*. Basic Books 2002. 404 pp.

From the Mountain. A quarterly published by the School of Theology at the University of the South. 1997 on.

Gaston, Paul M. *Man and Mission: E.B. Gaston and the Origins of the Fairhope Single Tax Colony*. Black Belt Press 1993. 161 pp.

Jakle, John A. *The Gas Station in America*. Johns Hopkins 1994. 272 pp.

Jakle, John A. *The Tourist*. Nebraska 1985. 382 pp.

Putney, Clifford. *Muscular Christianity: Manhood and Sports in Protestant America, 1880–1920*. Harvard 2001. 300 pp.

Schama, Simon. *Landscape and Memory*. Knopf 1995. 652 pp.

Schenck, Carl Alwin. *The Birth of Forestry in America*. Forest History Society 1974. Includes an 1898 lecture given at Sewanee and a proposed forest management plan.

Wright, Geoffrey. *The Stone Villages of Britain*. David & Charles 1985. 232 pp.

Phi Delt house is a top priority for renovation.

INDEX

Bold numbers indicate illustrations.

This book was designed by Latham Davis,
set into type by Latham Davis in Sewanee, Tennessee,
and printed and bound by Thomson-Shore
in Dexter, Michigan.

The text, captions, and display faces are Goudy
issued in digital form by Adobe Systems.

The text paper is a 70 pound Fortune Matt.